AQA History

A2
Unit 3

From Defeat to Unity: Germany, 1945–1991

55

Sally Waller

Nelson Thornes

Published in 2010 by:
Nelson Thornes Ltd
Delta Place
27 Bath Road
CHELTENHAM
GL53 7TH
United Kingdom

13 14 15 16 / 10 9 8 7 6 5 4 3 2

A catalogue record for this book is available from the British Library

ISBN 978 1 4085 0259 4

Illustrations by Angela Knowles and David Russell Illustration

Page make-up by Thomson Digital

Printed in China by 1010 Printing International Ltd

Contents

Introduction

Nelson Thornes

Nelson Thornes has worked hard to ensure that this book offers you excellent support for your A Level course. You can be confident that the range of learning, teaching and assessment practice materials has been checked and is matched to the requirements of your specification.

How to use this book

The features in this book include:

Timeline

Key events are outlined at the beginning of the book. The events are colour-coded so you can clearly see the categories of change.

Learning objectives

At the beginning of each section you will find a list of learning objectives that contain targets linked to the requirements of the specification.

Key chronology

A short list of dates usually with a focus on a specific event or legislation.

Key profile

The profile of a key person you should be aware of to fully understand the period in question.

Key terms

A term that you will need to be able to define and understand.

Did you know?

Interesting information to bring the subject under discussion to life.

Exploring the detail

Information to put further context around the subject under discussion.

A closer look

An in-depth look at a theme, person or event to deepen your understanding. Activities around the extra information may be included.

Sources

Sources to reinforce topics or themes and may provide fact or opinion. They may be quotations from historical works, contemporaries of the period or photographs.

Cross-reference

Links to related content within the book which may offer more detail on the subject in question.

Activity

Various activity types to provide you with different challenges and opportunities to demonstrate both the content and skills you are learning. Some can be worked on individually, some as part of group work and some are designed to specifically 'stretch and challenge'.

Question

Questions to prompt further discussion on the topic under consideration and are an aid to revision.

Summary questions

Summary questions at the end of each chapter to test your knowledge and allow you to demonstrate your understanding.

Study tip

Hints to help you with your study and to prepare for your exam.

Practice questions

Questions at the end of each section in the style that you may encounter in your exam.

Learning outcomes

Learning outcomes at the end of each section remind you what you should know having completed the chapters in that section.

Introduction to the History series

When Bruce Bogtrotter in Roald Dahl's *Matilda* was challenged to eat a huge chocolate cake, he just opened his mouth and ploughed in, taking bite after bite and lump after lump until the cake was gone and he was feeling decidedly sick. The picture is not dissimilar to that of some A Level History students. They are attracted to history because of its inherent appeal but, when faced with a bulging file and a forthcoming examination, their enjoyment evaporates. They try desperately to cram their brains with an assortment of random facts and subsequently prove unable to control the outpouring of their ill-digested material in the examination.

The books in this series are designed to help students and teachers avoid this feeling of overload and examination panic by breaking down the AQA History specification in such a way that it is easily absorbed. Above all, they are designed to retain and promote students' enthusiasm for history by avoiding a dreary rehash of dates and events. Each book is divided into sections, closely matched to those given in the specification, and the content is further broken down into chapters that present the historical material in a lively and attractive form, offering guidance on the key terms, events and issues, and blending thought-provoking activities and questions in a way designed to advance students' understanding. By encouraging students to think for themselves and to share their ideas with others, as well as helping them to develop the knowledge and skills they need, this book should ensure that students' learning remains a pleasure rather than an endurance test.

To make the most of what this book provides, students will need to develop efficient study skills from the start and it is worth spending some time considering what these involve:

▨ Good organisation of material in a subject-specific file. Organised notes help develop an organised brain and sensible filing ensures time is not wasted hunting for misplaced material. This book uses cross-references to indicate where material in one chapter has relevance to material in another. Students are advised to adopt the same technique.

▨ A sensible approach to note-making. Students are often too ready to copy large chunks of material from printed books or to download sheaves of printouts from the internet. This series is designed to encourage students to think about the notes they collect and to undertake research with a particular purpose in mind. The activities encourage students to pick out information that is relevant to the issue being addressed and to avoid making notes on material that is not properly understood.

▨ Taking time to think, which is by far the most important component of study. By encouraging students to think before they write or speak, be it for a written answer, presentation or class debate, students should learn to form opinions and make judgements based on the accumulation of evidence. The beauty of history is that there is rarely a right or wrong answer so, with sufficient evidence, one student's view will count for as much as the next.

▨ Unit 3

The topics chosen for study in Unit 3 are all concerned with the changing relationship between state and people over a period of around 50 years. These topics enable students to build on the skills acquired at AS Level, combining breadth, by looking at change and continuity over a period of time, with depth, in analysing specific events and developments. The chosen topics offer plentiful opportunities for an understanding of historical processes enabling students to realise that history moves forward through the interaction of many different factors, some of which may change in importance over a period of time. Significant individuals, societies, events, developments and issues are explored in an historical context and developments affecting different groups within the societies studied from a range of historical perspectives. Study at Unit 3 will therefore develop full synoptic awareness and enable students to understand the way a professional historian goes about the task of developing a full historical understanding.

Unit 3 is assessed by a 1 hour 30 minute paper containing three essay questions from which students need to select two. Details relating to the style of questions, with additional hints, are given in the accompanying table and helpful tips to enable students to meet the examination demands are given throughout this book. Students should familiarise themselves with both the question demands and the marking criteria which follow before attempting any of the practice examination questions at the end of each section of this book.

Answers will be marked according to a scheme based on 'levels of response'. This means that an essay will be assessed according to which level best matches the

Unit 3 (three essay questions in total)	Question types	Marks	Question stems	Hints for students
Two essay questions	Standard essay questions addressing a part of the specification content and seeking a judgement based on debate and evaluation	45	These are not prescriptive but likely stems include: To what extent … How far … A quotation followed by 'How valid is this assessment/view?'	All answers should convey an argument. Plan before beginning to write and make the argument clear at the outset. The essay should show an awareness of how factors interlink and students should make some judgement between them (synoptic links). All comments should be supported by secure and precise evidence.
One essay question	Standard essay question covering the whole period of the unit or a large part of that period and seeking a judgement based on debate and evaluation	45	As above	Evidence will need to be carefully selected from across the full period to support the argument. It might prove useful to emphasise the situation at the beginning and end of the period, identify key turning points and assess factors promoting change and continuity.

historical skills it displays, taking both knowledge and understanding into account. All students should keep a copy of the marking criteria in their files and need to use them wisely.

Marking criteria

Level 1 Answers will display a limited understanding of the demands of the question. They may either contain some descriptive material which is only loosely linked to the focus of the question or they may address only a part of the question. Alternatively, they may contain some explicit comment but will make few, if any, synoptic links and will have limited accurate and relevant historical support. There will be little, if any, awareness of differing historical interpretations. The response will be limited in development and skills of written communication will be weak.   *(0–6 marks)*

Level 2 Answers will show some understanding of the demands of the question. They will either be primarily descriptive with few explicit links to the question or they may contain explicit comment but show limited relevant factual support. They will display limited understanding of differing historical interpretations. Historical debate may be described rather than used to illustrate an argument and any synoptic links will be undeveloped. Answers will be coherent but weakly expressed and/or poorly structured.   *(7–15 marks)*

Level 3 Answers will show a good understanding of the demands of the question. They will provide some

assessment, backed by relevant and appropriately selected evidence, which may, however, lack depth. There will be some synoptic links made between the ideas, arguments and information included although these may not be highly developed. There will be some understanding of varying historical interpretations. Answers will be clearly expressed and show reasonable organisation in the presentation of material.   *(16–25 marks)*

Level 4 Answers will show a very good understanding of the demands of the question. There will be synoptic links made between the ideas, arguments and information included showing an overall historical understanding. There will be good understanding and use of differing historical interpretations and debate and the answer will show judgement through sustained argument backed by a carefully selected range of precise evidence. Answers will be well-organised and display good skills of written communication.   *(26–37 marks)*

Level 5 Answers will show a full understanding of the demands of the question. The ideas, arguments and information included will be wide-ranging, carefully chosen and closely interwoven to produce a sustained and convincing answer with a high level of synopticity. Conceptual depth, independent judgement and a mature historical understanding, informed by a well-developed understanding of historical interpretations and debate, will be displayed. Answers will be well-structured and fluently written.   *(38–45 marks)*

Introduction to this book

Fig. 1 *The ruined city of Cologne in 1945*

Fig. 2 *Cologne at the beginning of the 21st century*

For Germany, 1945 marked both an end and a new beginning. The unconditional surrender of Nazi Germany in May 1945 brought to an end 12 years of Nazi rule. It had been 12 years of right-wing dictatorship and submission to one man's distorted vision of German greatness. At first, some of Hitler's promises had won favour. He helped restore a German pride, which had been so deeply shattered after the war of 1914–18 and the vindictive Treaty of Versailles. There were, of course, some aspects of Nazism which were never widely approved; the racial fanaticism and the inhumanity with which opponents and outcasts were treated. However, while Hitler gave the German people a new faith in their future, the more sinister side of Nazism was overlooked. It was when he plunged Germany into a second and even more deadly war that the dream started to sour. The early victories of 1939–41 soon gave way to uncertainty, desperation and ultimately anger. By 1945 there were few illusions left. The end of the war meant seeing, for the first time, the grim reality of the extermination camps. Nazism had not only brought humiliation, defeat and a good deal of self-questioning, it had cost the lives of 60 million people. In 1945 the past was something most Germans wanted to put behind them and forget.

The need and desire to 'begin again' made 1945 the start of a new era in German history, but it was not to take the shape most would have expected in that year. The victorious allies' decision to divide Germany into four occupation zones proved to have long-lasting consequences as the eastern zone, apportioned to the USSR, developed in quite a different way from the three western zones, under the UK, the USA and France. While the Western powers cooperated in fostering the development of parliamentary democracy, leading to the emergence of the Federal

Republic of Germany (FRG) in May 1949, the USSR created a communist regime in the East, and the division of Germany was sealed when this became the German Democratic Republic (GDR) in October 1949.

The division steadily deepened through the 1950s as Cold War pressures put an end to hopes that national unity might be quickly restored. The young Federal Republic built up its ties with the Western democracies, becoming one of the founder members of the European Coal and Steel Community in 1951 and one of the six countries establishing the European Economic Community (today's EU) in 1957. It received American 'Marshall Aid' and joined NATO in 1955. For West Germany, the opening of the new era was a time of optimism and prosperity. This was a period of unparalleled economic growth which continued well into the 1960s. An 'economic miracle' (or, at least, so it seemed) transformed the West German wastelands of the Second World War into the booming, prosperous powerhouse of Europe. With the new-found prosperity came a high standard of living which, coupled with the absence of social tensions, helped give the FRG's post-war democracy the stability which the inter-war years had so grievously lacked.

In the East, it was a very different story. The communist regime created by the Socialist Unity Party (SED) in the GDR was firmly tied to the USSR and its ideological goals. 'Building Socialism' by means of a planned economy, involved the nationalisation of industry and collectivisation of agriculture. While East Germans were assured that their political masters were developing a 'peasants' and workers' paradise', the initial disruption caused by the drive to economic change caused resentments, which were made worse by mediocre living and working conditions, which compared unfavourably with those in the West. Workers' discontent peaked in an uprising in June 1953, which was crushed with the aid of Soviet tanks. Around 100,000 people left the GDR for the West each year and it was not until the SED resorted to the building of a wall to seal the border gap in Berlin on 13 August 1961, that the GDR finally achieved some measure of stability as a separate state.

The late 1960s were a time of transition for the Federal Republic with the emergence of a student-led protest movement and Willi Brandt, a new Social Democrat Chancellor, in 1969. After 20 years of federal government young people and intellectuals began to question how far West Germany had come, and in particular to query its pro-Americanism (at the time of the Vietnam War) and the country's failure to come to terms with its Nazi past. As the 1970s unfolded, the student movement gave way to the rather more sinister Red Army Faction, centred on Andreas Baader and Ulrike Meinhof, which sought to destabilise the government, economy and society through terrorist attacks and kidnappings. Protest reached a climax in the 1977 'year of terror', which concluded with the suicide of the leading gang members in prison.

The significance of Brandt's election was twofold. Acceptance of a socialist Chancellor showed how far West Germany had come in terms of its democratic development. However, Willi Brandt is remembered less for his reforming measures within the FRG – including educational reforms and the expansion of the social welfare system – than for his 'Ostpolitik' or policy towards East Germany and the states of the communist Eastern bloc. Brandt negotiated a series of treaties with eastern Europe, culminating in the Basic Treaty of 1972, which did much to improve relations between the two German states and enabled East Germany to benefit from favourable Western loans.

On the other side of the border, a new GDR leader was brought to power in 1971, when Erich Honecker succeeded the unmourned Walter Ulbricht. Honecker's arrival (aided by Brandt's Ostpolitik) marked a revival in East Germany's political and economic fortunes. Consumer goods became more widely available, cars and televisions became more common, services improved and life became a little easier, even if this was only a pale imitation of the West's 1950s 'miracle'. 'Real existing socialism' seemed for a short while to be beginning to work, although what everyone, particularly the SED elite, failed to see at the time was that the state was structurally unsound – living on Western loans, yet dependent on the USSR.

With a change of leadership in the USSR, the possibility of a 'third way' of running a successful state – neither capitalist nor hardline communist – opened up. From 1985, Gorbachev not only set an example of what a reformist leadership might be able to achieve through economic and social restructuring (*perestroika*) he, more crucially, withdrew the USSR from the commitment to maintain unpopular communist regimes in eastern Europe and advocated *glasnost* – openness and accountability. It took time for these messages to be fully understood, but new movements for democracy in Hungary and Poland created an atmosphere in which an East German opposition movement could come out into the open, gain in confidence and grow to the point where it would challenge the complacent regime.

By the 1980s the GDR was living on borrowed time. As opposition grew and the economy deteriorated, the SED leadership set its face against reforms. In 1989, some GDR citizens expressed their dissatisfaction by fleeing via Hungary and Czechoslovakia; others participated in the 'Monday demonstrations' in front of the Nikolaikirche in Leipzig. Such developments shook the SED confidence so powerfully that, following an internal coup, Honecker was forced to resign as SED General Secretary in October 1989. His successors, led by Egon Krenz, tried to rescue the regime, but their decision to allow the opening of the border controls on the Berlin Wall on 9 November 1989 opened the floodgates to reform and reunification.

Helmut Kohl had become Federal Chancellor in 1982 and his languishing political career was rescued by the chance of propelling another new beginning. The integration of the GDR into the Federal Republic which even Kohl believed to be 10 years away in November 1989, was to take place on 3 October 1990. Kohl worked tirelessly to achieve West Germany's long-declared aim within months, once he realised the strength of feeling in the East. A favourable vote in the GDR in March 1990, a currency union in May and the consent of the four victorious powers of the Second World War in the 'Two plus Four' talks in September, permitted a united Germany to gain full sovereign rights finally ending the territorial rights of the allies. Vindicated in the first all-German election of December 1990, Helmut Kohl became the first Chancellor of the reunified Germany.

The first year of reunification was to prove a difficult one. Undoing the differences arising from 40 years of division was never going to be easy and the citizens of the former GDR had perhaps hoped for (or even been promised) too much too soon. Internally, the country faced the daunting task of dealing with the burden of debts; cleaning up and modernising the industries of the old GDR; creating new ones, together with a new modern infrastructure; producing an efficient administration and legal system and trying to bring living standards into line. Fiscal changes, including a solidarity tax levied on all citizens, were introduced to help finance these demands and yet, despite all this, it proved impossible to avoid a good deal of hardship in the new eastern *Länder* – creating new sources of discontent in both East and West. Furthermore, another division – the cultural differences resulting from the division of the country – proved no less difficult to break down than trying to create an economic/social balance. By the end of 1991 the future still appeared uncertain, but hope rested on the fundamental principles underlying the political and social system in West Germany which had been well established during its 40 years of separate existence. Whatever the tensions, the underlying belief in the future of parliamentary democracy was sound and the decision, taken in 1991 (although not effected until 1999) to move the state capital from Bonn to Berlin helped set the path for future development.

As you read this book, think about the recurring themes which underpin this period of German history between 1945 and 1991 and look for continuities as well as changes. You should reflect on the interaction of political, economic and social developments and should try to assess the relative importance of the state and the people in driving change or allowing matters to remain the same. Understanding the driving forces of history will also require you to consider the importance of ideologies and individuals to the development of the country as well as the extent to which developments were propelled by external (as opposed to internal) forces.

As you read and comment on the period covered by this book, remember that it is easy to interpret the story of post-war Germany as the triumph of Western democratic ideas over the 'evil' communist system of the East. You are looking at history from the perspective of the present. You know that Germany has now been reunited for around 20 years, has a thriving parliamentary system and is a staunch supporter of the EU. However, Germans living in the 1950s, 60s and 70s did not know that this would be the case, and to portray the GDR as an unbearable and universally hated regime would be both naive and unfair to the millions of East Germans who enjoyed perfectly contended lives under that East German communist regime. To understand the development of the two Germanies in this period, it is necessary to understand the circumstances that created them, the ideologies that drove them, the leaders that moulded them and the people that lived in them. As you look at the past, try to open your mind to the hopes and fears of those that were there at the time and so reach your own judgements about the issues and events you read about.

US Presidents

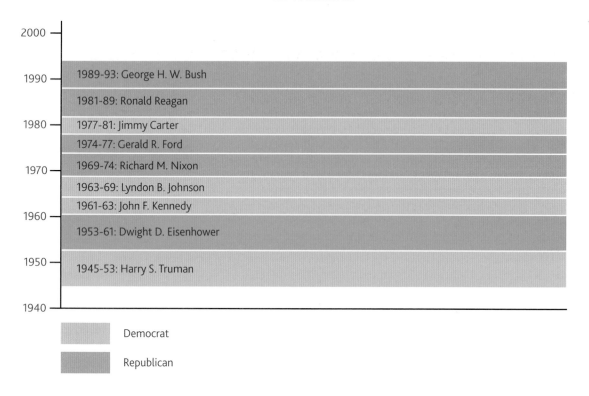

USSR Presidents

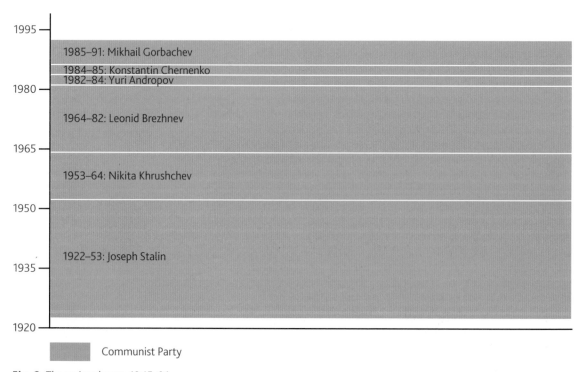

Fig. 3 *The major players, 1945–91*

FRG Chancellors

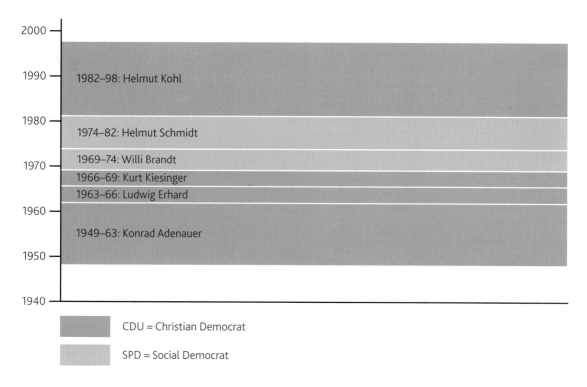

1982–98: Helmut Kohl

1974–82: Helmut Schmidt

1969–74: Willi Brandt

1966–69: Kurt Kiesinger

1963–66: Ludwig Erhard

1949–63: Konrad Adenauer

CDU = Christian Democrat

SPD = Social Democrat

GDR Chancellors

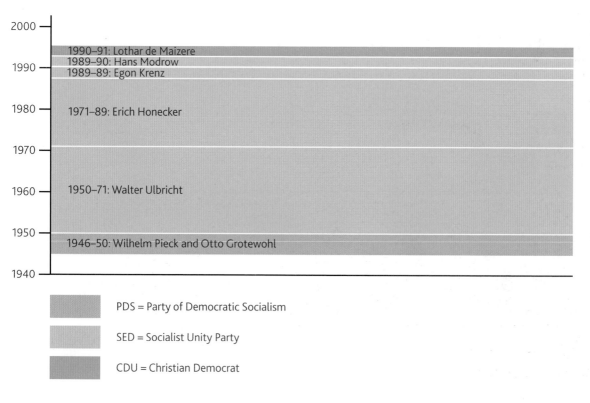

1990–91: Lothar de Maizere

1989–90: Hans Modrow

1989–89: Egon Krenz

1971–89: Erich Honecker

1950–71: Walter Ulbricht

1946–50: Wilhelm Pieck and Otto Grotewohl

PDS = Party of Democratic Socialism

SED = Socialist Unity Party

CDU = Christian Democrat

■ Timeline

The colours represent different types of events as follows: International, East Germany, West Germany, and Involving both East and West (jointly)

1945

4–11 Feb Yalta Conference

25 Apr Meeting of American and Soviet troops near Torgau on the River Elbe

30 Apr Adolf Hitler commits suicide

7–9 May Signing of the German surrender in Rheims and Berlin-Karlshorst

1–4 Jul Western troops enter Berlin

17 Jul–2 Aug Potsdam Conference

Aug–Sep The licensing of political parties begins in the western zones of occupation

1946

7 Mar Founding of the 'Free German Youth'

21–22 Apr Amalgamation of the KPD and SPD to form the SED in the Soviet zone of occupation and East Berlin

1 Oct Passing of sentences in the Nuremberg War Crimes Trials

20 Oct Elections to the state parliaments in the Soviet zone

2 Dec Washington Treaty on the economic unification of the British and American zones

1947

10 Mar–24 Apr Moscow foreign ministers' conference of the four victorious allies

5 Jun Announcement of a programme for the economic reconstruction of Europe by US Foreign Minister George C. Marshall

10 Jun Economic Council of the Bizone set up in Frankfurt am Main

25 Nov–15 Dec Foreign ministers' conference of the four victorious allies in London

1948

23 Feb–6 Mar and **20 Apr–6 Jun** Six Power Conference in London; adoption of the recommendations on the founding of a West German state

20 May Last meeting of the Allied Control Council

20–21 Jun Currency reform in the western zones

24 Jun Start of the Berlin airlift

10–23 Aug West German constitutional conference

1 Sep Setting up of the Parliamentary Council in Bonn

1954

25 Mar Declaration by the USSR recognising the sovereignty of the GDR

23 Oct Treaty of Paris allowed the Federal Republic to join NATO and permit West German rearmament

1955

14 May Founding of the Warsaw Pact, including the GDR

1956

18 Jan Decision by the People's Chamber to set up a 'National People's Army'

1957

25 Mar Signing of the Treaty of Rome establishing the European Economic Community

15 Sep Bundestag election, absolute majority for the CDU/CSU

1958

10 Nov 'Berlin Ultimatum' issued by the Soviet Union

1960

12 Sep Following the death of Wilhelm Pieck, the Council of State of the GDR is established under the chairmanship of Walter Ulbricht

1961

13 Aug Building of the Berlin Wall

1969

28 Sep Bundestag election, considerable gains made by the SPD

21–22 Oct SPD Chairman Willy Brandt elected Chancellor; formation of an SPD/FDP federal government

1970

19 Mar Meeting between Chairman of the GDR Council of Ministers Willi Stoph and Federal Chancellor Willy Brandt in Erfurt

21 May Return visit by Willi Stoph to Kassel

12 Aug Signing of the German–Soviet Non-Aggression Pact in Moscow

7 Dec Signing of the German–Polish Treaty in Warsaw

1971

3 May Erich Honecker replaces Walter Ulbricht as Secretary General of the SED Central Committee

3 Sep Signing of the Four Power Agreement on Berlin

10 Dec Chancellor Willy Brandt receives the Nobel Peace Prize

1972

17 May Ratification of the Moscow and Warsaw Treaties by the Bundestag

26 May Signing of transport agreement between the GDR and the Federal Republic

19 Nov Bundestag elections: SPD and FDP gain a clear majority

21 Dec Signing of the Basic Treaty between the GDR and the Federal Republic in East Berlin

1982

1 Oct Replacement of Chancellor Helmut Schmidt and the SPD minority government by a CDU/CSU/FDP coalition under Chancellor Helmut Kohl

1983

6 Mar Bundestag elections: the CDU/CSU and the FDP obtain an absolute majority; the Greens are represented in the Bundestag for the first time

29 Mar The German Bundestag re-elects Helmut Kohl as Federal Chancellor

1987

7–11 Sep Erich Honecker, Chairman of the Council of State of the GDR, visits the Federal Republic of Germany

1989

7 Oct 40th anniversary of the founding of the German Democratic Republic

Mass demonstrations in Leipzig for reform and democracy

18 Oct Erich Honecker is replaced as General Secretary of the SED

9 Nov Opening of the Berlin Wall, GDR citizens may travel freely

1949

4 May Agreement on the lifting of the Berlin Blockade on 12 May

15–16 May Elections to the Third German People's Congress in the Soviet zone

23 May Promulgation of the Basic Law for the Federal Republic of Germany

14 Aug Election of the first German Budestag

15 Sep Election of Konrad Adenauer (CDU) as Federal Chancellor

7 Oct Establishment of the German Democratic Republic

1950

16 Jan End of food rationing in the Federal Republic

8 Feb Ministry of State Security established in the GDR

29 Sep GDR joins the Council for Mutual Economic Assistance (COMECON)

1951

10 Apr Bundestag passes the law on co-determination in the steel and coalmining industries

18 Apr Signing of the European Coal and Steel Community Treaty in Paris

1952

9–12 Jul Decision by the Second Party Congress of the SED concerning the 'planned building of Socialism in the GDR'

23 Jul Division of the Länder in the GDR into 14 districts and 217 counties

1953

5 Mar Death of Joseph Stalin

17 Jun Uprising in East Berlin and East Germany

1962

14–28 Oct Cuban Missile Crisis

Oct–Nov Spiegel Affair, leading to the resignation of Federal Defence Minister Franz-Josef Strauss

1963

24–25 Jun Economic conference of the SED and the Council of Ministers concerning the 'New Economic System of Planning and Guidance'

15–16 Oct Resignation of Chancellor Konrad Adenauer, election of Economics Minister Ludwig Erhard as his successor

17 Dec First agreement on cross-border travel between the GDR and the West Berlin Senate

1964

24 Sep Willi Stoph becomes chairman of the GDR Council of Ministers following the death of Otto Grotewohl

1966

1 Dec Formation of a Grand Coalition between CDU/CSU and SPD under Chancellor Kurt Kiesinger

1968

11–17 Apr Murder of the student leader Rudi Dutschke, 'Easter Riots' in Berlin and other West German cities

21 Aug Troops of the Warsaw Pact invade Czechoslovakia

1973

18 Sep The Federal Republic and the GDR become members of the United Nations

Oct Start of the global oil crisis; Arab oil-producing nations restrict supplies and raise prices

1974

6 May Resignation of Chancellor Willy Brandt

16–17 May Election of Finance Minister Helmut Schmidt (SPD) as Chancellor; renewal of the SPD/FDP Coalition

4 Sep Establishment of diplomatic relations between the GDR and America

1975

1 Aug Signing of the CSCE Final Act in Helsinki

1976

16 Nov Wolf Biermann deprived of East German citizenship

1977

5 Sep–19 Oct Kidnap and murder of the president of the employers' federation, Hanns-Martin Schleyer; hijack of a Lufthansa plane; liberation of the hostages in Mogadishu; suicide of the terrorists Baader, Ensslin and Raspe

1980

30 Jun–1 Jul Visit by Chancellor Helmut Schmidt to Moscow

1981

11–13 Feb Visit by Chancellor Helmut Schmidt to East Germany

1990

18 Mar First democratic elections to the People's Chamber of the GDR

1 Jul Economic, monetary and social union comes into force between the Federal Republic and the GDR

3 Oct Accession of the GDR to the Federal Republic of Germany

2 Dec First all-German elections to the Bundestag; the CDU/CSU and the FDP retain their majority and form the federal government

1991

20 Jun The Bundestag decides by 337 to 320 votes to transfer parliament and the government to the capital, Berlin

20–28 Jun Slovenia and Croatia declare independence; civil war begins in Yugoslavia

17–23 Sep Attacks against asylum-seekers in Hoyerswerda in Saxony and in other towns

9–10 Dec EC summit meeting in Maastricht; signing of the treaties on economic and monetary union and political union

In this chapter you will learn about:

- the end of the war in Europe with the German surrender of May 1945

- the legacy of the war for Germany and the creation of the four zones of occupation

- the problems raised by the Potsdam Conference

- the prosecution of German war criminals in the Nuremberg Trials and the attempts at post-war denazification.

'If a British soldier met Hitler, would it be his duty to shoot him or take him alive?' asked Ivor Thomas, the Labour MP for Keighley, Yorkshire, in the House of Commons in March 1945. To the laughter and applause of the assembled MPs, Anthony Eden, the Foreign Minister replied, *'I'm quite satisfied to leave the decision to the British soldier concerned.'*

By March 1945, Eden could well afford to act the comic. Across the channel in the heart of Europe, British, American and Russian 'allied' soldiers were closing in, in a pincer movement, on Berlin. Hitler's war had been lost and it was clear that the German Führer's end was not far away. Germany's future was about to be changed in a way that few of those MPs joking with Eden would ever have been able to foresee.

◼ Occupied Germany

The German surrender

On 7–8 May 1945, representatives from the German High Command, led by Field Marshal Wilhelm Keitel, assembled at Berlin-Karlshorst where, in the presence of representatives of the USSR, America, Britain and France, they signed a document accepting Germany's unconditional surrender. The war in Europe was over. Hitler's dream of a thousand-year Reich had been shattered and the allies could celebrate a complete victory.

Although the war officially ended at 11.01pm on 8 May, in reality, this was only the formal recognition of events that had developed in a piecemeal fashion over the preceding months. Once British and American forces had crossed the Rhine at the end of February, German resistance in the West had begun to crumble and that crumbling had soon given way to a complete collapse. Indeed, many Germans, both soldiers and civilians, welcomed the allied advance and encouraged the British and Americans to march to Berlin and to occupy as much of the country as possible before the Russians, whom they feared far more, broke through in the East. However, it was the Soviet troops who were to reach the capital first. On 11 April, the Western allies halted their relentless advance at the River Elbe, 60 miles from Berlin, while the Soviet forces, under Marshals Zhukov and Konev, advanced across the Rivers Oder and Neisse.

The fall of Berlin

As the Battle for Berlin began at 5.00am on 16 April, with Soviet troops attacking along a 250-mile front to take the city, the National Socialist Führer of Germany, Adolf Hitler, remained isolated beneath 15 metres of concrete in his bunker under the Reich Chancellery. Here, he lived out a dreamworld, holding daily meetings of his military General Staff, barking out orders for non-existent armies and demanding that the German people lay waste their own country rather than surrender it. As the bombs and shells rained down above, Hitler continued to talk of victory. He celebrated his birthday on 20 April by receiving the good wishes of his generals and he denounced anybody who dared suggest that the Germans had been defeated. By 27 April Soviet troops had surrounded Berlin and joined with the American forces on the Elbe. Only when the Soviet soldiers were a few hundred metres from the Chancellery building, did Hitler face up to the reality that Nazi Germany was lost. On 30 April, as Soviet soldiers broke into the Reichstag (parliament) building itself, Hitler committed suicide. Some of his right-hand men, such as Göbbels, took the same path, while others fled. National Socialist Germany was at an end.

Fig. 1 *Berlin in ruins, 1945*

In those last two weeks of April, Berlin had been pounded with 40,000 tons of shells and the final week of war saw desperate fighting. The defiant city was taken, house by house and street by street, reducing it to hills of rubble with 75 per cent of its buildings uninhabitable. On the morning of 1 May, the red flag, bearing the Russian hammer and sickle, was symbolically unfurled by Soviet soldiers from the roof of the Reichstag building above war-torn Berlin. The following day at 3.00pm, the Berlin garrison under General Weidling surrendered.

In his journal entry for 3 November 1945, the newly returned American journalist William Shirer, who had been posted in Berlin in the years before the war, was to write:

> How can one find words to convey truthfully and accurately the picture of a great capital destroyed almost beyond recognition; of a once almighty nation that ceased to exist; of a conquering people who were so brutally arrogant and so blindly sure of their mission as the master race when I departed from here five years ago, and whom you now see poking about their ruins, broken, dazed, shivering, hungry human beings without will or purpose or direction.

The surrender

This continued fight to destruction was in large measure the result of Hitler's intransigence, but it was also due to the allies' insistence on 'unconditional surrender'. This had been agreed by the United States and Britain at the Casablanca Conference on 24 January 1943, and adopted by the Soviet Union on 1 May 1943. In the realisation of impending defeat, some sections of the Nazi leadership had sought to make a compromise peace in the last months of war, but such negotiations had won no favour. An 'Act of Military Surrender' had even been drawn up in July 1944, in preparation for the final showdown, and it was this that formed the wording for the final surrender of 8 May 1945.

Consequently, it was only after Hitler's suicide that any serious efforts were made to end the war and even then, the Admiral of the Fleet, Dönitz, whom Hitler had named as his successor, tried to avoid total surrender in order to continue the fight against the 'Bolshevik mortal enemy'. The end was therefore the result of a series of 'partial surrenders'.

■ 28 April: The German Army surrendered in Italy.

■ 4 May: The German armed forces in Holland, north-west Germany and Denmark surrendered to the British Commander-in-Chief, Field Marshal Montgomery.

■ 7 May: Surrender negotiations between Colonel-General Jodl of Germany and General Eisenhower, Commander-in-Chief of the allied forces, began in Rheims. However, Eisenhower had to threaten to resume air strikes and hand German prisoners of war to the USSR before the German negotiators accepted the need to make a full surrender to the Russians also.

■ 8 May: The act of full military surrender, coming into effect at 11.01pm, was agreed by Field Marshal Wilhelm Keitel before Marshal Georgi Zhukov at the Soviet headquarters at Berlin-Karlshorst. Since Stalin insisted on using the full text of July 1944 (rather than the abbreviated form used in Rheims), the official signing actually took place at 12.16am on 9 May.

■ **Cross-reference**

Eisenhower is profiled in Chapter 5, page 77.

The war legacy

It was not just in Berlin that the German people had paid dearly for Hitler's ambitions. The war had brought death, misery and physical destruction throughout the nation. Although, thanks to Germany's advanced economy and the spoils of war that Hitler had been able to tap, German civilians had not felt the impact of war too severely before 1944, the allied carpet-bombing and the merciless push of their armies from east and west in the final year of fighting shattered many German illusions. After the surrender of 8 May, the country was left in a state of chaos, shock and disarray. As its people grappled to come to terms with what had happened, a mixture of bewilderment and demoralisation left the country in a state of paralysis.

There was physical destruction everywhere. Towns and communities lay in ruins. Proud cities, such as Hamburg, Cologne, Düsseldorf, and Dresden were little more than rubble heaps, with blackened church spires emerging from the charred remains of hollow buildings. Communications had broken down as roads, railways and bridges had disappeared. Industrial plant lay smoking or idle and agricultural land was left barren or pock-marked by shells and other wartime debris. The industrial area of the Ruhr was described by one British observer as '*the greatest heap of rubble the world has ever seen.*' It was said that six months after the end of war, the ruins still smelled of fire and death.

Fig. 2 *Ruins of a German city*

The human costs had also been horrific. Around 6.5 million Germans had been killed and many more were unaccounted for; lost on the Soviet–German front. In the final months of war, millions of civilians had been among those who lost their lives. Half a million or more had perished in the burning cities while others, largely in the East, had been killed by the advancing troops.

George Kennan, an American diplomat, described the scene in his memoirs:

> The disaster that befell this area (eastern Prussia) with the entry of the Soviet forces had no parallel in modern European experience. There were considerable sections of it where, to judge by all existing evidence, scarcely a man, woman or child of the indigenous population was left alive after the initial passage of the Soviet forces. The Russians swept the native population clean in a manner that had no parallel since the days of the Asiatic hordes.

Death had been accompanied by the assault and rape of women living in the villages and towns taken by the Soviet army. Around 90,000 women in Berlin were systematically raped, mostly during the week of 2–7 May, as the war-weary and brutalised Soviet soldiers seized the city and inflicted punishment for the sufferings of their own families on the civilians they found there. Around 150,000 to 200,000 'Russian babes' were to be born to German women in what was to become the Russian zone of Germany in 1945–46 and this takes no account of the many thousands of abortions that took place, sometimes killing both child and mother.

For those that survived and escaped vengeance, there were still the problems of finding shelter, food and medication, in order to stay alive. Twenty million Germans, including 500,000 in Hamburg alone, were forced to live in cellars and ruins while many children, including 53,000 in Berlin by the end of 1945, lived parentless, homeless or simply 'lost' among the debris of war. Elsewhere, people survived in overcrowded, cramped living conditions, with several families sharing rooms and cooking and washing facilities. Since many husbands and fathers had been lost, women often had to bear the brunt of 'survival work', both feeding and caring for their families, as well as helping in the hard physical work of rebuilding their surroundings. The name *Trümmerfrauen* was given to the bands of women who stood passing stones and bricks from one to another in the reconstruction of ruined buildings.

Food was in short supply and even after peacetime was declared, people continued to die from hunger and infection. In June 1945, in the American zone of occupation, the average calorie intake for ordinary Germans was just 860 calories per day (compared with 2,445 in 1940–41). Looting and bartering on the Black Market became common, and basic luxuries such as cigarettes and chocolate, which the allied soldiers carried, were more eagerly sought than Germany's devalued paper currency. Those who could, went foraging in the countryside.

Health was another major issue. Damaged sewer systems and polluted water supplies brought an outbreak of dysentery in Berlin during July 1945 and raised the infant mortality rate to 66 deaths to every 100 live births. In October 1945, Robery Murphy, the American political adviser for Germany, reported that 10 people a day were dying at the Lehrter railway station in Berlin from exhaustion, malnutrition and illness. There was also the serious risk of disease posed by rotting corpses. In December 1945, it was reported in the British zone that one in four children under a year old were dying and that there were 1,023 new cases of typhoid and 2,193 cases of diphtheria that month.

To add to the distress, the country was swamped by ethnic Germans from countries such as Yugoslavia, Hungary, Czechoslovakia, Poland, the Baltic and the western Soviet Union who had fled westwards as the Red Army advanced. There were also refugees from the former eastern lands of Germany itself (Silesia, East Prussia, eastern Pomerania and

Cross-reference

The division of Germany into zones is described on pages 15–16.

This wartime legacy grew worse before it got better. Those Germans who did not leave voluntarily were often forcibly expelled from eastern Europe over the following year. In the 18 months from May 1945, nearly three million ethnic Germans were forcibly expelled from Czechoslovakia into Germany and approximately 267,000 died in the process. A further 623,000 were expelled from Hungary, 786,000 from Romania, 500,000 from Yugoslavia and 1.3 million from Poland.

Exploring the detail

Death marches

As the allied armies closed in on the Nazi concentration camps, many prisoners were marched, often pointlessly, back towards central Germany. They were forced to keep going over long distances in bitter cold, with little or no food, water, or rest. Those who could not keep up were shot. During one 'death march', 7,000 Jewish prisoners, of which 6,000 were women, were moved from camps in the Danzig area. On the ten-day march, 700 were murdered. Those still alive when the marchers reached the shores of the Baltic sea were driven into the water and shot.

Activity

Thinking point

Study Fig. 3. What feelings do you think these people are experiencing – relief, gratitude, hope, emptiness, fear, anger, sadness, despair? How would you account for these feelings?

eastern Brandenburg) and other ethnic peoples, including Poles, Ukrainians, Hungarians and Romanians who had fled westwards to escape the dual horrors of war and the prospect of communist domination. Returning Wehrmacht soldiers and allied soldiers newly released from prisoner of war camps; non-Germans who had fought in the German armies; the millions of men and women who had been brought to Germany to work as slave-labour on farms and in factories for the Nazis; and the often emaciated survivors of the concentration camps and the death marches added to the numbers seeking relief and the general sense of disorientation.

According to William Byford-Jones, an officer with the British army, there were 'displaced persons' everywhere:

> Women who had lost husbands and children; men who had lost their wives; men and women who had lost their homes and children; families who had lost vast farms and estates, shops, distilleries, factories, flour mills, mansions. There were also little children who were alone, carrying some small bundle, with a pathetic label attached to them. They had somehow got detached from their mothers, or their mothers had died and been buried by other displaced persons somewhere along the wayside.

3

For many Germans, the act of sheer physical survival prevented too much musing on the past or the future, but whether they feared or welcomed the consequences of defeat largely depended on where they lived and their experience of the allied armies with which they came into contact.

Fig. 3 *A German family seeking shelter*

The establishment of the four occupation zones

Various proposals for the post-war treatment of Germany had been put forward from 1942 onwards. Most assumed that there would need to be an initial occupation of Germany, but not surprisingly views varied as to what would happen beyond that. There were differences both between the attitudes of the various allied powers and between different leaders and groups within the individual allied countries.

Differing views of Germany's future

At one extreme there were those who believed that Germany should be broken up into a series of separate states with no heavy industry so that it could never again pose a threat to the peace of Europe. At the other were those who favoured the creation of a centralised federal state similar to the former **Weimar Republic**, and who wanted to see the country rebuilt as quickly as possible along democratic lines, in order to re-educate the people.

 Activity

Revision exercise

What would have been your recommendations for the future of Germany after the collapse of Nazism? Write down your own ideas and, as a group, consider the strengths and weaknesses of the suggestions made.

The allies' initial post-war planning involved the establishment of a military occupation and in September 1943 the 'Post-Hostilities Planning Sub-Committee' presented a map showing three zones – British, American and Russian – with roughly equal population densities. The proposal permitted the Russians to occupy a large eastern zone, which, being more rural, contained a sparser population. The USSR accepted the proposal in February 1944, and in September this decision was extended to include a shared control of Berlin, which would otherwise have lain in the Russian zone. It was also agreed that a Control Council should be set up to coordinate the allies' occupation policies.

There were discussions on the issues of both occupation and Germany's ultimate fate at Tehran (28 November–1 December 1943) and Yalta (4–11 February 1945).

The Yalta Conference, February 1945

The Yalta Conference, attended by Britain, America and the USSR, approved the plans for the occupation and administration of post-war Germany and it was also agreed that France should have its own occupation zone. However, while America and Britain had hoped that this zone would be carved out of the original Soviet allocation, Stalin adamantly refused to accept this and a zone was eventually created in the south-west of Germany, from former American and British-allocated territory.

It was also agreed that the northern half of East Prussia would be given to the Russians, while German territory to the east of the Rivers Oder and Neisse would go to the Poles, although there was some difference of opinion between the West and Russia as to exactly where this border should be placed. The longer-term future of Germany remained uncertain, although Stalin seemed to have accepted the probability of the eventual emergence of a neutral and disarmed united Germany, which was in sharp contrast to his 1943 pronouncement that Germany should be obliterated as a single central European state. The American view had

 Key terms

The Weimar Republic: this had been Germany's only experience of a genuine democratic constitution with a figurehead president, an elected central (federal) government and local state governments. This Republic had lasted from 1919 to 1933, although its multiplicity of competing political parties, encouraged by a system of proportional representation, weakened it and it was ultimately destroyed by Hitler's rise to power.

 Did you know?

American planning for the future of Germany divided Roosevelt's wartime government. One senior group, including Secretary Morgenthau of the Treasury and Harry Hopkins, the personal adviser to the President, favoured the harshest possible treatment for Germany, while Secretary Stimson of the War Department, and the foreign service favoured occupation followed by a swift return to an independent democratic state. General Lucius D. Clay, who became the military governor of the US occupation zone, complained that he had to deal with a home government which did not know what it wanted in Europe.

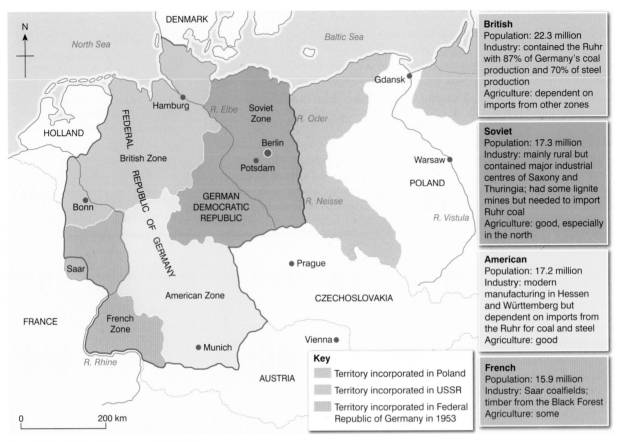

British
Population: 22.3 million
Industry: contained the Ruhr with 87% of Germany's coal production and 70% of steel production
Agriculture: dependent on imports from other zones

Soviet
Population: 17.3 million
Industry: mainly rural but contained major industrial centres of Saxony and Thuringia; had some lignite mines but needed to import Ruhr coal
Agriculture: good, especially in the north

American
Population: 17.2 million
Industry: modern manufacturing in Hessen and Württemberg but dependent on imports from the Ruhr for coal and steel
Agriculture: good

French
Population: 15.9 million
Industry: Saar coalfields; timber from the Black Forest
Agriculture: some

Key
- Territory incorporated in Poland
- Territory incorporated in USSR
- Territory incorporated in Federal Republic of Germany in 1953

Fig. 4 *The division of Germany after 1945*

also swung away from the programme of dismemberment (as promoted in September 1944 by Morgenthau) towards the idea of a democratic and economically sound Germany which could play its part in world trade. It was only the French, who were not present at the conference, who continued to press for the break-up of Germany. They wanted the Rhineland to be taken away and the Ruhr put under international control.

The Yalta Conference also saw general agreements on the principles of 'The Four Ds' – demilitarisation, decentralisation, denazification and democratisation – within post-war Germany. However, there were major differences of opinion over the level and type of reparations that might be exacted from a defeated Germany. As well as a huge monetary reparation, Stalin wanted control over 80 per cent of all German factories as recompense for the huge sacrifices made by the Russian people in order to repel the German invasion.

Table 1 *'The Four Ds'*

Demilitarisation	Decentralisation	Denazification	Democratisation
This would leave Germany as a neutral or non-aligned and disarmed country	This would remove a strong central government by placing power in the hands of the local states or Länder. It would be accompanied by decartelisation, breaking up huge industrial conglomerates	This would remove all Nazi influences from society, punishing those responsible for Nazi policies and forcing others to break with their Nazi past	This would restore the Germans' freedom to choose between political parties and be ruled by an elected government reliant on consent, debate, and a majority vote

The development of the zones

Despite Admiral Dönitz's brief attempt at government, from May 1945, after Hitler's suicide, Germany was effectively in the hands of the occupying armies, which assumed control within their allocated zones. The proposed Control Council was established on 5 June, when Berlin was also divided into four sectors.

Each occupying power began establishing its control in different ways, but the Russians acted with the greatest speed. On 9 June, the Soviet Military Administration in Germany (SMAD) began work in Berlin and the Anglo-American troops which had advanced deeper into Germany than originally expected and thus found themselves within the Soviet-allocated territory, were forced to withdraw between 1–3 July, before the Russians would allow the Western allies to take their allotted zones in Berlin.

By 9 July, five Länder (local state governments) had already been created within the Soviet zone.

The end of the Nazi past

The Potsdam Conference, August 1945

Fig. 5 *Attlee, Truman and Stalin at Potsdam*

The Potsdam Conference, held between 17 July and 2 August 1945 at the Cecilienhof, a small royal palace near Berlin and one of the few suitable buildings still left standing in the area, only served to reaffirm the disagreements between the allies. Decisions were not helped by France's non-attendance, nor by the replacement of Churchill by Attlee at the head of the British delegation during the course of the negotiations.

The allies failed to come to a joint agreement on reparations and although they agreed that Germany should be made to pay $20 billion, they disagreed on how or when that sum should be exacted. It was eventually decided that each occupying power should take reparations from their own occupation zone, with Russia being awarded a further

Did you know?

In July 1945, the Labour Party under Clement Attlee won a landslide victory in Britain and Attlee duly replaced Winston Churchill at the Potsdam Conference. Since Harry Truman had also replaced America's wartime leader Franklin D. Roosevelt, Stalin was left as the elder statesman, which probably gave him some advantage in the negotiations.

10 per cent from the British and American zones and an additional 15 per cent in exchange for the delivery of food and materials from their zone. This decision, which turned the four zones into separate economic units, was to make the earlier decision to provide political and economic coordination through the Control Council unworkable.

Similarly, although the decision to implement the four Ds was reaffirmed, and it was agreed that there should eventually be a united, although decentralised, Germany, little progress was made towards when or how this would happen. This left the four allied commanders who made up the Control Council (France having joined on 7 August) unable to put any sort of joint policy into effect. Consequently, each zone started to adopt different political and social systems, with each occupying power believing their system superior to that of the others.

The contentious issue of the German–Polish border was essentially decided before the conference by Soviet action. Poland's western boundary had been pushed westwards into former German land, with those Germans living there expelled and Poles resettled in the area. Stalin had unilaterally put these changes into effect in order to compensate Poland for the loss of land in eastern Poland and Königsberg that the USSR had taken from it under the Nazi–Soviet Pact of 1939 and was determined to retain. The remaining allies could only accept a **fait accompli** and since it was assumed that another peace conference would be held in due course, no final decision was taken. The Western allies tried to insist that the transfer of peoples from the area being taken by the Poles should be carried out in a humane fashion. However, in the following years, 6.75 million Germans were brutally deported and made to suffer for Germany's war crimes.

Exploring the detail

The Nazi–Soviet Pact of 1939

Hitler and Stalin had made a 'non-aggression' pact in August 1939 agreeing to divide Poland between them. This pact was broken when Hitler invaded the USSR in June 1941.

Key terms

Fait accompli: this is something that has already been done and which therefore has to be accepted.

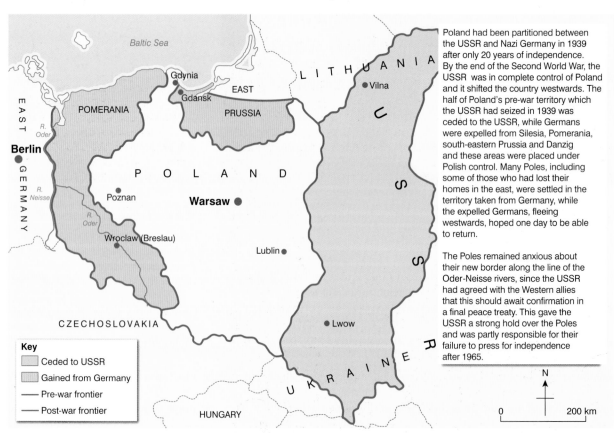

Poland had been partitioned between the USSR and Nazi Germany in 1939 after only 20 years of independence. By the end of the Second World War, the USSR was in complete control of Poland and it shifted the country westwards. The half of Poland's pre-war territory which the USSR had seized in 1939 was ceded to the USSR, while Germans were expelled from Silesia, Pomerania, south-eastern Prussia and Danzig and these areas were placed under Polish control. Many Poles, including some of those who had lost their homes in the east, were settled in the territory taken from Germany, while the expelled Germans, fleeing westwards, hoped one day to be able to return.

The Poles remained anxious about their new border along the line of the Oder-Neisse rivers, since the USSR had agreed with the Western allies that this should await confirmation in a final peace treaty. This gave the USSR a strong hold over the Poles and was partly responsible for their failure to press for independence after 1965.

Key
- Ceded to USSR
- Gained from Germany
- Pre-war frontier
- Post-war frontier

Fig. 6 *Poland's frontiers*

Activity

Thinking and analysis

Below are some of the main agreements in principle made at Potsdam. For each agreement, indicate the difficulties that might be encountered in carrying the principle out.

Political principles

1. Supreme authority in Germany will be exercised by the Commanders-in-Chief, each in his own zone of occupation, and also jointly in matters affecting Germany as a whole, in their capacity as members of the Control Council.

2. Uniformity of treatment will be given to the German population throughout Germany.

3. The complete disarmament and demilitarisation of Germany will take place.

4. The eventual reconstruction of German political life will be on a democratic basis.

5. The political structure in Germany will be decentralised. All democratic parties will be allowed. For the time being, no central German government will be established.

Economic principles

1. The German economy will be decentralised.

2. During the period of occupation, Germany will be treated as a single economic unit.

3. Payment of reparations should leave enough resources to enable the German people to subsist without external assistance.

The Nuremberg Trials, 20 November 1945–1 October 1946

Fig. 7 *American soldiers look over the defendants as the lawyers prepare their briefs*

Exploring the detail

The expulsions

The result of the change to the German–Polish border was that many Germans from the eastern provinces who had not already fled westwards before the Red Army advanced, found themselves expelled from their homelands. They were herded onto trains by the Soviets and sent westwards, with whatever they could carry. Even these meagre provisions were often looted en route in the many ambushes to which such trains were prey. In some areas of north Germany the displaced Germans formed 50 per cent of the local population and clashes with locals over differences in culture, religion, dialect and lifestyle ensued.

Did you know?

It was not until 1990, when the two Germanies were finally reunified, that the western border of Poland received official recognition.

Activity

Group task

Recreate your own Potsdam Conference with different class members representing Britain, France, America and the USSR. Others could act as journalists and write reports on the conference for their respective countries.

Although Stalin had shocked Churchill at the Tehran Conference in November 1943 by proposing a toast, '*I drink to the quickest possible justice for all German war criminals. I drink to the justice of the firing squad*', the allied powers reached an agreement on 8 August 1945 to try the leading Nazi war criminals before the International Military Tribunal. The trials were to take place in the Palace of Justice in Nuremberg, chosen because it had been the site of the huge Nazi Party rallies.

There were 13 trials in all and although these were only a small part of the wider drive to denazify Germany, the first, in which 21 of the most prominent Nazi leaders were interrogated and new and incriminating documents brought to light, received immense public attention. Those on trial had already been held for three months in Nuremberg Gaol and comprised four groups: military commanders; party men; civil servants; and those responsible for mass murder and slave labour.

■ **Did you know?**

Many rumours surrounded the disappearance of Bormann, who had been Hitler's secretary, and some believed, the most important man in the Reich, after Hitler, in its later years. He had last been seen in Hitler's bunker and was assumed to have been killed in his attempted flight from Berlin. Nevertheless, there were reported sightings of him in South America and the truth of his disappearance has never come to light.

■ Key terms

Final Solution: this was a euphemism for the extermination of the Jewish race, as practised in the Nazi gas chambers.

■ Activity

The defendants

Try to find out a little about each of the defendants given below. You might even like to hold your own 'mock trial' in which each defendant presents his own case and a panel of judges questions him and delivers a verdict.

The defendants were:

- **Military commanders:** Dönitz, Keitel, Jodl, Raeder
- **Nazi Party men:** Göring, Rosenberg, Streicher, Ribbentrop, von Schirach, Seyss-Inquart, Hess
- **Civil servants:** Schacht, von Papen, Speer, Neurath, Funk, Fritzsche, Frick
- **Mass murder/slave labour overseers:** Frank, Kaltenbrunner, Sauckel

There was a 22nd indictment, of Martin Bormann, but he was never found and was therefore tried 'in absentia'. There was also an attempt to try Gustav Krupp, the armaments manufacturer, but he was declared medically unfit. Many others such as Göbbels; Ley, the head of the Nazi Labour Front; and Himmler, head of the SS, had already committed suicide while others, such as Eichmann, who bore much responsibility for the '**Final Solution**', escaped and evaded justice – although he was eventually brought to trial in Israel in 1961.

The court was a military tribunal with four judges, one from each allied nation. There were also 250 journalists present. The British president of the tribunal, Justice Geoffrey Lawrence, opened proceedings on 20 November 1945 by referring to the trial as '*unique in the history of the jurisprudence of the world and of supreme importance to millions of people all over the globe*'.

The first trial lasted 218 days and began with the reading of the indictment. The prisoners were to be tried on four counts:

- Crimes against peace (preparing and initiating wars of aggression).
- War crimes (the ill-treatment of civilian populations and prisoners of war).
- Crimes against humanity (extremes of brutality against whole groups of nations).
- Conspiracy (involvement in a common plan to commit the above crimes).

The defendants, sitting in two rows and hemmed in by white steel-helmeted American soldiers, listened through headphones which were capable of providing simultaneous translations for all present in French, German, English and Russian. All pleaded 'not guilty'. The prosecution spent the next four months detailing their case, during which time much of what is now regarded as the standard history of Nazism was brought to light for the first time.

A closer look

Secrets disclosed

Among those crucial parts of Nazi history that were revealed – in many cases to the astonishment of the defendants as well as the public at large – were:

- the phone calls between Berlin and Vienna leading to the Anschluss with Austria in 1938
- Hitler's 'trick' of dressing up a dozen criminals in Polish army uniforms and leaving them dead at the German Gleiwitz radio station as 'proof' of Polish aggression in 1939
- the resistance activities within the Abwehr (counter-intelligence)
- the Hossbach meeting between Hitler and his army generals in 1937 at which he demanded 'Lebensraum' in the East
- the secret codicil to the Nazi–Soviet non-aggression pact that preceded the invasion of Poland which allowed for the division of Poland between those two nations. However, much to the relief of the Russians, this was discredited at the time because the prosecution lawyer refused to say how he had come by it
- Himmler's orders for the use of forced labour and removal of 'sub-humans' in the concentration camps
- Frank's 38-volume diary recounting the murder, starvation and extermination of concentration camp inmates
- details relating to medical experimentation
- the horrors of the concentration camps – as seen in an American film, shot when the camps were liberated.

Some of the defendants were visibly moved by the evidence and most gave way to tears. Fritzsche sobbed to the prisoners' American psychologist, *'No power in heaven on earth can take this shame away from my country'* and his words were echoed by Frank, who collapsed into religious hysteria declaring, *'a thousand years will pass and this guilt of Germany will not pass away'*. Dönitz and Funk muttered *'terrible, terrible'* over and over again and even Göring, the most composed and defiant of the group, admitted that things seemed to have got out of hand.

When Göring was given the opportunity to mount a defence, the deputy British judge said of him, *'It is obvious that a person of outstanding, though possibly evil, qualities has been seated there in the dock; suave, shrewd, adroit, capable, resourceful.'* The other defendants were less impressive and most denied knowledge of what had been going on. The defence lawyers tried to argue that it was really only Hitler that had been guilty but, in the final summing up in July 1946, the chief American prosecutor, Mr Justice Jackson was to say, *'If you were to say of these men that they are not guilty, it would be as true to say that there had been no war; there are no slain; there had been no crime.'*

A further month was devoted to indicted organisations – the cabinet, the party's leadership, the **SS** and **SD**, the **SA**, the **Gestapo**, the **General Staff** and the **High Command** – after which the first six were found

Key terms

SS: originally Hitler's personal bodyguard, these were the Nazi 'blackshirts' who ran the concentration camps.

SD: the Nazi security service under the control of the SS.

SA: a Nazi paramilitary force used to intimidate opponents – the 'brownshirts'.

Gestapo: the Nazi secret police – also a branch of the SS.

The **General Staff** and the **High Command** were the officers in charge of the armed forces.

guilty but the General Staff and High Command, not guilty. The final statements were heard on 31 August, the judgement on 30 September, and the sentencing on 1 October. The verdicts were:

Acquitted: Franz von Papen; Hjalmar Schacht; Hans Fritzsche

Death sentences by hanging a fortnight later: Joachim von Ribbentrop; Alfred Jodl; Julius Streicher; Hermann Göring; Fritz Sauckel; Hans Frank; Wilhelm Frick; Ernst Kaltenbrunner; Wilhelm Keitel; Alfred Rosenberg; Arthur Seyss-Inquart; Martin Bormann (in absentia)

Life imprisonment: Rudolf Hess (who remained in Spandau until his death in 1987); Walther Funk (released early because of ill health); Erich Raeder (released early because of ill health)

Shorter sentences (10–20 years): Karl von Dönitz (released 1956); Konstantin von Neurath (released 1954); Baldur von Schirach (released 1966); Albert Speer (released 1966)

A closer look

The defendants' reactions to the sentencing

Schacht, relieved to be acquitted, could never understand why he had been tried at all. Funk, who had expected hanging, wept with relief. Hess, whose sanity and consequent ability to understand the trial had been in question throughout, appeared not to listen. Sauckel could not accept the verdict and insisted there had been a mistranslation. However, the most dramatic reaction was from Göring who, on the night of 15 October, when the scaffold had already been erected in the prison gymnasium in preparation for the executions a few hours later, committed suicide by swallowing a cyanide capsule. The prison guards saw his convulsions and burst in, only to see him die. How he obtained and retained the capsule has remained a mystery. The other executions proceeded smoothly, although Streicher, who had refused to get dressed, went to the scaffold crying 'Heil Hitler'. The bodies were subsequently cremated and, according to the official announcement, the ashes scattered in a river 'somewhere in Germany'.

Further trials continued to April 1949 and included more party men, especially those associated with the concentration camps, as well as industrialists and doctors. Of these, the one that attracted the most interest was the Doctors' Trial, which heard evidence against 23 German physicians who conducted experiments on concentration camp prisoners. The impact of the trials on the German people is difficult to assess. Although many were appalled by the details that came to light and some felt events deeply, the majority are likely to have felt detached, accepting that the accused were responsible and feeling no degree of complicity.

A closer look

More recent Nazi war trials

In 1958 a Central Office of the Justice departments of the various states of Germany was set up near Stuttgart to coordinate further investigations into alleged Nazi war crimes, and by 1964 it had gathered evidence for 700 cases – most of which reached courts in the late 1960s. The Simon Wiesenthal Centre, set up by a Jewish man determined to find justice, was particularly active in helping

Activity
Stretch and challenge

Were the Nuremberg trials fair? Although the answer is 'yes' insofar as the verdicts were not decided in advance, the Nuremberg trials posed a number of moral questions. Consider these in groups:

■ By what law were the Nuremberg criminals judged?

■ Can people be punished for actions which were not a crime at the time they were committed?

■ Had the victors any right to punish Germans, while ignoring wartime behaviour on the allied side?

■ Does 'punishment' of this sort serve any purpose?

gather evidence for such trials. In 1969 a German law, by which prosecutions for murder had to be brought within 20 years, was repealed in order to enable Nazi war trials to continue and they still occasionally occur in the present day.

At the time of writing in April 2009, Ukrainian-born John Demjanjuk, aged 89 years and a retired car mechanic from Cleveland, Ohio, is in the process of being extradited to Germany. He was a member of the Red Army, captured by the Germans and then trained by the Nazis to help run the death camps. In February 2009, details of Aribert Heim, a 'wanted' Nazi doctor who had performed operations on prisoners without anaesthesia, removed organs from healthy inmates, injected poison into hearts for experimentation and taken the skull of at least one victim as a souvenir, were brought to light. He had been able been able to live out his life under an assumed name in Egypt, where he had died in 1992. However, since there can be few remaining survivors of the era and most of the remaining witnesses will now be very elderly, it is very unlikely that there will be many more prosecutions for crimes committed during the Third Reich.

Denazification

Initially the allied soldiers were under orders for strict non-fraternisation (not mixing or socialising) with the German populace. An official warning issued to British soldiers read:

> There will be no brutality about a British occupation, but neither will there be softness or sentimentality. You may see many pitiful sights. Hard luck stories may somehow reach you. Some of them may be true but most will be hypocritical attempts to win sympathy. For, taken as a whole, the German is brutal when he is winning, and is very sorry for himself when he is beaten. When you meet the Germans you will probably think they are very much like us. But they are not really so much like us as they look. The Germans have, of course, many good qualities, but for centuries they have been trained to submit to authority. That is one reason why they accepted Hitler. He ordered them about, and most of them liked it. All they had to do was obey and leave the thinking to him. It also saved them, they thought, from responsibility. The vile cruelties of the Gestapo were nothing to do with them. That is the tale that will be told over and over again by the Germans. But the German people cannot slide out of their responsibility quite so easily.

4

Activity

Source analysis

This source makes a number of assertions and generalisations. Identify these and suggest evidence that might a) support and b) disprove this opinion.

However, non-involvement was clearly impractical when it came to addressing the many problems facing Germany and as early as June 1945, the prohibition against speaking to German children was made less strict. In July it became possible to speak to German adults in certain circumstances. In September, the whole non-fraternisation policy was dropped in order to involve the Germans themselves in the process of getting basic services running again and dealing with the refugee problem. Nevertheless, most Germans, in allied eyes, remained tainted by their Nazi past and those who had held positions of authority and who were most needed to help, all the more so.

Although the Wehrmacht (the German army) was disbanded, the Nazi Party dissolved and the Nuremberg Trials set up to deal with the most important Nazis, transforming a whole society that had been 'Nazified' over the previous 12 years was a far more complex task. While the Russians saw Nazism as part of a complete social and economic system that had to be destroyed, the Western powers were more inclined to see it as an individual and perhaps psychological problem linked to the recent history of Germany.

Denazification in the Russian zone

In the Russian zone, denazification became part of a major restructuring of society, replacing old class distinctions and effecting changes in the running of industry and business. Nazis in prominent positions, for example in political, administrative, educational and judicial posts were purged and altogether approximately 520,000 Nazis in government and industry were removed up to 1948, although the medical profession was less thoroughly 'cleansed'. The need for trained professionals was a major handicap to the denazification programme and lessened its thoroughness. Essentially, the Russians denazified where it suited them, keeping some Nazis in high positions and treating others brutally in prisoner camps, or deporting and executing them without trial.

A closer look

Denazification in Berlin in 1945

In Berlin, which remained under Soviet control for two and a half months before the four-power administration could be installed in mid-July, arrests and dismissals began immediately. In the Municipal Authority's report of July 1945 it was stated that:

- 1,677 people had been dismissed from the municipal administration
- 7,631 from the postal and telecommunications service
- 1,102 from the Higher Fiscal Board
- 903 from BEWAG, the electric power supply company.

All Nazi teachers and administrators in schools were also dismissed and by September 1945, there were over 4,000 teachers' assistants and new trainee teachers. Old textbooks were withdrawn and new education guidelines established.

Ex-Nazi employees and party members were given the lowest level of ration card and pay and were only employable as 'reconstruction and conscription workers'.

'Nazi property' had to be reported and was confiscated and 1,400 businesses belonging to 'active Nazis' were closed. Furthermore, all swastikas had been removed from the city, street names changed (by December, 677 streets had been renamed), postage stamps and official seals changed. A committee was also set up to help the 'Victims of Fascism' although this mainly helped those who had actively fought fascism, rather than simply suffered at its hands.

In 1947 the Russians offered a general amnesty to all those who, whatever their past, were prepared to help further the socialist society in East Germany. In 1948–49 restrictions on the activities and rights of former Nazis were removed and in 1952 full citizenship rights were given to all former Nazis who were not war criminals. All this was accompanied by an intense 're-education' campaign to promote socialism.

Fig. 8 *All references to Nazism disappeared*

Exploring the detail

Internment camps in the Soviet zone

Eleven internment camps, modelled on the Soviet gulags, were established in the Soviet occupation zone. Some, like Sachsenhausen and Buchenwald, were former concentration camps. Although officially for 'Nazi criminals', in practice these housed a variety of political opponents, members of the intelligentsia, bourgeoisie, aristocrats, and capitalists. Prisoners included children aged from as young as 14. Conditions were appalling and worsened when food rations were reduced in November 1946. Beatings, sleep deprivation and psychological torture were accompanied by rape from sadistic guards, inadequate clothing and insanitary living conditions. Around 154,000 Germans were interned in these special camps and approximately 43,000 died in them.

Denazification in the western zones

Initially, there was a similar mass internment of those associated with Nazism. The SS were rounded up, along with Foreign Office diplomats, generals, industrialists and others who had supported the Nazi cause. According to the US Directive JCS 1067 of April 1945:

> All members of the Nazi Party who have been more than nominal participants in its activities, all active supporters of Nazism or militarism and all other persons hostile to allied purposes will be removed and excluded from public office and from positions of importance in quasi-public and private enterprises such as (1) civic, economic and labour organisations, (2) corporations and other organizations in which the German government or subdivisions have a major financial interest, (3) industry, commerce, agriculture, and finance, (4) education, and (5) the press, publishing houses and other agencies disseminating news and propaganda. Persons are to be treated as more than nominal participants in Party activities and as active supporters of Nazism or militarism when they have (1) held office or otherwise been active at any level from local to national in the party and its subordinate organisations, or in organisations which further militaristic doctrines, (2) authorised or participated affirmatively in any Nazi crimes, racial persecutions or discriminations, (3) been avowed believers in Nazism or racial and militaristic creeds, or (4) voluntarily given substantial moral or material support or political assistance of any kind to the Nazi Party or Nazi officials and leaders.

5

However, the three zones interpreted 'more than nominal support' for Nazism in slightly different ways and by the end of 1945, while 117,512 had been interned in the American zone, only half that number had been found in the British zone.

After this initial programme, the approach of the Western powers was generally different from that of the Russians. In the West it was not considered necessary to restructure society to eliminate Nazism. The emphasis was therefore more on looking at individual cases on their merits.

From June 1945, those dismissed from their jobs could appeal to an arbitration tribunal and present a testimony of good behaviour from priests, pastors, neighbours and colleagues to plead their case. These testimonials became known as 'Persilscheine' or 'Persil certificates', after the well-known brand of washing powder. Citizens arrived at the tribunals sullied – or in the 'brown shirt' of the Nazis – and emerged 'shining white' – with a clean record! The tribunals could hardly keep pace with the number of cases brought and long waiting lists soon built up.

The Americans took the lead in introducing the 'Fragebogen' – questionnaires asking about

Fig. 9 *The Persil machine in action – in brown and out white!*

all aspects of life under the Nazis. This system was copied, with varying degrees of thoroughness in the French and British zones.

As a result of responses, individuals were placed in a category and dealt with as follows:

- Major offenders – imprisoned.
- Offenders – imprisoned and re-educated.
- Lesser offenders – fined and re-educated.
- **Followers** or fellow-travellers – restricted in activities and employment and re-educated.
- Exonerated – given the right to return to the community as free citizens.

In March 1946, the 'Law for Liberation from National Socialism' (*Befreiungsgesetz*) established new tribunals, staffed by Germans but supervised by the allies, to investigate ex-party members. Around 3.6 million people came before these tribunals but the system was cumbersome and the easiest cases were addressed first, so by the time the more difficult ones gained a hearing, the treatment had become more lenient anyway. In the British zone nearly 90 per cent emerged as 'exonerated' but only just over a third in the American zone and a half in the French zone were pardoned. Furthermore, in the British zone only a tenth were deemed 'followers', compared to over half in the American zone and just under half in the French zone.

It was above all the practical problems that led to the abandonment of denazification by the early 1950s, when there was a swing back in the other direction. Until 1951 former civil servants were not allowed to stand for elected political posts, but in that year this was changed and they were given the opportunity to have their jobs back – or to retire on full pensions.

The effects of the denazification and re-education programme in the West

The effects of the denazification programme, rather like those of the war crime trials, are difficult to gauge. In all, it has been estimated that, within the western zones, around 870,000 people lost their jobs, at least temporarily, and 230,000 were detained, some for several years. However, most of those who were condemned in the 1945–47 period regained positions consistent with their social and educational background after this temporary interruption, simply because there was no alternative elite to replace them. In this sense denazification was a failure.

Despite this, there was no immediate re-emergence of Nazism in German society and certain groups and individuals took it upon themselves to renounce Nazism openly. The Protestant Church in Germany issued the 'Stuttgart Declaration of Guilt' in October 1945 which said, *'We accuse ourselves of German guilt and more importantly of the failure of the Churches to protest more courageously'*. However, the Nazi 'witch-hunt' helped increase resentment against the occupying powers among those in the middle classes who had suffered the most. This resentment may have helped encourage Germans to think of themselves more as victims of the Nazi regime than as complicit in it, and therefore needing to renounce it. Mary Fulbrook has claimed, *'the effects of the Western allies' policies were to feed the collective **amnesia** evident in much of post-war West German history and to compound the difficulties many West Germans experienced in coming to terms with their past'*.

Re-education was similarly confused in its execution. The school system was not radically restructured in the west and within the universities, academics and administrators with links to Nazism often retained their posts. There was very little formal attempt to change attitudes, although films such as *Todesmühlen* (about the concentration camps) no doubt shocked their audience. The new press, which accepted its duty to discredit Nazism and inculcate new values, probably did the most to 're-educate', but no doubt the most effective re-educator of all was the revival of the economy, which accompanied Germany's new political arrangements and ensured there was no desire to return to the past.

 Cross-reference

The revival of the economy is discussed in Chapters 2 and 3.

 Activity

Thinking point

How would you set about constructing an education system to 'denazify' the Germans after the years of propaganda during the Third Reich? How might new values be taught at a) primary, b) secondary and c) university level?

Further stretch and challenge

Is the purpose of education political?

Debate

Was the ambition to denazify and re-educate necessary? Was it too ambitious? Could it have been carried out more effectively? Discuss your ideas with a partner and then present your views to the rest of the class to consider.

Summary question

To what extent was the Nazi legacy eradicated in Germany in the years 1945 to 1946?

2 The Emergence of the Two Germanies

In this chapter you will learn about:

- the political developments that took place after 1945 and how Konrad Adenauer emerged as a leader in the West

- the differing economic developments of the eastern and western zones

- the breakdown in relations between East and West in 1948–49

- the impact of the currency reforms and the experience of the Berlin Blockade

- the creation of the FRG and GDR.

A shadow has fallen upon the scenes so lately lighted by the allied victory. Nobody knows what Soviet Russia intends to do in the immediate future, or what are the limits, if any, to their expansive tendencies. From Stettin in the Baltic to Trieste in the Adriatic, an iron curtain has descended across the continent. Behind that line lie all the capitals of the ancient states of central and eastern Europe – Warsaw, Berlin, Prague, Vienna, Budapest, Belgrade, Bucharest and Sofia. All these famous cities are subject to a very high and increasing measure of control from Moscow. The Communist parties are seeking everywhere to obtain totalitarian control.

Our difficulties and dangers will not be removed by closing our eyes to them. They will not be removed by merely waiting to see what happens, nor will they be relieved by a policy of appeasement. What is needed is a settlement, and the longer this is delayed the more difficult it will be, and the greater our dangers will become. From what I have seen of our Russian friends and allies during the war, I am convinced there is nothing they admire so much as strength, and there is nothing for which they have less respect than military weakness.

1

Winston Churchill's famous 'Iron Curtain' speech, delivered at Fulton, Missouri, America on 5 March 1946, illustrates the breakdown in trust that took place between the allied powers in the years immediately after 1945. It was in Germany, more than anywhere else between 1946 and 1949, that this breakdown was to have its greatest impact.

The allied occupation

Political developments

Fig. 1 *Boundaries were established between the occupation zones*

While the allies had been united in their fight against Nazism and committed to the eradication of what had been Germany's only political party for the previous 12 years, they were far less united, or even certain in themselves, as to how Germany should develop politically. Although they all, except France, initially envisaged a united Germany, they wanted it on their own terms. When the first military governors of occupied Germany, the three victorious allied commanders, Zhukov, Montgomery, and Eisenhower left the country, future developments were supposedly in the hands of the Allied Control Council in Berlin. Here, the leaders were General Vassily Sokolovsky (USSR), General Sir Brian Robertson (UK) and General Lucius D. Clay (US).

However, political and economic decisions were often made within the four separate zones, and influenced by the occupiers' ideologies, irrespective of the other allies. Consequently, there was a considerable discrepancy in the way the zones developed.

The USSR undoubtedly had the firmest idea of what it wanted and political development in the Russian zone was shaped by **Marxist-Leninism**. Indeed, it is likely that Stalin believed that if he could establish communism quickly and firmly in the East, this would then become the dominant government when Germany re-emerged as a single united country.

The Western powers, however, while favouring 'democratic' government, were anxious to avoid strong centralisation or to permit any resurgence of Nazism or even more emphatically the spread of communism in their zones.

The Russians had the advantage in establishing their political ideas in that they controlled Berlin between April and July 1945; before the other allies finally arrived to take up their joint control there. Consequently, SMAD – the Soviet Military Administration in Germany – was able to gain a headstart in the establishment of a communist-dominated government in the East.

The Soviet zone

Key terms

Marxist-Leninism: the German philosopher Karl Marx had put forward the view that history was the product of class struggles, from which would emerge a society in which all were equal. Lenin had adapted Marxist theory to emphasise the need for the Bolshevik/Communist Party to lead the proletariat in bringing about this state of equality. It is this Marxist-Leninist theory that is generally implied in references to the practice of communism.

Fig. 2 *Soviet soldiers entering Frankfurter Allee*

On Monday, 30 April 1945, the day of Hitler's suicide, ten German communists led by Walter Ulbricht were flown from the Soviet Union to join Zhukov's army just outside Berlin. A further ten were similarly attached to Marshal Konev's armies near Dresden, while a third group was sent to the Soviet armies in Mecklenburg. Each was given the task of setting up a local government in their area as soon as the fighting stopped.

Walter Ulbricht, 1893–1973

Walter Ulbricht came from Leipzig. He joined the SPD and, in turn, the German Communist Party, studied at the International Lenin School in Moscow and in 1928 was elected as a deputy for Potsdam and served as a Reichstag deputy until 1933. When Hitler came to power, Ulbricht went abroad, fought in the Spanish Civil War with the International Brigade and, from 1937–45, lived in the Soviet Union. He returned to Germany in 1945 and helped to found the SED. He became deputy chairman of the GDR Council of Ministers in 1949. He was much favoured by Stalin and in 1950 became General Secretary of the SED Central Committee (a title changed to First Secretary in 1953). In 1953 Ulbricht suppressed a workers' uprising in East Germany and in 1968 he applauded the Soviet crushing of the Prague Spring in Czechoslovakia. However, he never got on well with Leonid Brezhnev and on 3 May 1971 was forced to resign from virtually all of his public functions, officially because of poor health.

■ **Did you know?**

'It is crystal clear: it must appear democratic, but we must have all the strings in our hands.' Ulbricht's comment was reported by Wolfgang Leonhard, who was one of Ulbricht's deputation but who later defected to the West in the early 1950s and published *Die Revolution Entlässt Ihre Kinder* (The Revolution Casts Its Children Aside). Leonhard was the son of a German communist mother, and grew up in the Soviet Union in the 1930s and 1940s. He returned to Germany in 1945 but defected to Yugoslavia in 1948. His first-hand account gives us insight into communist plans and policy during the 1945–48 period.

The Ulbricht group in Berlin began action as soon as the city surrendered at the beginning of May, arranging the installation of local German mayors and other officials for all Berlin boroughs. Ulbricht ordered communists to stand as mayors in the four workers' boroughs of Wedding, Neukoelln, Friedrichshain, and Lichtenberg and 'anti-Fascist bourgeois' mayors to stand elsewhere, with a communist as their deputy mayor. In addition, communists were installed as heads of education and the police in each district. Ulbricht stated, '*It is crystal clear: it must appear democratic, but we must have all the strings in our hands.*'

By mid-May 1945, a German language radio station had been set up under communist control and a city-wide government had been installed. Dr Arthur Werner, an independent 'anti-fascist', was named Lord Mayor of Berlin, but Karl Maron, a veteran German communist and one of the Ulbricht group, was named as the First Deputy Lord Mayor. Of the 18 city officials working under the mayor, nine were former KPD (German Communist Party) members.

The Soviets sent Wilhelm Pieck from Moscow in June 1945, to establish political parties to form an 'Anti-Fascist Democratic Bloc'. He was also responsible for seeing that land reforms were carried out, while Erich Honecker was given the task of setting up the 'Free German Youth' (FDJ).

Wilhelm Pieck, 1876–1960

Wilhelm Pieck came from eastern Germany and had trained as a carpenter. He had joined the SPD before World War I and the KPD in 1918. In 1933, when Hitler became Chancellor, he left Germany and in 1935 moved to Moscow. From 1938 to 1943, he was General Secretary of the Communist International. In 1943, Pieck was among the founders of the National Committee for a Free Germany (NKFD) and returned to Germany in 1945 with the victorious Red Army. In 1949 Pieck was elected president of the newly established German Democratic Republic (GDR). Pieck served as the only president of the GDR until his death in 1960.

■ **Cross-reference**

Erich Honecker is profiled in Chapter 5, page 74.

Although America, Britain and France had prohibited all political activity in their own occupation zones, in the Soviet zone, SMAD unilaterally licensed the official formation of political parties in June. This was primarily undertaken to legitimise the activities of the German Communist Party (KPD). A number of political parties consequently emerged, as well as the KPD and socialist SPD and other Communist Party 'puppet' parties. These included the conservative Christian Democratic Union (CDU), the German Liberal Party (LDPD), the more right-wing National Democratic Party of Germany (NPDP) and the Democratic Peasants' Party (DBD).

By the time the Americans, British and French arrived in Berlin at the beginning of July 1945, they could do little other than approve the Soviet arrangements, although they were probably unaware of the full implications of the developments.

Since the KPD proved not to be strong enough to win local elections alone, the Soviets put pressure on the SPD to merge with this party, and in April 1946 the SED or Socialist Unity Party of Germany was created. This party was to become the dominant power in political development of the Soviet zone and other left-wing parties were forced to support it in an 'anti-fascist bloc'. In November 1946, the SED drew up plans for a German Democratic Republic as an independent east German state, but while there was still a chance of the creation of a neutral single German state friendly to the USSR, the Russians were reluctant to go down this route. It was only as it became clear, in the course of 1947, that the British and Americans were set to revive the German economy within a capitalist framework, that Stalin began, cautiously, to strengthen the Soviet zone.

The western zones

Political activity in the US and British zones of occupation started later than in the Soviet zone. Despite their commitment to democratisation and denazification, the allies suppressed the German 'antifas' or anti-fascist groups that sprang up in the final months of war to combat the Nazis, since they were fearful of any German 'political organisations'. Their chosen path to democracy was by re-educating Germans in responsible administration at a local level only, leaving the occupying powers in firm overall control.

To permit this, licences to form parties to participate in local elections were made available, from September 1945, but these were only for parties believed to be democratic in type. As a result, four major parties emerged: the socialist SPD, the Christian Democrats (CDU/CSU, the latter being the Bavarian party), the communist KDP, and the Liberal Democrats (LDP), which later became the Free Democrats (FDP) combining liberal principles with support for business. Many smaller parties also received licences, such as the *Bund der Heimatvertriebenen und Entrechteten* or BHE (The League of Expellees and Refugees). In some respects, the emerging political scene in the West looked as though it might echo the days of Weimar!

However, in the local and **Land** elections the CDU/CSU led by Konrad Adenauer and the SPD led by Kurt Schumacher were overwhelmingly the most successful parties. The Communists and Liberal Democrats gained some representation, but seldom won overall control, while most of the smaller parties were unsuccessful and were subsequently disbanded.

Activity

Thinking point

Draw a timeline to show the steps by which the USSR ensured communist domination in the eastern zone.

1. Why do you think communists were placed in the position of deputies rather than made mayors in most districts of Berlin?

2. Why do you think the SPD was reluctant to merge with the KPD in 1946?

Cross-reference

The Weimar Republic is outlined in Chapter 1, page 15.

Key terms

Land (plural Länder): a German state.

Exploring the detail

The July 1944 Bomb Plot

The July Bomb Plot of 1944 was an abortive attempt to blow up Hitler, led by a group of army officers under Count Stauffenberg.

Key profiles

Konrad Adenauer, (1876–1967)

Konrad Adenauer was a Catholic who trained as a lawyer and joined the Centre Party. He was Mayor of Cologne (1917–33) and strongly opposed Hitler and Nazism. He was imprisoned in 1934, released but rearrested in September 1944, after accusations of involvement in the July Bomb Plot. He only avoided being sent to Buchenwald concentration camp by feigning a heart attack. In 1945, he re-entered politics and helped form the Christian Democratic Union (CDU). In 1949 he became the first Chancellor of the Federal Republic of Germany (West Germany), a post he held until 1963.

Kurt Schumacher, (1895–1952)

Kurt Schumacher was a Prussian who fought in World War I but was discharged in 1915, having lost an arm. He studied law and economics and joined the SPD, working as a journalist. In 1930, he was elected to the Reichstag but was arrested by the Nazis in 1933 and remained in Dachau, where he lost a leg, until 1943. He was briefly rearrested after the July 1944 Bomb Plot, released again but marked for execution. He went into hiding in Hanover until the British arrived. He wanted to rebuild the SPD to protect Germany from political extremism and was elected chairman in 1946.

The emergence of Adenauer

Fig. 3 *Adenauer leaving Allied Military Headquarters in Berlin*

Konrad Adenauer had been Mayor of Cologne (Köln) before the war and when American troops seized the area, he was offered his old post back. Although 69 years old, he had a reputation as a good administrator and opponent of Nazism. However, when the British replaced the Americans, he was dismissed (supposedly for negotiating with the French about the possibility of a separate Rhineland state) and he turned instead to reviving his old political party – the German Centre Party – which had been a conservative Catholic party. He believed it needed to broaden its base to include all faiths that supported democracy.

In January 1946, Adenauer called a political meeting which led to the foundation of the new political party – the Christian Democratic Union (CDU) which was committed to combining socialism with Christianity. Since he was the oldest man in attendance, Adenauer was informally confirmed as its leader and he worked diligently to build up support for the new party. He stressed that his party stood for 'the dignity of the individual' and he condemned both left-wing socialism and right-wing Nazism as political ideologies based on materialistic values, which violated human dignity.

With the backing of the Catholic Church and influential Cologne businessmen, Adenauer rapidly advanced from head of the local CDU to chairman of the party for the British zone (1946). He was favoured by the occupying powers as a conciliator and in 1948 he was elected President of the Parliamentary Council, a body chosen that year to draw up the political foundations for a new German Republic.

The success of democratisation

'Re-education' in the ways of democracy was not always easy. For older Germans 'democracy' was associated with the disasters of the Weimar Republic and its continuation by those who were 'occupiers' was regarded with suspicion. It posed problems for the occupiers too.

- The Americans, for example, were uncertain what to do when an ex-Nazi mayor was elected by a democratic vote!
- The French, based on their fears, rivalry, and long history of conflict with Germany, controlled political activity for much longer than the other three occupation powers and were very suspicious of the revival of German political activity.
- The British encountered problems when they tried to replace the traditional German proportional representation system with their own 'first past the post' electoral system.

However, gradually, working local governments were established in the western allied zones and German politicians, elected by the German people, rather than appointed by the occupying powers, came to play an important part in the reconstruction of Germany.

Economic developments

The allies were faced with the enormous task of rebuilding the war-torn German economy and, at the same time, satisfying the allied demand for 'punishment' and reparations to help their own people. Each sector reshaped the economy according to its own ideas, but once again, it was the Soviets that had the more determined and consistent idea of what they wanted to achieve.

The Soviet zone

Although the Soviet zone had faced rather less war damage than the western zones and its loss of productive capacity was roughly 15 per cent compared with 21 per cent in the West, the Soviets' initial policy was to take the maximum amount of reparations (possibly as much as three times what had originally been agreed at Potsdam). They aimed to take their occupation costs from the zone while dismantling what productive capacity was left. This provides some evidence that the Soviets were not expecting the occupation and division of Germany to last and that they were anxious to take what they could while they could. Productive

Activity

Making a summary chart

Make a summary chart to illustrate the main differences between approaches to the revival of politics in the Russian and British/American zones.

■ Cross-reference

To recap on the agreements reached at the Potsdam Conference, look back to Chapter 1, pages 17–18.

capacity in the Soviet sector was reduced to around 50 per cent of that of 1939 and whole industrial plants were shipped, with varying degrees of success, to the USSR.

In July 1945, a new system of centralised state banking was introduced to replace private banks, and private insurance companies were merged into five public corporations – one for each Land within the Soviet sector.

From September 1945, the Soviets began to nationalise mines and factories and in June 1946, 25 Soviet-owned joint-stock companies *Sowjetische Aktiengesellschaften* (SAGs) were formed by amalgamating 213 firms. Any enterprises that had belonged to Nazi activists were taken over and in April 1948, these expropriated enterprises became *Volkseigene Betriebe* (VEBs). VEBs and SAGs controlled 60 per cent of industry by 1948, and the remaining private sector was gradually worn down through taxes and price and planning measures.

Fig. 4 *The break-up of a former landed estate in East Germany*

■ Key terms

Junkers: the traditional aristocratic landlords who lived in eastern Germany.

The Soviets also sought to get rid of the **Junker** landowners and in September 1945, 7,000 large estates of over 100 hectares (247 acres), as well as those which had belonged to Nazi activists, were seized. The land was turned into large collective state farms (*Volkseigene Güter*). However, to avoid creating unnecessary antagonism, peasants and landless refugees were permitted to work smallholdings. These were nevertheless kept deliberately small so that their recipients would be dependent on state support.

In June 1947, in response to economic developments in the western zones, the Soviets set up the German Economic Commission to coordinate economic policy and produce a development plan for the Soviet zone. This Commission was made up of the heads of the ministries and chairmen of the trade unions and farmers' association within the zone and all were controlled by the SED. In essence this was to be the nucleus of a new East German state, although at the time, the Russians played down its significance and emphasised that it was under the control of the Soviet military government.

The western zones

Initially, the occupiers in the western zones adopted quite a tough approach, intending to eliminate Germany's war potential and provide reparations while permitting sufficient reconstruction to satisfy the immediate needs of the German people.

The Level-of-Industry Plan, agreed by the Four Powers in March 1946, suggested that:

- Germany's standard of living should be kept to its 1932 level and should not exceed that of other European countries
- industrial capacity should be reduced to 50–55 per cent of the 1938 level
- approximately 1,546 plants should be dismantled in the western zones
- there should be limits on the output of industries
- armaments and war-related industries should be banned
- coal output (alone) should be expanded to provide for reparations and reconstruction.

However, the Russians refused to accept the American proposal that the Germans should only pay reparations once Germany had become economically self-supporting and that the Russian seizures of plant in the eastern zones should be deducted from the total reparations due to that country.

In May, the American governor, Lucius D. Clay, announced that America would no longer provide the Russians with goods from their zone until the Russians stopped acting independently and started treating Germany as one economic unit. The Soviet Union, in turn, broke its agreement to deliver agricultural products from its eastern zone to the western ones and began obstructing the administrative work of all four sectors.

This failure to cooperate over reparations, coupled with the spread of communism in eastern Europe, led the Americans to believe that any weakening of the western German economy would leave it open to a communist takeover and consequently the Western powers came to adopt a new approach.

At the Paris Conference of 1946, the Americans invited the other zones to work together in an economic union, but only the British were in favour. They had already suggested the development of an economically united western 'partial state' in the 'Bevin Plan' of February 1946, as a way of reducing the costs of their German occupation and helping a western European economic recovery. The Americans also favoured this as the best way of resisting a communist-dominated central government.

In a speech given in Stuttgart on 6 September 1946 by the US Secretary of State, James Byrnes, it was announced that heavy industries would no longer be dismantled if they were necessary for a German peacetime economy and that America was ready to merge its zone economically with other zones in the interest of the growth of trade and communications. Both the Soviets and the French rejected this proposal, the former on ideological grounds and the latter because it wished to see Germany develop into a loose confederation of states and feared moves towards stronger centralisation.

Bizonia

America and Britain went ahead and united their zones on 1 January 1947, creating a Bizone (soon to be known as Bizonia), to allow for a more efficient joint economic administration. It was headed by a joint Economic Council and an executive committee which acted on behalf of the eight Länder and was staffed by Germans. There were six boards to manage economic activity: Economics, Food and Agriculture, Transport, Communications, Civil Service, and Finance. The British and Americans went to great lengths to avoid French and Soviet charges that they were forming any type of political unification, so these boards had their headquarters in four different cities and worked under the supervision of the Bipartite Control Office, headed by General Lucius D. Clay for America and General Brian Robertson for Britain. However, since the members of the boards were elected and the elected representatives were chosen from the political parties already established in the West, it was hard to see these developments as anything other than steps towards a new political unit.

Beyond these developments, there was little actual transformation of the economic structure in the western zones, although subtle pressure was used to weaken communist and socialist influences in the trade unions. Union activity was strictly limited to economic matters regarding wages and conditions, even though this went against the West's professed democratic principles.

Decartelisation made limited progress. Some trusts and cartels were broken up. The Deutsche Bank, Dresdner Bank and Commerzbank, for example, were split into 30 different groups and I. G. Farben and some large steel and coal conglomerates were broken down. Such rationalisation as took place, however, was not undertaken for punitive reasons, but to reduce 'bureaucratic unwieldiness' and help German economic activity by making German production, according to the historian Ralph Willett, *'leaner and more efficient than it had been'*.

> Decartelisation was thwarted by large American firms seeking a strong industrial system. Much more could have been done to transform the German economy into a system of decentralised competitive forms and to encourage a new class of entrepreneurs, untainted by monopoly capitalism and a Nazi past, had these been the priorities of the occupying powers. Small wonder that Kurt Schumacher, leader of the SPD should describe the motivation of the US as 'a mixture of misplaced reformist zeal, shrewd power politics and plain greed'.

2

On 12 March 1947, with a clear allusion to the way the USSR was trying to dominate the eastern states of Europe, President Truman gave his famous speech to the US Congress, in which he declared *'I believe that it must be the policy of the United States to support free peoples who are resisting attempted subjugation by armed minorities or by outside pressures'*. This 'Truman Doctrine' to 'contain' communism and prevent Soviet expansionism was the final straw for any attempt at cooperation in Germany.

A council of Foreign Ministers meeting in Moscow in March to April 1947 failed to agree on a German peace treaty or on ways forward to German unification. Consequently, Clay was instructed by the US government, in April 1947, *'to proceed vigorously with the strengthening of the bizonal organisation in conjunction with Robertson [the British Military Governor], and to expedite the upward revision of the level of bizonal industry to ensure the self-sufficiency of the area.'*

On 5 June 1947, the US Secretary of State George Marshall, in a speech at Harvard University, called for a European recovery programme. He promised large sums of money, so-called 'Marshall Aid', on American terms. This plan was unsurprisingly rejected by the USSR (and its east European satellite states) in July, because it was based on a free market economy and would benefit American exports. However, the offer of Marshall Aid was to mark an important step forward in western German economic

Did you know?

The Cold War

The years 1946–47 witnessed a breakdown in relations between the USSR and the Western democracies which became known as the Cold War. This was a period of conflict and competition between two very different ideologies. While America believed in democracy and capitalism, embracing personal freedom and freedom of the media, the USSR was a communist autocratic dictatorship, with a commitment to equality, but a society controlled by secret police and strict censorship. The rivalry between the two superpowers was played out in a variety of ways including military and technological developments, including the space race. It involved costly defence spending; a massive conventional and nuclear arms race; and, at times, actual conflict through other countries, such as Korea.

Fig. 5 *Poster promoting the Marshall Plan. What is the message of the poster?*

recovery. While America accepted that *'an orderly and prosperous Europe requires the economic contribution of a stable and prosperous Germany'*, the decision to seek Marshall Aid on behalf of Bizonia necessitated changes to improve economic efficiency and output.

Consequently, the 'Level-of-Industry' Plan was revised in August 1947 and production in the American/British zones was permitted to increase to 70–75 per cent of the 1938 level.

The preamble to the revised plan stated:

> Experience has shown the necessity for revision of the plan which was based on specific assumptions that have not been fulfilled. Neither the bizonal area nor all of Germany can regain economic health under the plan as it now stands. Moreover, it has become increasingly apparent that under present conditions Germany cannot contribute her indispensable part to the economic rehabilitation of Europe as a whole. Consideration has been given throughout to the necessity for ensuring that the bizonal plan be assimilated into a plan for Germany as a whole. The offer to the other occupying powers to join the bizonal area in developing a unified German economy still stands. The plan has been developed with due regard to the hope that this offer will be accepted.

 3

In 'How Germany was Divided', published by the Ministry of Foreign Affairs in East Germany in 1966, the Soviets gave a very different picture of what happened:

> In 1946–47 the Western powers were stubbornly opposing the Soviet proposal to form a central German government. They pursued, in their occupation zones, an ever sharper course towards the division of Germany, at first by forming the bizone from the American and British zone. They knew they were in full accord with the West German big industrialists and their political spokesmen in the West German CDU, in particular, Konrad Adenauer.

 4

As is openly admitted in his book *Decision in Germany* by General Lucius D. Clay, it had already been decided by the USA on 26 May 1946 – ten months after the Potsdam Agreement – *'to approach the British in order to learn of their readiness to unite their occupation zone with ours'*. Clay added that he had already discussed essentials of the bizone fusion with US Secretary of State, Byrnes, in the spring of 1946.

In the same year, on 2 December, the Foreign Ministers of America and Britain, Byrnes and Bevin, signed in New York the agreement on the economic merger of the American and British zones and the establishment of the bizone, soon to be known as 'Bizonia'. With their signatures, Byrnes and Bevin took a major step towards the division of Germany.

 Activity

Source analysis

Identify the ways in which Source 4 differs from Source 3 in relation to the development of Bizonia. Can you explain these differences?

 Activity

Revision exercise

Make a revision chart. On the left, list the actions of the Western powers between 1946 and 1948 and on the right, the Soviet reaction to these.

Exploring the detail

The development of Bizonia

By February 1948 Bizonia had its own supreme court and its economic council had the right to raise money by taxation. When, in April, the OEEC (Organisation for European Economic Cooperation) was set up to organise the distribution of Marshall Aid, Bizonia was one of the 17 European states represented on it. It also developed its own central bank (see the section on pages 39–40 on currency reform).

Cross-reference

Walter Ulbricht is profiled on page 30.

The division of 1948–1949 and the influence of the Western powers

The Council of Foreign Ministers which met in London in November to December 1947 proved no more successful than that held in Moscow earlier in the year in reaching an agreement on Germany's future. The Americans and British therefore decided to go forward with their plans for further political reorganisation in the west regardless of the other powers, although they invited the French to reconsider their position.

In February to March 1948 (and in a subsequent session in April–May) the United States, UK and France (together with Belgium, Luxembourg and Holland) held a conference in London to discuss German affairs. The outcome was an agreement in favour of developing a federal form of government in western Germany, which the French accepted, in return for an agreement to detach the Saar economically. However, they initially held back from merging their zone with the rapidly developing Bizonia.

The USSR protested vehemently throughout the period of these conference meetings and the actions of the Western powers were repeatedly attacked by the German communist press and radio. In December 1947, Ulbricht, the first Secretary of the East German SED called the first of two 'People's Congresses' – the *Volkskongresse* – to try to win over public opinion against division in eastern and western Germany. Around a third of the delegates attending came from western Germany, but they were overwhelmingly from KPD-dominated areas. The second congress of March 1948 elected a German People's Council (*Volksrat*) of 400 delegates to draw up a new constitution, and prepare for a referendum on German unity. However, it was by then clear that hopes of a compromise had passed and the main purpose of these deliberations was to ensure that eastern Germany had a government structure prepared, should they need to declare an independent East German State.

There were also a number of incidents, many centred on Berlin, which escalated in the course of the year.

Table 1 *Clashes between the Soviets and the Western powers, January–June 1948*

Month	Incident	Result
January	Soviet guards stopped a British military train and detached two cars carrying German passengers travelling under British permission.	Petty interference increased tension.
February	Soviets delayed a US military train travelling to Berlin at the Soviet zone border, on a technicality.	Ill-feeling led to some angry exchanges at the Allied Control Council meetings, making its work more difficult.
11 February	The Western powers protested that they had been denied access to a political meeting in the Soviet sector of Berlin to which they had been invited by Germans. Sokolovsky claimed Berlin was part of the Soviet zone.	Tension increased over the future of a divided Berlin.
20 March	Sokolovsky demanded details of all agreements on western Germany reached by America, Britain and France in London in February and March. He was told he would receive a conference report when it had been considered by the home governments. Sokolovsky declared, '*I see no sense in continuing this meeting, and I declare it adjourned,*' and the entire Soviet delegation walked out.	Sokolovsky (the Allied Control Council chairman for March) did not call another meeting. This effectively ended the existence of the Allied Control Council for Germany.

Month	Incident	Result
31 March	Soviet order that baggage and personnel on military trains to and from Berlin had to be checked by their inspectors. Freight on military trains departing Berlin had to have a permit from the Soviet commander in Berlin.	The British/Americans rejected the regulations and ordered guards on military trains to proceed through the checkpoints and prevent Soviet personnel entering the trains.
31 March, evening	Three US military trains entered the Soviet zone. One guard allowed Soviet personnel to board the train and was allowed to continue. The other two trains refused Soviet entry and the Soviets had the trains shunted to a siding where they remained until morning (when they were backed out to the US zone). Two British military trains were treated similarly.	All US military trains to and from Berlin were cancelled and replaced by an airlift – the 'Little Lift' which lasted only about ten days. The US Air Force Europe (USAFE) flew in about 300 tons of supplies for the military garrison.
5 April	A Soviet fighter plane 'buzzed' and then collided with a British transport plane approaching the Berlin–Gatow airfield in the British Sector. Both aircraft crashed, killing the Soviet pilot and 14 passengers and crew of the British plane, including two Americans. The British demanded an inquiry and ordered fighter escort for unarmed planes until the Soviets could ensure their safety.	The Soviets expressed regret but denied intentional molestation of British aircraft in the Berlin corridor and claimed the British plane had violated air safety regulations and was to blame for the accident.
10 April–18 June	The Soviets eased their restrictions on allied military trains but intermittently interfered with rail, road, and barge traffic.	Unsuccessful attempt to dissuade the Western powers from their plans for a provisional West German government and a currency reform.

The currency reforms

Fig. 6 *Exchanging the old Reichsmark for the new Deutschmark in 1948*

Activity

Revision exercise

Convert the chart shown above into a labelled line graph of the months January to June 1948, showing graphically the comparative levels of tension across these six months.

Before the American and British plans for the creation of a western German government could become a reality, they felt it was necessary to create a central bank and undertake some reform of the grossly devalued German currency.

The *Bank Deutscher Länder* (which became the Bundesbank in 1958) was established early in 1948, to serve as the central bank for the three western zones. It was placed temporarily under the supervision of the

The currency reform

The Deutschmark became the basic unit of the new currency (replacing the Reichsmark) and every inhabitant was permitted to exchange 60 Reichsmarks on a 1 to 1 ratio, but any additional Reichsmarks were to be converted at 100 to 6.5. The currency reform was not a simple revaluation, but a comprehensive and complicated set of changes to wages, prices, public and private debt, involving exchange rates and banking reform. It took several years to have full effect, and in 1952, those who had lost savings through the war or currency reform were given compensation.

■ **Did you know?**

The Western allies discussed the option of allowing the Eastmark to become the sole currency for the whole of Berlin, subject to the control of a Four Power financial commission, but the talks broke down. It became obvious that the dispute was about more than currency reform and that the Soviets wanted to drive the Western powers from Berlin and force them to abandon their plans for a separate West German state.

Allied Bank Commission but was given authority to issue money and control foreign exchange. Discussions on currency reform followed, in consultation with German economists, and these developments finally forced the hand of the French. Since the Russians had refused to discuss the possibility of a currency reform for the whole of Germany and the United States was placing pressure on the French by refusing to offer any Marshall Plan funds for a separate French zone, they agreed, on 17 June, to include their zone in the plan for the establishment of a provisional West German government and the currency reform. Trizonia had been created.

The currency reform became effective in the three western zones on 20 June. It did not, however, apply to the western sectors of Berlin which were still considered to be under the Four Power Accord.

The Berlin Blockade

The Soviet authorities declared that the western currency reform had broken the Potsdam Agreement, which stipulated that Germany should be treated as a single economic unit, and that the new currency would not only be invalid in the Soviet zone and Berlin, but even possession of it would be considered a criminal offence.

To reinforce their disapproval, road and railway passenger traffic to and from Berlin was suspended and freight traffic reduced, officially to protect the Soviet zone from an influx of the old devalued currency.

Furthermore, on 23 June 1948 the SMAD issued an order proclaiming a currency reform for the Soviet zone and all sectors of Berlin, to commence the following day. The US, British and French commanders countered this by proclaiming that the western Deutschmark would come into use in the three western sectors of Berlin from 25 June, although they would allow the new Eastmark and Soviet zone postage stamps to be used there, unlike the East Berlin authorities, who outlawed West German currency and refused to handle mail with West Berlin stamps.

The tightening of restrictions on traffic entering West Berlin put the future of western control there in doubt. The only way the West could maintain their half of the city (comprising 2 million people) was to use the air. Initially this looked far from easy. Both the American Air Force and the Royal Air Force had been much reduced since the ending of the Second World War and the French had almost no planes available. There was also the fear that such an extreme measure might lead to further retaliation, perhaps even war with the USSR.

Nevertheless, Clay and Robertson, supported by President Truman, pressed ahead with a temporary airlift, hoping that this display of Western resilience might, after a few weeks, force the Soviet authorities to back down.

The first planes began arriving in Berlin on Saturday, 26 June and a joint Anglo-American military meeting on 29 June agreed that an airlift could supply 2,000–2,500 tons a day – sufficient to meet Berlin's food needs, even if the delivery of fuel might still fall short of requirements. Little did they realise that the airlift would last 11 months and would turn into a very efficient operation which, by April 1949, was supplying West Berlin with 7,845 tons per day.

The first month of the airlift was marked by considerable brinkmanship as each side attempted to outpace the other in threats and actions. One of the tenser moments came with the stationing of American B-29 bombers in England in July. These were known to be capable of delivering the atomic bomb and had Moscow within their range.

A closer look

The Berlin airlift

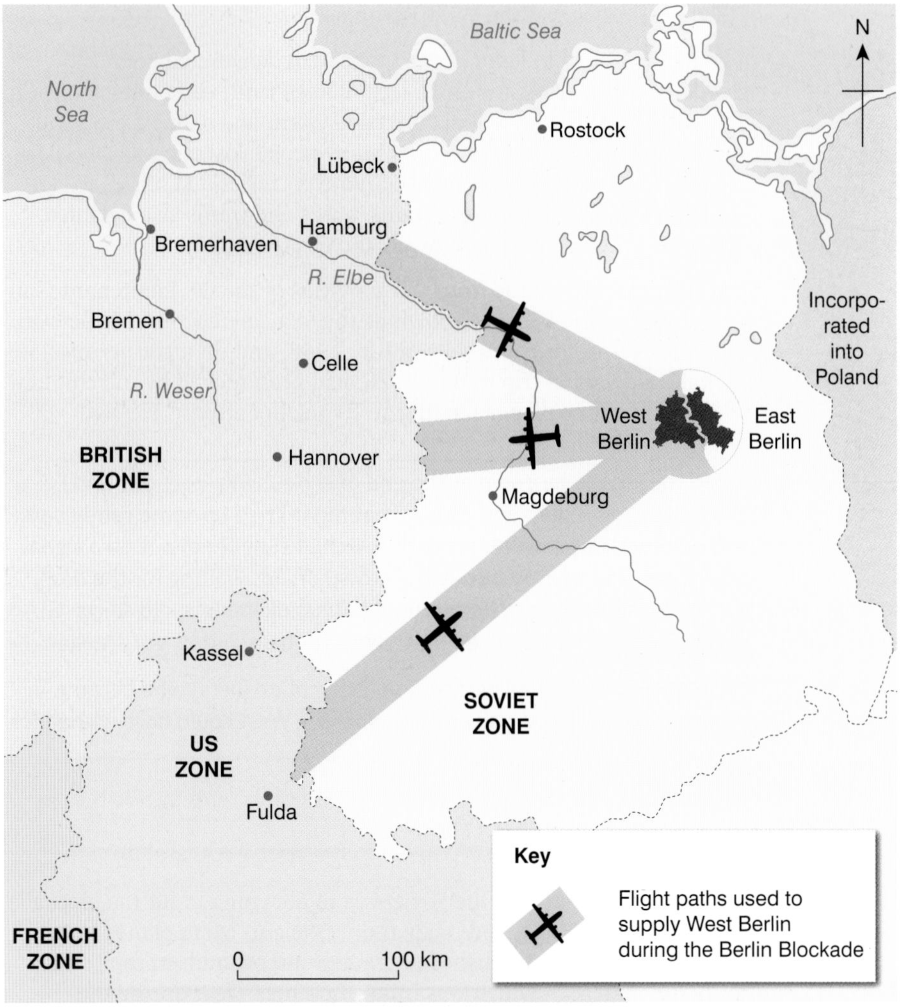

North Sea

Baltic Sea

N

● Rostock

Lübeck ●

Hamburg

Bremerhaven ●

● Bremen

R. Elbe

● Celle

R. Weser

**BRITISH
ZONE**

● Hannover

West
Berlin

East
Berlin

Incorpo-
rated
into
Poland

● Magdeburg

Kassel ●

**SOVIET
ZONE**

**US
ZONE**

Fulda

**FRENCH
ZONE**

0   100 km

Key

Flight paths used to
supply West Berlin
during the Berlin Blockade

Fig. 7 *The Berlin airlift routes*

At the beginning of the airlift, enthusiasm was high, but confusion often reigned as pilots who had not flown for some time were enlisted to fly ill-equipped planes and land on poor West Berlin runways. The work was demanding and dangerous as pilots and crews had to make two or more round trips a day, seven days a week, in all kinds of weather. For the West Berliners, too, it was a tense time. Although the Western powers promised protection, the communist press and radio constantly printed and broadcast reports and rumours of imminent allied departure, together with threats that those Berliners who supported allied policies would be

Fig. 8 *Berliners watching a US aircraft approaching Tempelhof Airport*

harshly dealt with when the allies left. However, for the most part, there was a positive response to the airlift and, perhaps for the first time since the war, a shared sense of comradeship between the allied personnel and the West Berliners.

The Berliners had to learn how to cope with dehydrated potatoes, powdered milk for infants and a lack of fresh fruit, vegetables and meat. They also battled with a dual currency system and reduced electrical supplies required severe rationing. Many people lost their jobs because the restricted power supplies forced many factories and offices to close. Underground and overground trains, buses and trams also operated restricted timetables because of gas and electric rationing.

A lighter moment came from the activities of the US Lieutenant Gail S. Halvorsen who became known as the 'chocolate flyer'. He flew on the 'Vittles' run for two weeks in July 1948, and then got permission to make a personal trip to Berlin. He had been moved by the children who waved to the planes landing at Tempelhof airport. He said:

'I told the kids to be down at the end of the runway next day and I'd drop them some gum and candy. That night I tied up some candy bars and gum in handkerchiefs and had my chief sling them out on a signal from me next day. Day by day the crowd of kids waiting for the drop got bigger, and day by day my supply of handkerchiefs, old shirts, GI sheets, and old shorts, all of which I use for parachutes, got smaller.'

Halverson was followed by a series of 'chocolate fliers', who became some of the best good-will ambassadors the West could have wished for.

Once it became apparent that the Soviets were not going to lift the blockade, the operation was expanded and made more efficient. More planes were found, a joint command established and a new airport built in the French sector of Berlin at Tegel – which was in itself no mean feat during the circumstances of the blockade. This became operational in December 1948, together with another new airport in the British zone at Celle-Wietzenruch.

The tonnage delivered to Berlin increased each month and despite some setbacks in the early winter months, by January 1949, there was even sufficient to begin stockpiling. It was obvious that the blockade had been broken and furthermore, a counter-blockade by the West, cutting off steel, chemicals, and manufactured goods from western Germany and western Europe to Soviet eastern Europe, from mid-1948, had begun to have an adverse economic effect on the Soviet zone.

Nevertheless, despite various diplomatic attempts to end the blockade and appeals to the United Nations, it was not until May 1949 that an agreement was finally reached. The Soviet Union lifted the blockade of Berlin and the Western powers ended their counter-blockade from midnight on 12 May 1949. In an attempt to settle the Berlin issue without any further military action, it was also agreed that another Council of Foreign Ministers would meet in Paris on 23 May 1949.

The creation of the FRG and GDR

By mid-1948 it was clear that Germany was heading for division. America and Britain continued to press ahead with their plans for the unification of the western zones, with the underlying hope that the successful

Activity

Creative thinking

Write a newspaper editorial on the Berlin Blockade from a) a Western perspective and b) a Soviet perspective. Try to justify the view taken in each.

development of West Germany would act as a 'magnet' to the citizens of the east and lead to an eventual unification on western democratic lines.

The Russian attitude was less certain. Even in the summer of 1948, the Russians were prepared to negotiate for a weak, demilitarised but united Germany, rather than see the strongly industrialised western half of Germany enter America's 'capitalist camp'. However, the Western allies feared that the Soviets would produce a communist-dominated Germany. In any case, many West German leaders, not least Konrad Adenauer, saw the advantages for themselves of integrating into western Europe.

The Federal Republic of Germany (FRG)

Despite the Berlin Blockade, moves towards the political unification of the western zones continued. The decisions of the London Conference (February–March 1948) were announced on 1 July and put to a meeting of the Minister-Presidents (prime ministers) of the western German Länder in Koblenz on 8 July 1948. They were asked to prepare a new **constitution** for West Germany; however, they argued that since Germany was still under an occupation statute, it could not have a separate constitution. The compromise solution was to create a *Grundgesetz* (Basic Law), which allowed for a provisional constitutional arrangement which could become official after a peace treaty had been signed and full unification taken place.

Fig. 9 *The new Basic Law*

A Parliamentary Council – made up of 65 delegates chosen by the Länder and under the chairmanship of Adenauer – was formed to draft this Basic Law in August. It was approved by the Western military governors and came into effect on 23 May 1949, with only Bavaria voting against it.

Following the creation of a new electoral law, the first national elections for the Federal Republic of Germany (known as the FRG in English and BRD – Bundes Republik Deutschland – in German) were held on 14 August 1949. There was a 78.5 per cent turnout and the first West German parliament was created. The results are shown in Fig. 10.

Fig. 10 *Seat allocation in the first West German parliament*

- 139 — Christian Democrats (CDU/CSU) conservative
- 131 — Social Democrats (SPD) socialist
- 52 — The Free Democrats (FDP) liberal
- 17 — The German Party (DP) right-wing conservative
- 15 — The Communists (KDP) Marxist

Key terms

Constitution: a set of laws by which a country is governed.

Did you know?

The creation of the FRG on 14 August 1949 was exactly four years after the dissolution of the Third Reich.

Cross-reference

More detail on each of the parties can be found in the glossary.

Key terms

Council of Europe: an organisation founded in 1949 to develop common and democratic principles throughout Europe based on the European Convention on Human Rights.

OEEC: the Organisation for European Economic Cooperation, which came into being on 16 April 1948. It emerged from the Marshall Plan and the Conference for European Economic Cooperation, which sought to establish a permanent organisation to continue work on a joint recovery programme and in particular to supervise the distribution of aid.

Cross-reference

The Volksrat is introduced earlier in this chapter, on page 38.

Cross-reference

Wilhelm Pieck and Walter Ulbricht are profiled in this chapter on page 30.

The office of Federal Chancellor, elected by the parliament, went to Konrad Adenauer by a majority vote of one and as a trade-off for their willingness to join Adenauer's coalition, Theodor Heuss, leader of the FDP, was elected by a parliamentary committee as the first West German president.

Military government ceased and was replaced by the Allied Commission consisting of John McCloy (America), Sir Brian Robertson (Britain – formerly the British military governor) and André François-Poncet (France).

Although the German politicians who drafted the law were disappointed that West Berlin was not to be part of the Federal State, they nevertheless went on to win several further concessions. In November 1949, the new federal government was admitted to the status of associate member of the **Council of Europe** and given direct representation on the **OEEC** and consular representation abroad. The allies also agreed to abandon the dismantling of industrial plants, although West Germany had to accept that control over the coalfields of the Ruhr would remain under a separate independent commission.

The German Democratic Republic (GDR)

The Soviet authorities were swift to react to these political developments in the West by taking corresponding measures. The Volksrat of March 1949 had already drawn up a constitution and in May, elections for a third Volkskongress were held. Voters were given a single list of candidates and also asked if they were 'for or against German unity and a just peace' which was actually a disguised way of asking for their support for an East German State which purported to support both of these. Two thirds voted in favour but the new state was not actually established until after the elections in the West in August had made it clear that there would be no last-minute compromise.

On 7 October 1949, the Volkskongress proclaimed the establishment of the German Democratic Republic (known as the GDR in English and DDR in its German form), *'as a powerful bulwark in the struggle for the accomplishment of the National Front of Democratic Germany'*. The Volksrat became the provisional government. Wilhelm Pieck, the communist hardliner, was 'elected' as president and Otto Grotewohl as prime minister on 12 October, despite having been a former Social Democrat. However, the real power lay with the deputy prime minister, Walter Ulbricht, who also held the post of Deputy of the Central Committee of the Socialist Unity Party (SED).

Key profile

Otto Grotewohl, (1894–1964)

Otto Grotewohl was a former member of the German SPD and had served in the Reichstag between 1925 and 1933 when he was forced into hiding. In 1945 he re-emerged and became chairman of the Central Council of the SPD. He played an important role in the merger of the KPD and SPD to form the SED in 1946, but he was really only a puppet prime minister with a figurehead role.

The SMAD changed its name to the Soviet Control Commission and most of its responsibilities were transferred to the new German state. Huge celebrations were ordered to mark the launching of the new Soviet state, in stark contrast to the creation of the FRG which was a fairly low-key affair. To the accompaniment of bands performing martial music, Pieck, Grotewohl and Ulbricht reviewed contingents of the People's

Police (the KVP), which had been set up in May 1948 and was comprised of 50,000 men and 20,000 border police by October 1949. It looked as though the one-party dictatorship was set to remain.

Activity

Thinking points

Who was most responsible for the division of Germany in 1949?

Look back over this chapter and in pairs, copy and complete the following table with as many ideas as you can think of. Compare your findings with the rest of your group.

Western powers	USSR	Germans

Learning outcomes

In this section you have seen how a war-torn and devastated Germany was set on the path of its future development in the years 1945 to 1949. You have learnt how the relationship between the four occupying powers broke down at the end of the war and that this was already apparent in the Potsdam Conference of July to August 1945. You have also seen how the four former allies adopted differing approaches to key aspects of the peace, such as denazification, and to the political and economic development of their respective zones. Finally, you have learnt how the struggles of 1948–49 and the failure of the Berlin Blockade led to the creation of two quite separate states – the FRG and GDR. How those two states developed in the years after 1949 will be the subject of the next two sections.

Practice question

How far were the years of allied occupation in Germany between 1945 and 1948 a period of 'missed opportunities'?

(45 marks)

Study tip In order to answer this question you will need to consider what is meant by 'missed opportunities'. It might be helpful to think of the 4 Ds – demilitarisation, denazification, decentralisation/decartelisation, and democratisation – since these were the avowed aims of the allied occupation. Plan your answer by making a list of the successes and failures of each of these 'aims' with separate columns for the western and eastern zones of Germany which addressed the issues in different ways. You may wish to add in other ideas too, particularly the opportunity to develop a unified Germany or even to reduce Cold War tension through cooperation in Germany. Before beginning to write, decide which way you will argue and whether you wish to blame anyone or anything in particular for the 'missed opportunities' or whether you feel that there were no 'missed opportunities' in the first place. Try to sustain a clear argument in your essay so that your conclusion grows naturally out of the supported views you have put forward.

In this chapter you will learn about:

- ■ the structure of government in the FRG

- ■ Adenauer's chancellorship

- ■ Erhard and the 'economic miracle' in the West

- ■ the results of economic and social change.

Fig. 1 *The German eagle emblem*

Cross-reference

Election results for 1965–89 are provided in Chapter 7, page 108, and for 1990 in Chapter 10, page 170.

Any visitor travelling to the city of Bonn today might find it hard to imagine that this was where the capital of the Federal Republic of Germany found its home. Despite its former historic associations, not least as Beethoven's birthplace, it was a comparatively small sleepy city in the British zone. It hardly compared with the more imposing Frankfurt but it was the wish of Adenauer, who came from that area. Some contemporaries joked that it was the *Bundeshauptdorf* (the federal main village). The later Chancellor Helmut Kohl rather more poignantly spoke of it as *'a symbol of conspicuous modesty'* and indeed, when the new German parliament convened there, it met in a building of a plain style and small scale that seemed to suit the sober mood of post-war Germany. Michael Stürmer commented, *'On the front wall, a symbol was fastened, an eagle with spread wings, less reminiscent of imperial glory than Churchill's wartime dictum that he wished the future Germany to be like a turkey, fat and impotent.'* However, under the careful chancellorship of Konrad Adenauer, the German turkey began to take flight, the name 'Bonn' assumed a new importance and decisions made there were to have repercussions for the rest of the world.

■ Political developments

The new governmental structure

The new Basic Law which established the framework of government for the FRG guaranteed freedom of expression, assembly, association and movement. It also committed the FRG to work for the full unity of Germany and to recognise all people of German descent (including those under Soviet or Polish rule) as citizens of the Federal Republic.

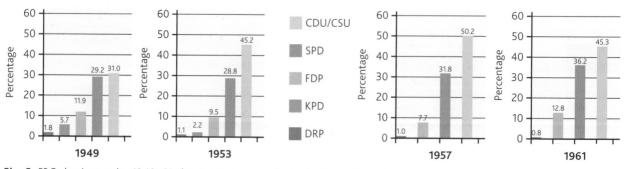

Fig. 2 *FRG election results, 1949–61, showing percentage of votes for the major parties*

The details of the governmental structure are outlined in Fig. 3.

The Federal Republic of Germany is a democratic and federal constitutional state.
The constitution is guarded over by the Federal Constitutional Court and includes
a statement of basic rights.

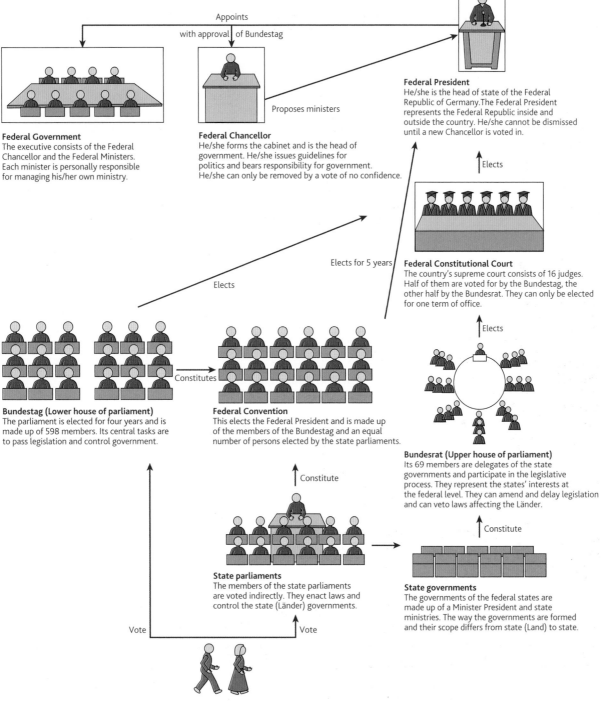

Appoints

with approval of Bundestag

Proposes ministers

Federal Government
The executive consists of the Federal
Chancellor and the Federal Ministers.
Each minister is personally responsible
for managing his/her own ministry.

Federal Chancellor
He/she forms the cabinet and is the head of
government. He/she issues guidelines for
politics and bears responsibility for government.
He/she can only be removed by a vote of no confidence.

Federal President
He/she is the head of state of the Federal
Republic of Germany. The Federal President
represents the Federal Republic inside and
outside the country. He/she cannot be dismissed
until a new Chancellor is voted in.

Elects

Elects for 5 years

Elects

Federal Constitutional Court
The country's supreme court consists of 16 judges.
Half of them are voted for by the Bundestag, the
other half by the Bundesrat. They can only be elected
for one term of office.

Elects

Constitutes

Bundestag (Lower house of parliament)
The parliament is elected for four years and is
made up of 598 members. Its central tasks are
to pass legislation and control government.

Federal Convention
This elects the Federal President and is made up
of the members of the Bundestag and an equal
number of persons elected by the state parliaments.

Bundesrat (Upper house of parliament)
Its 69 members are delegates of the state
governments and participate in the legislative
process. They represent the states' interests at
the federal level. They can amend and delay legislation
and can veto laws affecting the Länder.

Constitute

Constitute

State parliaments
The members of the state parliaments
are voted indirectly. They enact laws and
control the state (Länder) governments.

State governments
The governments of the federal states are
made up of a Minister President and state
ministries. The way the governments are formed
and their scope differs from state (Land) to state.

Vote

Vote

Electorate
All German citizens vote in general, direct, free, equal and secret elections. Each elector has 2 votes;
one for a party and one for a named local constituency representative.

Elections
Held every 4 years parties have to gain 5% of votes for a seat. A mixture of proportional representation
with seats allocated by the percentage of votes cast and first past the post in each constituency.

Fig. 3 *The constitution of the Federal Republic of Germany – as laid down in the Basic Law of 23 May 1949*

Question

Identify the 'safeguards' in this governmental structure.

Adenauer's 'Chancellor democracy'

Fig. 4 *Adenauer's government in approximately 1951. He is shown third from the left, with Erhard second from the left*

Although elected Chancellor by a majority of only one, Adenauer was to prove an extremely successful first Chancellor for the new Federal Republic. He was both skilful in his dealings with other countries and adept in holding together a political coalition of many varying interests and using it to his advantage at home. He was 'gentlemanly' in manner as his press spokesman, Felix von Eckardt, recalled:

> His upright composure made him look much younger than his age. The first characteristic that I noticed was his extraordinary politeness, including to his subordinates. In political or official exchanges, he could, on occasion, be very outspoken, but he would never be impolite. During those 10 years I must have entered his study a thousand times or more. Always, he would rise to greet me and always, at the end of every conversation, he would rise again and accompany me all the way to the door to say goodbye. I am convinced he did the same to every visitor.

1

However, this did not mean that Adenauer was not also an adept politician who could 'read' his audience and force doubters into line. Eckardt also praised Adenauer's 'political instinct', his ability to manage conferences and party meetings and his intolerance of those whose command of the facts was inadequate. Furthermore, while he was realistic in his ambitions, he never displayed the faintest trace of an 'inferiority complex' in his dealings with America or the USSR. It was well known that, on taking office and making a formal visit to the allied High Commissioners, he was warned not to step on the carpet reserved for them. However, Adenauer not only deliberately did just that; he made sure there were plenty of press photographers there to record the incident.

Adenauer's first two terms of office (1949–53 and 1953–57)

Increasing political stability

Adenauer's CDU/CSU party enjoyed a period of unbroken rule between 1949 and 1966, although it was in the first two terms of office that the government was at its most dynamic. Although the CDU/CSU came to power with only 31 per cent of the vote in 1949 and it had seemed likely that it would be ousted by or forced into coalition with the SPD at that stage, it survived and grew, so that in September 1957 it gained 50.2 per cent of the vote and had an absolute majority.

The stability of the political system had certainly not been guaranteed in the early years. The first elections had seen political extremists on the left and right competing for influence and, with 12 parties represented in the Bundestag, the trend towards political fragmentation was a real cause for concern. However, two extremist parties whose views were anti-democratic were soon outlawed under the terms of the constitution – the right-wing Socialist Reich Party (SRP) in 1952 and the left-wing Communist KPD in 1956 – and a rapid economic upturn, in addition to the five per cent rule, whereby parties had to poll at least 5 per cent of the vote to be represented in the Bundestag, helped to halt this tendency.

Furthermore, although Adenauer's own coalition had been forced to rely on a number of smaller parties and a good deal of political pressurising in 1949, it showed itself capable of integrating a wide range of political views and had soon built up an effective national party organisation. While Hans Globke, the Secretary of State between 1953 and 1963, ran an efficient party machine within the Chancellery, Adenauer ensured that his coalition was able to offer something to both urban and rural communities and to the workers as well as the middle/upper classes.

Since just over half the West German population was Catholic (the strongly Protestant regions of Brandenburg-Prussia and Saxony were part of the eastern zone), Adenauer was able to make the most of the CDU's Catholic Centre Party heritage. Furthermore, in Bavaria, home to his CSU partner, conservative Catholics made up the larger part of the electorate. However, he was careful to ensure that the CDU was perceived as an ecumenical Christian, rather than an exclusively Catholic, party, since he wanted the maximum amount of appeal. He also worked to get the support of those groups which were the most politically motivated, namely former Nazi voters and war veterans, the large group of nearly 9 million ethnic Germans expelled from eastern Europe and the refugees from East Germany who fled to the West in a steady flow. By promoting policies which suited a variety of interests, he was able to build up a genuine trans-regional appeal.

By 1953, it was clear that parliamentary democracy in the FRG was working, with just three major parties (CDU/CSU, SPD and FDP) dominating the political scene and the central CDU/CSU coalition showing flexibility and success. The Swiss political author, Fritz René Allemann, consequently wrote a book with the apt title *Bonn is not Weimar*.

The policies of Adenauer's governments, 1949–57

One of the main tasks facing the administration was the reconstruction of towns and cities destroyed by war, and the provision of housing for the refugees, expellees and those victims of bombing still living in temporary accommodation. In April 1950 the construction law began a generous system of grants to the Länder and cities for large-scale building projects and the government-assisted housing and apartment building scheme soon bore dividends, providing over 4 million new dwellings by 1957.

Cross-reference

Election results for this period are provided on page 46.

Cross-reference

For more on the flow of refugees from East Germany, look ahead to Chapter 6, page 50.

Summary question

Explain why hopes for political stability in the FRG changed between 1949 and 1953.

The refugees and expellees, who often spent long periods in 'holding camps' without work, were also gradually integrated into German society with the help of government programmes. The success of Adenauer's efforts was such that in the 1957 election, the BHE (Alliance of Expellees and Disenfranchised Persons) failed to clear the five per cent hurdle and ceased to be represented in the Bundestag.

The government also arranged for compensation to be paid to individuals – the victims of Nazi crimes – particularly against the Jews, and the 1953 Equalisation of Burdens Act offered compensation to victims of the wartime bombing campaigns. This went some way towards integrating expellees and other wartime victims back into German society and consisted of grants and pensions for those whose claims could be verified by a new government committee. The money was to be raised from a 50 per cent levy, paid over 30 years on land, building and capital assets held within West Germany, based on their 1948 values. By 1978, 110.4 billion Deutschmarks had been redistributed, although economic growth and inflation made the amount less than had originally been envisaged.

The economic policies of Adenauer's government also offered sustained economic growth and improvements in standards of living. Good labour relations were maintained through the Collective Bargaining Law on Industrial Relations (April 1949) and systems were set up from 1950 which allowed for 'co-determination' – the participation of workers in decision-making processes within factories and firms. By 1951, all joint stock companies in the coal and steel industries with over a thousand employees had to have workers' representation at managerial level while the 1952 Works Constitution Law extended workers' consultative councils throughout industry for enterprises with more than 20 employees. This created a framework for peaceful Labour relations and supported the work of Adenauer's Finance Minister, Erhard, in rebuilding the German economy.

The government was also able to introduce significant measures of welfare reform, including a new pensions act in 1957 which provided for index-linked state pensions and an initial rise of 60–75 per cent in pension payments.

A more controversial policy, which involved a revision to the Basic Law, was the decision to create a new German 'Citizens' Army', the *Bundeswehr*, in 1956. Although there was some initial hostility, not least from supporters of the SPD, public opinion was won round for an 'army' of 'citizens in uniform', defending the democratic values of the state. A Parliamentary Chief Commissioner was appointed to take overall control and an advisory committee was set up to review the appointment of senior officers, with the result that the Bundeswehr could never develop into an independent and politically influential organisation like the old **Reichswehr**.

There was also much debate within the Bundestag, and outside, about the orientation of foreign policy and rearmament and on the degree to which the goal of national unity should be sacrificed in favour of greater integration with the West. Adenauer's stance that the advancement of the FRG was, for an unspecified period, attainable only at the expense of unity, eventually won the day and on 26 and 27 May 1957 the Bonn Conventions were signed, by which the Federal Republic became a sovereign state and the FRG joined the European Defence Community (EDC).

Cross-reference

Labour relations are discussed further on page 54.

Fig. 5 *Setting up the new Bundeswehr*

Key terms

The Reichswehr: this was the German Army of the inter-war years. It was a proud and powerful, independent force. In a famous incident in 1920, some Reichswehr soldiers refused to fire on others that were staging a coup, known as the Kapp putsch. The army had been virtually beyond the control of the civilian authorities.

Cross-reference

Foreign policy is discussed in Chapter 4 on pages 58–66.

Activity

Revision exercise

Prepare a chart which identifies the main political, economic and social problems faced by the Adenauer government and identifies the responses to these.

The reasons for Adenauer's longevity as Chancellor

Clearly the way Adenauer built up his coalition and the attractions and success of his government's policies go some way towards explaining his longevity as Chancellor. However, there were other factors too.

Adenauer's cautious, pragmatic approach to politics, symbolised in his election slogan, *'Keine Experimente'* (no experiments) proved popular. In the early years of the republic, many Germans were happy enough to enjoy a quiet family and private life leaving politics to the politicians and only turning out at election time to further the continuance of a party with a track record of success. This attitude is sometimes described as *'ohne mich'* (count me out). Non-involvement was, no doubt, a reaction to the enforced politicisation of the Nazi years and the lack of a democratic tradition in Germany, but it worked to Adenauer's advantage. According to historian Ralph Willett, surveys taken at the time showed that 60 per cent of the population, *'preferred property, jobs and the possibility of a substantial income to all democratic freedoms.'*

Fig. 6 *Konrad Adenauer*

Adenauer and his party were also helped by the strong anti-communist sentiment of the 1950s, encouraged by the Americanisation of West German society and the fears engendered by the Cold War. The KPD had not put in a strong performance in 1949, receiving just 5.7 per cent of the vote, and developments in eastern Europe diminished its appeal further, reducing its support to just 2.2 per cent of the vote in 1953. The KPD was banned by the West German Constitutional Court under the terms of the Basic Law because of its non-democratic beliefs in 1956. The SPD was also, rather unfairly, smeared with the same 'red brush' despite its detachment from the SED in East Germany and its commitment to democracy. Despite its 19th-century Marxist constitution, it had worked within a democratic framework since the early 20th century.

Adenauer's success was partly attributable to other SPD weaknesses. While its leader, Kurt Schumacher, had many admirable qualities and a solid record of anti-Nazism which included an insistence that Germany should acknowledge its war crimes, he made the mistake of opposing Adenauer's moves to align West Germany firmly with the West, and further the cause of European union. Under Schumacher, the socialists put the unification of Germany into a single but neutral state at the top of their agenda and this was a prospect which grew increasingly unrealistic. Furthermore, the socialists' prediction that the conservative capitalist policies of the CDU/CSU would bring economic disaster were so clearly proven wrong; it left the socialists with nothing new to offer to the electorate. Indeed, as Tony Judt has written, *'So long as Germany's Social Democrats maintained their principled opposition to most of Adenauer's policies, they contributed inadvertently to the stability of the West German Republic.'*

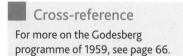

Cross-reference

Schumacher is profiled on page 32.

The SPD also suffered internal division over the issue of rearmament and remilitarisation and had the problem of being seen as working class at a time when the country was growing increasingly affluent and middle class. Although it eventually changed its image in the Godesberg programme of 1959, Erich Ollenhauer, who succeeded to the SPD leadership after the death of Schumacher in 1952, was a colourless character and the party's fortunes were slow to revive.

Cross-reference

For more on the Godesberg programme of 1959, see page 66.

The most controversial factor behind Adenauer's dominance was the way he rehabilitated and used former Nazis within his administration and in the country as a whole. By turning a blind eye to their past, Adenauer could draw on the talents of capable administrators and politicians, and it may be argued that this was the only practical policy in the circumstances.

Mary Fulbrook has provided the following overview of Adenauer's Germany up to 1957:

> The fundamental task of restructuring German society was missed as neither structure nor personnel were changed in an era of conservative 'restoration'. Against all this it can be asserted that without the integration of former Nazis, and without the startling economic success, Bonn democracy might have had as little chance of survival as Weimar democracy. Radical anti-system opposition on the part of a few activists would have combined with mass discontent based on economic misery and uncertainty to provide powerful forces for political destabilisation. The argument can be mounted that the end, retrospectively, might have justified the means: actions which can be criticised on moral grounds might have had consequences which even the critics would applaud.
>
> **2**

Activity

Source analysis

1 Summarise Mary Fulbrook's argument in one sentence.

2 Do you agree with Mary Fulbrook's conclusions? Explain your answer.

A closer look

The rehabilitation of former Nazis

When Adenauer's new foreign ministry was created in 1949, 39 out of 49 senior members were former Nazi Party members. Furthermore, his Minister for Refugees was Theodor Oberländer, a former SS man, who was ultimately forced to resign in May 1960. Hans Globke (author of the official commentary on the Nuremberg Race laws of 1935) was Secretary of State and Adenauer's chief aide in his Chancellery, while Herbert Blankenhorn, an ex-Nazi Party member, was Adenauer's personal adviser. From 1953, Adenauer's Minister of the Interior was another ex-party member, Gerhard Schröder, who was responsible for the banning of the KPD.

Cross-reference

To recap on the process of denazification, refer back to pages 23–27.

Activity

Research task

Try to read a biography of Adenauer and/or use the web to find some of Adenauer's speeches or to look at contemporary newspaper accounts of his government. Based on the information you find, make an illustrated character and career profile.

Under a series of amnesties, war criminals were steadily released back into civilian life and many crimes were never investigated. Although a central office of the Land Justice Department was set up in Stuttgart in 1956, investigations were undertaken at a slow pace and with little real commitment before the 1960s. Under the 1951 Reinstatement Act many ex-Nazis were re-employed in the civil service and in the early 1950s, 40–80 per cent of officials, including most members of the judiciary, were former NSDAP members. Entrepreneurs too were allowed to use the capital they had amassed in the Nazi period to expand their businesses, and others who had impeccable anti-Nazi credentials sometimes found themselves pushed out.

Adenauer's own attitude is difficult to gauge, although he no doubt saw the advantages of keeping the support and services of the often well-educated and well-trained ex-Nazi Party members. According to Judt, '*he clearly felt that a prudent silence was better than a provocative public recital of the truth. Germans of that generation were too morally compromised for democracy to work, except at this price.*' He was prepared to run the political risk of making an agreement of compensation, amounting to 100 billion DM (Deutschmark) with the Israeli Prime Minister Moshe Sharett in 1952, but he preferred to play down the Nazi past as much as possible and to concentrate energies on building prosperity for the future.

■ Economic recovery

Erhard and the social market economy

Just as the political outlook appeared uncertain in 1949, so too did West Germany's economic future. After a brief boom, when the economy grew by 30 per cent between March and August 1948 as a result of the currency reform and the end of price controls, there were, by 1950, signs that the economy was slowing down again. Unemployment had reached over 2 million (8.1 per cent) and with rising prices came more inflation. The situation did not look at all promising, despite the arrival of Marshall Aid which, in 1950, provided for 37 per cent of imports and was being used to improve railways and for investment in the electrical and steel industries.

The social market economy

■ Key profile

Ludwig Erhard, 1897–1977

Erhard came from Bavaria and studied economics at Munich University where he became head of an economics research institute before and during the war. In 1945 he became Professor of Economics at Munich University and chairman of the Economic Executive Council of the US-British zone of occupation. As Economic Director of the Bizone, he was responsible for the merger of the British and American zones in March 1948. He entered the Bundestag as a Christian Democrat in 1949 and became Federal Minister of Economics. He held this office until 1963, assisting in the country's 'economic miracle' during which the GNP trebled. He succeeded Adenauer as Chancellor in 1963 but resigned in November 1966.

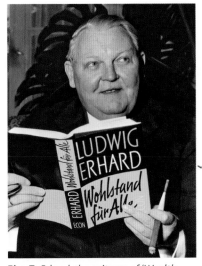

Fig. 7 *Erhard, the epitome of 'Wealth for all'*

Professor Ludwig Erhard, the Finance Minister, was a strong supporter of the 'free market' and believed that, provided the economy was guided in the right direction, market forces could be relied upon to bring about an economic transformation. His policy is referred to as the 'social market economy'. This implies a 'third way', somewhere between a completely free and unregulated market and a state-controlled socialist economy. Businesses would be left free to develop independently, setting their own prices and wages at a competitive level, but the state would assume a role in 'policing' developments, ensuring fair competition and intervening when necessary to protect the weaker members of society.

Consequently, Erhard's reaction to the situation by 1950 was to produce a limited work creation scheme to address problems of unemployment, but otherwise to allow the market to take its own course. Fortunately for Germany, the outbreak of the Korean War in June 1950 brought a sharp rise in demand for German exports and industrial production rose, although the cost of importing essential raw materials meant there was a **balance of payments** deficit in 1951.

In December 1951, Erhard again intervened to promote economic development through the Investment Aid Law by which a government subsidy of 3.2 billion DM was offered to manufacturing industry. Other government measures during the 1950s included a halving of Germany's protective tariffs, laws to prevent monopolies forming – for example the 1957 Anti-Trust (or decartelisation) Law and tight banking controls to ensure Germany had a strong currency.

■ Did you know?

The term 'social market economy' was first used by the Freiburg School of Economists in the 1930s. They were also known as the Ordoliberal economists and included Franz Bohm and Walter Eucken.

■ Key terms

Balance of payments: this refers to the difference between payments made by a country for imports and the money earned by that country in exports (and through services and overseas investments). If the former is lower than the latter there is a balance of payments surplus. If not, there is a deficit.

Cross-reference

Adenauer's policy of co-determination is outlined on page 50.

Exploring the detail

The DGB

The German Confederation of Trade Unions (*Deutscher Gewerkschaftsbund*, DGB) was founded in Munich in October 1949 as an umbrella organisation for German trade unions. Its job was to represent the member unions in any contact with the government authorities, the political parties and employers' organisations, as well as to coordinate their joint demands and activities.

Key terms

Real income: this is the income received after any price changes are taken into account and indicates a person's standard of living.

However, in other respects, Erhard avoided undue state intervention. He gave the manufacturing industries the task of allocating raw materials through their own associations, while Adenauer's policy of co-determination ensured that trade unions remained modest in their wage demands. The structure of the unions – with one union per industry and the German Confederation of Trade Unions (DGB) as a single umbrella organisation – helped foster the idea of a 'social partnership' between employers and employees and West Germany was to benefit from a low strike record.

The policy seemed to pay off and by the autumn of 1951, a global boom, with a fall in raw material prices, meant that Germany's export industries began to grow strongly.

Fig. 8 *Celebrations at the Volkswagen factory for the successful production of the Beetle*

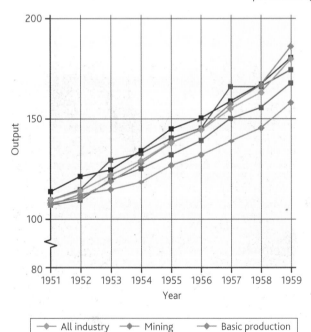

Fig. 9 *Increasing productivity in the FRG, 1951–59*

The first half of the 1950s was to witness a period of sustained economic growth and although the growth was slightly more variable from 1955 until the early 60s, the growth rate averaged 8 per cent per year and the unemployment rate fell to 0.5 per cent, despite the constant influx of eastern refugees. Exports were strong and as **real incomes** began to rise from 1952–53, consumer demand also grew to boost the internal market. Investment increased, partly under the government schemes and partly through the reinvestment of profits, from 19 per cent in 1950 to 24 per cent by 1960. Old firms like Krupp and Thyssen in steel manufacture and Bayer in chemicals thrived, while new industrial centres developed and the transport network was overhauled.

The rebuilding of cities and homes led to the furnishing and provision of comfortable lifestyles and as demand encouraged production, wages rose again. Erhard could take pride in more than fulfilling his slogan '*Wohlstand für alle*' – 'wealth for all'.

Of course, not all this flurry of economic expansion can solely be credited to Erhard or his ideas of a social market economy. West Germany's economic expansion was based on solid foundations that pre-dated the Second World War. The country enjoyed inherent natural advantages with good seaports and communications, including the River

Rhine, abundant coal and other raw materials, and a well-educated and highly-skilled workforce, that was to be augmented in the West after 1945 by refugees from the eastern sector. Germany had already been the world's second largest economy (after America) by 1939 and, despite the carpet bombing and the dismantling of factories by the allies, there was a secure economic base on which to build. The loss of some of the older factories actually proved a blessing in disguise, as new complexes were erected from scratch and could incorporate all the latest technology.

West Germany was also helped by the fact that it did not have to lay aside large amounts of money for rearmament, as was the case elsewhere, although some money was saved in a contingency fund for this from 1952. The Marshall Plan funds, although quite modest at $1.5 billion over the 1948–52 period, were also a help in buying essential equipment and expanding heavy industry, but their importance should not be overrated. West Germany spent more money itself in helping eastern refugees than it received in Marshall funds. However, it did give a boost to economic confidence, as it emphasised America's commitment to West German recovery.

Erhard has been hailed as the man behind an 'economic miracle' but this should not obscure Adenauer's contribution. His policy of reintegrating the FRG into Europe and working within the European Coal and Steel Community (and, from 1957, the European Economic Community – EEC) helped West Germany gain the maximum advantage from growing world trade. It should also be remembered that the social market economy was not fully applied everywhere. Agriculture remained heavily subsidised and despite the anti-Trust legislation, loopholes allowed big businesses to flourish. Nevertheless, by the 1960s West Germany had the third largest economy in the world, after America and the USSR. This was certainly impressive, whatever the reason.

Cross-reference

Adenauer's policy of reintegration and working within the European communities is discussed in Chapter 4, page 58.

A closer look

The German car industry

The rise of the German car industry is one of the most obvious signs of Erhard's 'Wirtschaftswunder' or 'economic miracle'. Among the cars that were churned off the production lines was the Volkswagen Beetle from Lower Saxony in the British zone, which cost under 2,000 Deutschmarks. BMW was revived under Herbert Quandt, a half-blind entrepreneur who believed in sports cars and motor travel. Friedrich Carl von Oppenheim, a banker from Cologne, brought the engineers, designers and managers from the destroyed Audi works in Saxony to Ingoldstadt in Bavaria, where they set up a new factory to produce high-quality cars for the world market. Daimler Benz in Stuttgart was reestablished and not only provided Adenauer with a black limousine, but also produced a Mercedes 300S which sold well around the world. Ford in Cologne and General Motors' Opel factory in Russelsheim produced cars for the mass market.

Fig. 10 *The German car industry boomed during the 1950s*

Activity

Construct a spider diagram to show why the FRG experienced such rapid economic growth in the 1950s. Differentiate between internal and external factors.

Activity

Thinking point

Was Erhard personally responsible for West Germany's 'economic miracle'?

The impact of economic and social developments

Despite the intention that the social market economy would work to the advantage of 'society' as a whole, the economic policies adopted in the 1950s actually served to widen the gap between rich and poor, although this was masked by the overall rise in living standards. There was a marked decrease in the number of self-employed workers in agriculture, trade and commerce, while the industrial workforce steadily grew. The general prosperity and resulting mass consumption narrowed the gap in the lifestyles of the classes, so although workers' wages remained low and a large proportion of the nation's wealth was concentrated in a few hands, there was a feeling of affluence. The average income of a West German household increased by 400 per cent between 1950 and 1970 and in comparison with the immediate post-war period, most Germans felt satisfied that they were living in a land of plenty. People could find jobs, live in relatively comfortable homes, obtain sufficient food and increasingly as the 1950s progressed, they were increasingly able to enjoy luxuries such as fridges, cars, holidays and TVs too.

Fig. 11 *West German households were filled with the latest electrical gadgets, like the food processor shown here in 1958*

Mary Fulbrook has noted:

> Being well-fed and well-housed mattered more to most Germans than the seemingly more academic question of whether theirs was becoming a more unequal society. Interestingly the percentages supporting democratic – rather than monarchical or Nazi – political views in opinion polls of the 1950s and early 1960s grew in close correlation with the increase in the average weights of ever more satiated West Germans.

3

West German society in the 1950s certainly had an air of prosperity and this reinforced commitment to the CDU/CSU and to democracy in general. Some writers, such as Heinrich Böll, were later to complain that the growth of greater prosperity made the Germans self-satisfied and too ready to suppress the past. However, it also helped reinforce an anti-communist standpoint and made most people happy to accept Western integration at the expense of reunification.

Economic recovery made it easier to reintegrate the expellees and refugees into German society, although it also created an 'underclass' of *Gastarbeiter* (guest-workers) from southern Europe. Around 8 million

travelled to Germany from Italy, Yugoslavia and Turkey under the
Gastarbeiter scheme of the late 1950s. The scheme encouraged workers
to take up jobs in shortage areas; some, such as mechanical and electrical
engineering required particular skills, but most were of the unskilled and
low-paid variety, for example in textiles and shipbuilding. Although it
had originally been envisaged that these workers would eventually return
home, many were joined by their families and settled permanently. While
there were just 150,000 of these in 1959, by 1966 there were 1.2 million
and they made up 10 per cent of the West German workforce by the 1970s.

Cross-reference

For more on the situation of the
Gastarbeiter in the 1970s, look ahead
to Chapter 7, page 120.

Summary question

To what extent was the domestic policy pursued in West Germany in the
period 1949–57 an unqualified success?

4 Foreign Policy and the End of Adenauer's Chancellorship

In this chapter you will learn about:

- the emergence of NATO and the EEC and their importance to West Germany

- the Hallstein Doctrine

- Western reactions to the building of the Berlin Wall

- events leading to Adenauer's resignation.

We live in disturbed times. New problems arise every day, developments never stand still. Despite the number and variety of problems, every responsible person must realise that for the present and coming generation there is now only one main problem, and that is this: the world has seen the formation of two power-groups. On one side there is the group of powers led by the United States of America and united in the Atlantic Pact. This group defends the values of Christian and Western civilisation, freedom and true democracy. On the other side there is Soviet Russia with her satellites. The line dividing these two groups of powers runs right down the centre of Germany. Twenty million Germans live under Soviet rule; about forty-three million in the orbit of the Atlantic bloc.

1

(From a speech by Konrad Adenauer, Chancellor of the FRG, 23 March 1949)

Key chronology

October 1949	West Germany became a member of the Organisation for European Economic Cooperation (OECC)
November 1949	the Petersberg Agreements allowed the FRG to join the Council of Europe as an associate member
April 1951	West Germany entered the European Coal and Steel Community (ECSC)
May 1951	West Germany became a full member of the Council of Europe
July 1951	the Western powers ended the occupation of West Germany
March 1952	Stalin's 'note' proposing a neutral united Germany
May 1952	the General Treaty recognised the sovereignty of the FRG and a treaty to set up a European Defence Community was signed
May 1952	the Inner German border was sealed
1954	Germany and Italy were admitted to the Brussels Pact and the name Western European Union was adopted
May 1955	West Germany became a full member of NATO
September 1955	the Hallstein Doctrine was announced
March 1957	West Germany became a founder member of the EEC in the Treaty of Rome
November 1958	Khrushchev issued the Berlin ultimatum
August 1961	the start of construction of the Berlin Wall and the final sealing of the East–West border

Germany's reintegration into the western world

In fewer than 10 years West Germany changed from an embryonic state under an occupation order into a major player in Europe and the Western alliance system.

Adenauer recognised that the best way of reaccommodating his country was to win the support of the western world and bring about a reconciliation with Germany's age-old enemies, the French. Reintegration was also supported by America, who saw a strengthened West Germany as a bulwark against communist expansionism, while reliance on the US would prevent a resurgence of German nationalism and militarism which would have unsettled Europe.

Adenauer's first important step in this 'Westpolitik' was made in the Petersberg (West Germany) Agreements of November 1949, which allowed the FRG to join the Council of Europe as an associate member. The FRG was also given the right to set up consulates in other countries and to have direct representation on the OEEC, the organisation which administered the Marshall Plan, and the Board of the International Authority of the Ruhr.

The emergence of NATO, April 1949

In the immediate aftermath of war, it had been far from certain that America would commit itself to the long-term defence of western Europe.

Fig. 1 *Germany's rehabilitation into Europe: Erhard at the OECC*

Consequently, on 17 March 1948, in the Brussels Pact, Britain, France, Belgium, the Netherlands and Luxembourg had formed a European Defence Organisation (EDO). Its declared aim was to prevent any German resurgence that might threaten the security of post-war western Europe. However, given Germany's divided state, the true motive seemed to be protection against the advance of communism. This made the US reassess their own position. In the eyes of the US:

- western Europe was vulnerable to the ideological expansionism of the Soviet Union
- the EDO was 'too European' and too small to protect western Europe
- joining the EDO would give the US little direct input into policy making while committing them to the duty of western European protection
- an Atlantic alliance, rather than a regional European alliance, would permit them to have real influence and provide greater certainty for European defence against the march of communism
- a US-led alliance would send a message to the USSR, highlighting the United States's determination not to accept any further expansion of Soviet influence into Europe
- membership of a new alliance had to extend beyond that of the European Defence Organisation.

As a result, in April 1949 the North Atlantic Treaty Organisation (NATO) was established as a political defence system. Its original members were the US, Canada, Britain, France, Belgium, the Netherlands, Luxembourg, Italy, Portugal, Denmark, Norway and Iceland. However, only months after NATO's formation, the Soviet Union successfully tested its first atomic bomb and NATO's initial political role very quickly transformed into a military stance.

Cross-reference

The establishment of the Bundeswehr is introduced in Chapter 3, page 50.

■ **Exploring the detail**

The historiography of the reunification proposals of 1952

At the time, criticism of Adenauer's refusal to consider Stalin's note was led by Schumacher of the SPD, Jakob Kaiser, the Minister for All German Affairs and Paul Sathe, the editor of the *Frankfurter Allgemeine* newspaper. More recently the same attitude has been taken by Rolf Steininger in *The German Question, the Stalin Note of 1952* (1990) and Willy Loth, although it has been rejected by Hans-Peter Schwarz, author of Adenauer's biography written in 1995, and by Gerhard Wettig writing in 1994.

Fig. 2 *The creation of the Bundeswehr aroused protest from France. Can you explain why?*

This left the FRG in an ambiguous position. On the one hand, Germany was the 'vanquished' nation which the other powers were committed to keeping in check, but on the other, West Germany lay in the front line against the advance of communism, which was seen as a far bigger threat.

In 1950, Adenauer began to argue for the creation of an 'armed security police' or Bundeswehr, capable of combating internal attempts at revolution, as well as for a West German contribution to the European defence system. The outbreak of the Korean War in June 1950, when communist North Korean forces attacked the US-backed South Koreans on a divided peninsula, made such a suggestion appear all the more reasonable and urgent since, unlike the GDR, the FRG was still completely unarmed.

Stalin, however, was anxious to prevent any US-supported West German rearmament taking place and put forward a series of proposals for German reunification from 1950, the most important of which was that of 10 March 1952. This offered the prospect of a united, neutral Germany following free elections, supervised by a Commission of the four former occupying powers. Stalin's proposals seemed remarkably liberal. He even suggested that whatever form of government the German people chose should be accepted and that this Germany should be freed from reparations and permitted its own small army. Whether it was a serious proposal or merely sent as a propaganda exercise to destabilise Adenauer's pro-Western policies is unclear. If it was a genuine proposal, Adenauer, who no doubt felt that he had too much to lose from breaking his profitable agreements with the West, can be accused of abandoning his commitment to reunification, despite his official support for it. Certainly, Schumacher at the time and a number of historians since, have suggested that he feared the creation of a united, SPD-dominated German state with a predominance of Protestants. However, Adenauer's supporters have doubted the honesty of the proposal, pointing out that Stalin would never really have risked a free political choice in Germany because of the repercussions this would have had on the other eastern satellite states.

Although America wanted West Germany in NATO, France at first resisted, and when the Foreign Secretaries of America, Britain and France met in New York in September 1950, the French put forward an alternative proposal, the 'Pleven Plan'. This plan, named after the French Foreign Minister René Pleven, would have allowed West Germany a limited number of troops, but only as part of a western European army, within a new European Defence Community. The US, Britain and France approved, in principle, a German contribution to the defence of the West in December 1950, although the British were unhappy with the French scheme. Furthermore, a General Treaty was signed in Bonn in May 1952, followed by another to set up a new European Defence Community (EDC), which was successfully concluded in Paris in May 1954.

The General Treaty abolished the statute of occupation and recognised the full sovereignty of the Federal Republic, although a pledge to work for the future reunification of the whole of Germany was also included.

■ **Exploring the detail**

The Brussels Pact

The Brussels Pact was originally signed by France, the Netherlands, Belgium, Luxembourg and Britain in March 1948 in order to set out terms for economic, social and cultural cooperation, as well as collective self-defence. West Germany and Italy joined the pact in October 1954 and its name was changed. It was regarded as an anti-communist organisation and eventually became part of the broader European Union.

All restrictions on the German economy and on German scientific research were lifted and Germany was allowed to set up a Bundeswehr to give a guarantee of security. However, the EDC arrangements collapsed when the French National Assembly refused to ratify the treaty in August 1954. Adenauer, desperate to keep German involvement alive, voluntarily agreed to renounce nuclear weapons and to keep the West German army limited in size and under strict civilian control. As a result, the British plan, to admit Germany and Italy to the Brussels Pact and rename the European Defence Community the 'Western European Union', was adopted.

Fig. 3 *The NATO alliance agrees to accept German membership*

Thus the way was opened for West German rearmament. Since a proposed Four Power summit to discuss German reunification had been delayed after the power struggles following Stalin's death in 1953 and the GDR riots of the same year, the French reluctantly gave in to American pressure to accept West German membership of NATO. West Germany was admitted as a member in May 1955. In retaliation, the USSR recognised the sovereignty of the GDR and created the Warsaw Pact with the GDR as a member.

■ Exploring the detail

The remilitarisation of the FRG

Membership of NATO brought its own fears. Some were worried about the stationing of American nuclear weapons in West Germany and feared that the Americans merely sought the alliance for their own ends. In July 1956, the Basic Law had to be changed to allow for a system of compulsory military service for 15 months which had to be introduced to provide for the FRG's contribution to the NATO forces. This also provoked controversy. By 1961 the FRG had 350,000 soldiers and was the second strongest force in NATO. There was also criticism that some of the officers had formerly served in the Nazi Wehrmacht (army).

■ Cross-reference

The GDR riots of 1953 are detailed on pages 75–78.

■ Exploring the detail

USSR reunification proposal, 1953

After Stalin's death in 1953, Churchill proposed a Four Power summit to reconsider the issue of German reunification, while Beria, the deputy Soviet prime minister, actually considered 'selling' the GDR to the West for $10 billion provided that the reunited Germany was a neutral state. However, the GDR riots of 1953 and Beria's own fall from power delayed the proposed Four Power summit until after West Germany had been admitted into NATO in May 1955. It met in Geneva in July 1955 when East–West relations were at a low ebb and Khrushchev effectively ruled out reunification.

■ Activity

Creative thinking

Suggest some contrasting newspaper headlines, from America, the USSR, FRG and GDR, announcing West Germany's entry into the NATO alliance.

Fig. 4 *The French saw the EEC as a way of harnessing Germany within western Europe*

Cross-reference

The crisis in Berlin of 1958–61 is described on pages 91–92.

Activity

Thinking and analysis

Produce a report outlining the FRG's position with regard to Europe, the USSR and America in 1950. Include an assessment of West Germany's options in foreign affairs and recommend a strategy, explaining why it is appropriate in terms of the FRG's national interests.

The European Economic Community

The French Foreign Secretary, Robert Schuman, produced a plan, based on the ideas of the French economist, Jean Monnet, to merge the western European coal and steel industries under a supranational control in 1950. This provoked some fierce debate within the Bundestag. Adenauer thought this a concession worth making in the interests of reducing Franco-German rivalry, while Schumacher and the SPD believed this was 'selling out' to the Western powers and derided him as 'Chancellor of the allies'. However, an agreement was negotiated and the Treaty of Paris was signed in April 1951. This established a single authority, merging the coal, iron and steel industries of West Germany, France, Italy, Belgium, the Netherlands and Luxembourg, eliminating tariffs and creating a free labour market. Britain refused to take part. The ECSC (European Coal and Steel Community) began to function in July 1952 and although this was primarily an economic agreement, merging Germany's and France's industrial potential, in some ways, it signified a 'peace treaty' between the two powers.

The FRG joined the International Monetary Fund (IMF) in 1952 and Adenauer was solidly behind the negotiations that led to the March 1957 Treaty of Rome; this set up the European Economic Community (EEC or Common Market) which began to function in January 1958. The ECSC was merged into this new organisation along with EURATOM (the European Atomic Energy Commission) and the members agreed to establish common policies for agriculture, transport, capital and labour, and to establish common external tariffs. It envisaged that ultimately some form of political integration might take place, but in the shorter term its concerns were economic.

The establishment of the EEC came at a time when America was beginning to adopt a more flexible policy towards the USSR. This alarmed Adenauer, who began to pull Germany closer to France, even though the hardliner General de Gaulle came to power there in 1958. The two countries still had very different outlooks, with de Gaulle seeing Europe as a loose confederation of states free from US influence, and Adenauer welcoming American support and involvement; their relationship was strengthened during the crisis over Berlin (1958–61), despite their differences. In January 1963, Adenauer gave his approval to de Gaulle's veto of Britain's application to join the EEC and the Elysée Treaty – a Franco-German treaty of friendship – was signed the same month. Although Adenauer was at pains to emphasise to the Bundestag that this did not mark a shift in his foreign policy, it led to fierce debate between those like Erhard and Schröder who looked to America and wanted Britain in the EEC, and the 'Gaullists' like Adenauer himself and his Minister of Defence, Franz-Josef Strauss, who favoured an integrated western Europe independent of America.

Key profiles

Gerhard Schröder, (1910–89)

Gerhard Schröder (not to be confused with the later Chancellor of the same name [see Chapters 7 and 10] was a West German politician and member of the CDU. He held office as Minister of the Interior (1953–61) and as Minister of Foreign Affairs (1961–66) in Adenauer's and Erhard's cabinets. He served as Minister of Defence under Kiesinger (1966–69).

Franz-Josef Strauss, (1915–88)

Strauss was the son of a butcher; he was academically gifted and won a scholarship to the prestigious Maximilianeum in Munich. He was taken prisoner during the war, but after this he entered Bavarian politics and was a founder member of the CSU, where he remained chairman from 1961 to 1988. He joined the economic council of Bizonia in 1948 and entered the Bundestag in 1949. He was Defence Minister from 1957 until his resignation in 1962, during which time his profound anti-communism and strong sense of nationalism were a cause for some concern. Although disgraced over the *Der Spiegel* affair, he returned as Finance Minister in 1966.

The Hallstein Doctrine

Ever since the founding of the FRG in 1949, Konrad Adenauer had insisted that his state represented *'the sole legitimate state organisation of the German people.'* The GDR was regarded as an illegitimate Soviet puppet state, but under Walter Ulbricht the GDR had adopted a similar stance, claiming to be the only true state representing the German people. However, it was the FRG that was recognised by nearly all UN members and only the countries within the Soviet bloc recognised the GDR government instead.

By 1955, the GDR had changed its stance and began to describe itself as a 'second German state', which should be recognised alongside the Federal Republic. In September 1955, Adenauer's government inadvertently appeared to support this view when it established diplomatic relations with the Soviet Union (which of course 'recognised' the GDR and had an East German embassy) as part of an agreement on the repatriation of German prisoners of war. However, Adenauer was anxious to make it clear that his position had not changed, not least because widespread recognition of the GDR as a second German state would harden Germany's division and raise doubts about Adenauer's claim that the Western integration of the FRG had not harmed the cause of German unity.

In his address to the Bundestag on 22 September 1955, Adenauer therefore made his position clear. His 'threat' which, when repeated in a press conference in December 1955, became known as the 'Hallstein Doctrine' was that the FRG would break off diplomatic relations with any country which established diplomatic relations with the GDR (the USSR excepted). Walter Hallstein, the state secretary at the foreign ministry from 1950–58, gave his name to the doctrine, even though he was only one of a number of officials involved in developing the policy.

The Hallstein Doctrine was to prove an effective deterrent. When Yugoslavia established diplomatic ties with the GDR in October 1957, Bonn immediately broke off relations with Belgrade. This example, and that of Cuba in January 1963, enabled the FRG to prevent recognition of the GDR. However, because the Warsaw Pact states and the People's Republic of China had recognised the GDR in 1949–50, the FRG was prevented from establishing diplomatic relations with those countries. In some respects this was to hinder the FRG's freedom of action, and while the doctrine suggested Western commitment to reunification, it had the effect of making the GDR even more dependent on the USSR. Consequently, in the ensuing years, the Hallstein Doctrine met with a good deal of criticism within West Germany and it was eventually to be loosened by Willi Brandt in the 1960s and ended in 1972.

Cross-reference

Brandt's foreign policy in the 1960s is covered in Chapter 8, pages 135–138.

Activity

Creative thinking

Write an article commenting on the Hallstein Doctrine for a) a West German newspaper and b) an East German newspaper.

■ **Cross-reference**

More detail on the Berlin Crisis, including the building of the Berlin Wall, can be found in Chapter 6. This chapter examines events from the standpoint of the FRG.

■ **Key terms**

Status quo: the existing state of affairs.

The Berlin Crisis of 1958–61

By 1958, the situation in the GDR had reached a crisis point since the open boundary between East and West Berlin was permitting more and more skilled workers to leave for the West. This was severely weakening the East German economy and Ulbricht was desperate to win Soviet support to drive the West from Berlin or, failing that, for a wall to seal the Berlin border.

Initially Khrushchev was not keen to disturb the **status quo**. However, a deteriorating relationship with China, combined with fears that West German membership of NATO might lead America to deploy nuclear missiles in West Germany and concerns about the Hallstein Doctrine, worked together to encourage Khrushchev to try once again to persuade the West to withdraw from Berlin.

Fig. 5 *The western allies were not prepared to see the Russian bear swallow up Berlin*

In November 1958, Khrushchev issued the Berlin Ultimatum, giving the West six months to recognise the existence of the GDR and accept Berlin as an independent 'free city'. If they failed to comply, Khrushchev threatened to hand its eastern zone of Berlin to the GDR, so giving the East Germans control over access from the FRG to West Berlin. This, in turn, would force America to recognise the GDR as an independent state and accept the permanent post-war division of Germany.

The Western allies rejected the ultimatum, but agreed to hold a Foreign Ministers' conference in Geneva in the summer of 1959. This development alarmed Adenauer, who produced the Globke Plan, named after Hans Globke, the state secretary. He proposed that the FRG and GDR should recognise each other's sovereignty and turn Berlin into a free city, but only so that a referendum on unification could be held which, if supported, would lead to free elections for a united German parliament.

These proposals were never seriously discussed because, when news reached Khrushchev that an American U-2 spy plane had been shot down while on a mission over the Soviet Union, he walked out of the Paris summit meeting in May 1960, thus deferring any decision over Berlin.

The arrival of John F. Kennedy as the new US President in November 1960 increased tensions further. Khrushchev believed that Kennedy was a young and politically vulnerable leader whom he could easily manipulate, while Kennedy told the American people that '*The immediate threat to free men is West Berlin but that isolated outpost is not an isolated problem. The threat is world wide.*' He refused to compromise on the status of Berlin, increased defence spending, called up army reservists and reactivated ships about to be scrapped. In July 1961 Kennedy called for a build-up of NATO forces and declared:

> We cannot and we will not permit the Communists to drive us out of Berlin, either gradually or by force. The fulfilment of our pledge to that city is essential to the morale and security of West Germany and to the faith of the entire free world.

2

The stage was thus set for Khrushchev to give Ulbricht the support he had been looking for and permit the erection of the Berlin Wall.

The Berlin Wall, August 1961, and the West's reaction

On 13 August 1961, Soviet troops and East German police began to seal off East from West Berlin. The border was closed, a wall constructed (initially of barbed wire) and all telephone lines from West Berlin cut.

John F. Kennedy, was aboard a yacht in the Atlantic when the news reached him. He gave a statement to the press declaring that, *'The Blockade of East Berlin is a visible sign of the defeat of the Communist system for all the world to see. Ulbricht's East German regime bears responsibility to the world for the inhumane imprisonment of its own population.'* However, there was no further ultimatum and he later explained to his aides, *'The other side panicked – but not we. We are going to do nothing now because the only alternative is war. It's all over. They are not going to overrun Berlin.'*

Adenauer also failed to make any immediate move, although strong protests were made. He was in the middle of an election campaign and waited nine days before even visiting Berlin.

The population of Berlin was less quiescent. There were incidents along the border and the Western press poured out denunciations and condemned the inaction of the Western allies. On 16 August, a day when 300,000 Berliners demonstrated in the front of the Schöneberg city hall, the home of the West Berlin government, the *Bild-Zeitung* ran the headline, 'The West does NOTHING'.

The same day, Willi Brandt, the Mayor of West Berlin, delivered a speech to a tense crowd of West Berliners in front of the City Hall:

Fig. 6 *Willi Brandt, Mayor of Berlin, denounces the Berlin Wall, 16 August 1961*

> An unlawful regime has committed another injustice; one worse than any before. The East bears responsibility! It bears the full responsibility for what may follow as a result.
>
> We are not able to lift this burden that weighs upon the shoulders of our fellow citizens in the sector and our countrymen in the zone these days, and that is the hardest part for us! We can only help them to bear it by showing that we are big enough for this hour! They ask if we are writing them off now. There is only one answer: No! Never!
>
> Our people are being put to a test. Our people will be judged by History, and heaven forbid out of indifference, convenience, sluggishness or moral weakness, that we don't rise to the occasion! Because then the Communists won't stop at the Brandenburg Gate. They also will not stop at the zone border and not at the Rhine.

3

Finally, on 19 August, Kennedy sent Vice President Lyndon B. Johnson to Berlin, and General Lucius D. Clay, hero of the Berlin airlift, together with 1,500 troops to reinforce the Berlin garrison. They received a rapturous welcome but it was clear that America was determined to maintain **détente** with the USSR. Although in September 1961,

Key terms

Détente: an easing of Cold War hostilities. Working together.

■ Did you know?

Communication between West Germany and West Berlin

There were eight border crossings between East and West Berlin although these were closed to West Berliners until December 1963. Western foreigners were, however, allowed to cross. There were four motorways which West Germans could use to reach West Berlin and the FRG paid the GDR a lump sum to maintain these. There were also four railways routes and some canals and rivers.

■ Activity

Thinking point

Had Kennedy broken his pledge given in Source 2 on page 64? Do you feel Kennedy's actions were honourable and/or justifiable?

■ Activity

Thinking point

Was the outcome of the Berlin Crisis a victory for East or West?

■ Cross-reference

Election results throughout this period are presented on page 46.

■ Cross-reference

Willi Brandt is profiled in Chapter 7, page 113.

■ Exploring the detail

The Godesberg Programme of November 1959 was drawn up at an SPD party convention in the town of Bad Godesberg, near Bonn, and was notable because, for the first time, the SPD broadened its appeal by abandoning Marxist ideas and accepting the existing economic system.

the Americans sent a further 40,000 soldiers to Europe, a compromise was effected. The Americans demanded the right for the Western powers to remain in West Berlin, with their own troops, they demanded free access for them by land and air, and self-determination for the inhabitants of Berlin's western sectors. A newspaper article from a disillusioned West Berliner later recorded:

> We could have expected more from the allies on 13 August than we did. We still had the power to do many things even in the following days. If the first eastern deserters to the West had been promptly put in front of a microphone and had talked to their comrades and had destroyed the political propaganda; if they had assured them that they would not be returned and would be free; that the border was a breach of international agreements, then something might have been achieved.

4

Willi Brandt also expressed his disillusionment with the West when he observed, '*the curtain went up and the stage was empty.'*

The Four Power agreements had virtually broken down, and by tolerating the building of the wall, America had effectively acknowledged the GDR's right to exist and this, of course, forced the FRG to recognise the fact also. Nevertheless, war had been avoided.

Khrushchev, remembering the Berlin Crisis in later years, claimed:

> Thus the West tested our nerve by prodding us with the barrels of their cannons and found us ready to accept their challenge. They learned they couldn't frighten us. I think it was a great victory for us, and it was won without firing a single shot.

5

Adenauer's later years and resignation, 1957–63

Adenauer's third term in office had begun promisingly. He was elected with 50.2 per cent of the vote and an absolute majority and, although 81 years of age, had built up a formidable reputation and was held in high popular regard. However, his last six years in office were far less successful than his first two terms had been.

- In 1956, the majority of the FDP, which had up until then supported Adenauer's coalition, broke away under Thomas Dehler. They disagreed with Adenauer's rigid attitude to the GDR and the USSR. At a local level some of the break-away FDP parties cooperated with the SPD (and in North Rhine-Westphalia a CDU-led government was pushed out by a FDP/SPD coalition).

- The SPD reacted to its defeat in 1957 by a complete change of approach. Following the 1959 Bad Godesberg programme, it declared its support for Western integration, dropped opposition to membership of NATO and accepted Erhard's social market economy. It also abandoned that part of its constitution which committed it to the overthrow of capitalist society and so became far more electable. In August 1960, it chose Willi Brandt, the young charismatic and dynamic Mayor of West Berlin, as the party's Chancellor candidate.

In 1959, Adenauer put himself forward for the Presidency of the FRG on Theodor Heuss's retirement, but then withdrew, partly because the constitution would not allow him to combine the two roles and he had no obvious protégé to replace him as Chancellor. In the end, he put his weight behind his Minister of Agriculture, Heinrich Lübke, but Adenauer's arrogant behaviour weakened his authority within his own party.

Cross-reference

Franz-Josef Strauss is profiled on page 62.

Adenauer made a serious political miscalculation when he delayed visiting Berlin until nine days after the wall went up. Brandt accused him of indifference and in the 1961 elections, the CDU/CSU vote fell to 46 per cent, while the FDP increased its vote from 7.7 per cent to 12.8 per cent and thus held the balance. Adenauer managed to negotiate another coalition but he had to promise that he would resign in favour of Erhard after another two years.

Adenauer finally lost credibility over the *Der Spiegel* affair, when he supported the Defence Minister, Strauss, in his high-handed action against the news magazine *Der Spiegel*. Strauss had ordered the arrest of the editors of *Der Spiegel* for an article which had been printed concerning the inefficiencies of the Bundeswehr. Furthermore, the night-time arrest had been accompanied by some heavy-handed police action, reminiscent of scenes from Nazi Germany. There was a press outcry and student demonstrations and the five FDP ministers in the cabinet resigned in protest on 19 November on the grounds that the FDP Minister of Justice had not been consulted before the arrests took place. Adenauer immediately tried to negotiate an alternative coalition with the SPD, whereupon the FDP agreed to return provided Strauss was dismissed and Adenauer promised to step down no later than October 1963. Both requests were granted and Adenauer retired on 15 October, 1963.

A closer look

The *Der Spiegel* Affair, 1962

Der Spiegel was Germany's leading weekly political magazine with a readership of around five million. A controversial article of 1961 accused Franz-Josef Strauss of recommending the Fibag construction company for the construction of apartments for the US military in Germany. They claimed this deal had been made because his friend, Hans Kapfinger, was a share-holder in the company. An investigating parliamentary commission found Strauss not guilty of misconduct, but it soured his relationship with the paper and its owner Rudolf Augstein.

On 8 October 1962, the paper published an article, *'Bedingt abwehrbereit'* ('Partially prepared for defence'), in which it suggested that the Bundeswehr was under-funded and ill-equipped to deal with a communist threat from the East. This was an attack on Strauss's Defence Department.

The magazine was accused of treason and on 26 October 1962, its Hamburg offices were seized and the houses of its journalists searched by 36 policemen. Documents were taken away and the offices not allowed to reopen until 26 November. Augstein and fellow editors Claus Jacobi and Johannes Engel plus seven others were arrested, while Conrad Ahlers, who had written the article, and was at that time on holiday in Spain, was arrested at his hotel during the night and jailed for 103 days.

Fig. 7 *In Frankfurt, protesters decorated the statue of justice with signs calling for the freedom of the press and protesting against the night-time raids. The wording on the signs reads, 'Press freedom' and 'At night, when the criminal police came'*

The affair provoked the first mass demonstrations and public protests to be seen in post-war Germany, and although Strauss initially denied involvement, he was finally forced to admit that he had phoned the German military attaché in Madrid and urged him to seize Ahlers. Not only was such an action an infringement of personal freedom and therefore illegal, Strauss had also lied to parliament. Adenauer, who had known of the actions, was implicated by association and accused of using state resources to support the suppression of the press. The affair is regarded as having destroyed the values of the *Obrigkeitsstaat* (authoritarian state) and ensured that the FRG would remain a modern liberal democracy.

Overview of Adenauer's chancellorship

A question mark still hangs over interpretations of the development of the FRG under Adenauer's chancellorship. Nick Thomas, in *Protest Movements in 1960s West Germany* (2003) described the 'Chancellor Democracy' as:

> An immature new democracy in which the multiplicity of opinions, the active participation, and the critical stance toward those in authority that is essential for a watchful and balanced democracy, were often seen as dangerous. Protestors portrayed it as unrepresentative, rigid, dominated by the authoritarian personality of the Chancellor and frustratingly unresponsive to opposition by parliamentary means. The presence of many former Nazis in government and enduring Nazi sympathies, a pervasive intolerance of dissent and consensus politics meant the left equated Chancellor democracy with the restoration of totalitarianism by stealth.

6

Professor R. L. Merritt in *Democracy Imposed* (1995) highlighted the detrimental effect of the continuation of the German inclination to *'equate authority with obedience'*. He stressed Adenauer's inflexible approach to political dissent, which led to a number of outcries such as that accompanying the Schwabing Riots, involving young people in West Germany. He also pointed to the generational difference between those who were happy to ignore the past and so thrived under Adenauer, and the new generation that saw the republic as too complacent.

However, Philip Windsor wrote in 1970:

> The party which governed West Germany from 1949 and 1969 had very little in common with its ancestors, the conservative parties of the Weimar Republic. [...] They have worked towards a combination of democracy and internationalism. [...] West Germany today has had an astonishingly successful record, not only in the obvious field of economics, but also in the development of a stable, sophisticated society and a working parliamentary democracy. Part of the success is Adenauer's, but a great deal must be attributed to the fact that the German people, given the opportunity of partnership in an international society, have made a remarkable effort to deal with their own terrible history and develop along the lines of their own best traditions.

7

■ **Exploring the detail**

The Schwabing Riots

In the summer of 1962, harmless buskers were a catalyst for violent clashes between youths and the Munich police forces that lasted for several days. These events inspired the city and the police to rethink their hardline policy on police intervention.

Adenauer encouraged the development of a Western, American consumer society (as detailed in Ralph Willett's *Americanisation of Germany*, 1989), adopted American industrial techniques to boost the economy, and furthered European integration. He also led a regime dominated by conservative attitudes, one which allowed former Nazis to retain office and which accepted and perhaps even welcomed the *'ohne mich'* (count me out) attitude of the population.

Learning outcomes

From your study of this section you should now be in a position to evaluate how an apparently stable democracy was able to emerge in West Germany in the years 1949 to 1963, and the parts played by Adenauer and Erhard in that development. You have seen the effects of structural change within the government and the continued economic growth bringing unparalleled prosperity to the whole population in the 'economic miracle' and you have also examined the constraints and supports provided by changing external circumstances. You have witnessed West Germany's rehabilitation as a sovereign state in Europe and have considered the ways in which West German development built on past achievement and some of the ways in which it followed a new course. The picture you have built up of the FRG by 1963 is one of stability and success. In the third section of this book you will discover how this seeming stability was actually rather misleading, but before that you will look at developments in the GDR, where the same years saw very different developments.

Activity

Thinking and analysis

On the basis of what you have read in this chapter and any additional research you can undertake, write a critical appraisal of Adenauer as Chancellor. Try to indicate his strengths and weaknesses and whether you feel he was a 'good' Chancellor for Germany at this time.

Practice question

'Adenauer's contribution to foreign policy far outweighed his achievements at home.' To what extent do you agree with this view of the chancellorship of Konrad Adenauer?

(45 marks)

Study tip
You would be advised to plan your answer to this question by making a table. On one side list Adenauer's achievements at home and on the other, his foreign policy achievements. You would also find it helpful to list his failures in both areas at the bottom of each column. You will then need to decide your argument on the basis of the achievements and failures you have recorded. Try to adopt a definite viewpoint and, in arguing your case, refer to both sides. You may wish to stress the integration of Adenauer's foreign policy and domestic achievements. His commitment to Western integration, for example, might be seen as a way of ensuring that Germany developed as a stable democracy.

5 The Development of the GDR

In May 1953, Walter Ulbricht, leader of the SED, attended the opening ceremony of Stalinstadt, the first new socialist city to be built in East Germany. The nucleus of the town was the impressive new *Eisenbüttenkombinat Ost* (Ironworks Combine East) supplied by coal from Poland and iron ore from the Ukraine. The long straight *Leninallee* led from the ironworks to the community itself and the town was said to convey *'the harmonic satisfaction of the human need for working, living, culture and recreation'*. Three- and four-storey houses, described as 'palaces for workers', accommodated the majority of the inhabitants and social discrimination had been carefully avoided by placing factory workers, doctors and teachers in the same block. 'Palaces' was, however, something of an overstatement. Ulbricht would have looked at endless streets of flat-roofed, yellow-grey buildings, economically built by keeping the ceilings low and not one with any central heating. The deputy architect who had helped design the site later recalled: *'My wife was horrified when she first visited me in Stalinstadt, despite the fact that she came from the bombed Chemnitz and so wasn't used to anything special. She doubted whether we could ever feel at home here and raise our daughter. But eventually she got used to it.'* And, indeed, that is probably how most East Germans adapted to SED rule.

■ Political developments

The establishment of SED rule

Fig. 1 *The formation of the National Front group of parties, addressed by the new president Wilhelm Pieck*

According to the provisions of the East German constitution, the newly established German Democratic Republic (GDR) was a liberal state, which guaranteed fundamental rights, a **separation of powers** and a democratically elected parliament. The government that had been formed in October 1949 was a temporary coalition government pending elections. The SED party was certainly the most dominant political grouping within it, but it shared power with two important 'bourgeois' parties – the East German CDU and the LDP. This was a state of affairs that was not to last. Under Soviet pressure, elections were delayed for a year, to give the favoured SED time to build up its power-base. The East German Supreme Court and Department of Public Prosecutions were set up in December 1949, together with a Ministry of State Security, responsible for developing a secret police force (the Stasi), in February 1950. These enabled political dissidents, hostile to SED dominance, to be hunted out and prosecuted, some in public show trials. Heavy-handed terror tactics were employed and among those persecuted for their political beliefs were not only members of the CDU and LDP, but former SPD supporters whose commitment to the new party was suspect.

The SED also infiltrated the mass organisations, such as the Free German Trade Union Federation (FDGB) and the Free German Youth (FDJ), which had representation within the government. Before the elections were held in 1950, the SED persuaded the CDU and LDP to join with it in a 'National Front' in order to show solidarity. These three parties drew up a list of candidates offering the same policies, so that when the voters went to the polls there was really little choice. 99.72 per cent of voters (according to the official statistics) voted for the 'unity list' and while the SED only won 25 per cent of the vote outright, 30 per cent was won by the mass organisations and 15 per cent by the Peasants' Party and National Democratic Party – both of which had links to the SED. The bourgeois parties were carefully pushed to the political fringes and when, in 1952, the five Länder in the GDR were abolished and replaced with 14 *Bezirke* (districts), central SED-dominated control was extended still further.

The leadership of Walter Ulbricht

Walter Ulbricht became Party Secretary in 1950 and through this post, which was renamed 'First Secretary' in 1953, he dominated politics in the GDR until 1971.

However, in the early years of the GDR's existence, his position was far from certain. He not only had 'big brother' USSR watching his every move and regarding the East Germans as an inferior and 'defeated' people, there were also internal disputes within his own party and some challenges to his leadership.

It is perhaps not surprising, therefore, that the late 1940s and early 1950s saw the brutal suppression of those who suggested different paths for the future of the GDR.

Those Social Democrats who had remained within the SED were particularly vulnerable and despite the mass purge of 1948, a further purge took place in the first half of 1951. German-bred communists who had not made the journey to Moscow during the war years also came under suspicion, even when they had spent the Nazi years in prison camps, and any who had associated with the Americans were sought out for trial. Although the show trials in the GDR were not as drastic as those in neighbouring Czechoslovakia, such suspected 'deviants' were subject to social and political exclusion or worse.

Key terms

Separation of powers: this refers to the separation of the law-making or legislative body (parliament) from the executive (which carried out the laws) and the judiciary (which judged people according to the laws).

Cross-reference

The formation of the government of 1949 is outlined in Chapter 2, page 44.

More detail on the Stasi can be found in Chapter 8, pages 128–130.

Fig. 2 *Walter Ulbricht*

Cross-reference

Walter Ulbricht is profiled on page 30.

Cross-reference

For the purge of 1948, look back to Chapter 2, pages 30–31.

State and party in the GDR

GDR Government – democratic centralism

State Council

The Council of State consisted of the Chairman, his deputies and 16 members, elected by the *Volkskammer* (People's Chamber) for five years. Its tasks included issuing decrees which had the force of law, representing the country abroad and ratifying and terminating treaties; overseeing elections; maintaining defence with the assistance of the National Defence Council; proclaiming amnesties and pardons and administering the activities of the Supreme Court.

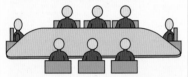

Council of Ministers

Known as the *Ministerrat* this consisted of 18 ministers under a chairman (PM) who, with the key ministers, made up the Präsidium. (Until 1960 there was a separate president.) Ministers were formally elected by the Volkskammer for five years (although in practice they were nominated by the Politburo). Officially, their legal drafts had to be approved by the Volkskammer but in practice they were always accepted. The Council discussed proposals put forward by individual ministers (who got most proposals from the Politburo and the Central Committee). The Council met weekly, while the Präsidium governed on a daily basis. The Council was responsible for directing and planning the national economy; working with COMECON; coordinating social policy; instructing and controlling lower levels of government and carrying out foreign policy.

How the state reflected the party

The government and SED Communist Party were closely interlinked. The main government officials were members of the SED (or at least from within its 'national bloc' of parties) and senior members of the government were usually members of the SED Politburo. The government bodies were therefore a means whereby the wishes of the party could be carried out.

SED Communist party

The Politburo

This was elected by the Central Committee and consisted of the General Secretary and 15 members of the secretariat and met once a week. The agenda was drawn up by the General Secretary. The 'first secretaries' directed other SED officials in district government and the army. This was the party's leading decision-making body and was highly influential.

The Central Committee (ZK)

This was elected by the SED Congress and most members remained indefinitely. The mass organisations also had representation here.
It comprised 51 full members and 30 candidate members awaiting vacancies in 1950. It met four times a year and its resolutions were passed to the Council of Ministers and the State Council, where they were turned into law. It ran party affairs when there was no Party Congress sitting and discussed and voted on key party issues.

Fig. 3 *The GDR Constitution and the SED*

Democracy in the GDR

GDR Government – democratic centralism

The Volkskammer

This consisted of 400 members elected every five years. Elections were supervised by local party officials and voters were given a 'single list' consisting of National Front (i.e. SED-supporting) parties which they had either to accept (and place unmarked in a ballot box) or reject (only then entering a booth to cross off the official list). The mass organisations (e.g. Free German Youth, Free German Trade Union Federation and the Democratic Woman's Federation) were also represented. The Volkskammer received reports and formally 'passed' legislation although it was really only a rubber stamp and voting was usually unanimous. It only met for a few days each year.

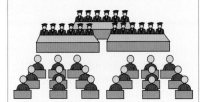

Judiciary

Legal and judicial bodies served as agents of the state. The Ministry of Justice was merely a formal body. The Supreme Court directed lower courts and the Office of the Prosecutor General was responsible for supervising 'strict adherence to socialist legality'. The Supreme Court was responsible to the People's Chamber and the Council of State. There were also community courts influenced by party officials at a local level.

The SED's claim to democracy rested on the concept of 'democratic centralism' whereby there was a 'chain of authority' from the 'people' upwards. The people elected the Volkskammer which elected the Council of Ministers and State Council. Similarly party delegates were 'elected' by party members to attend the Party Congress; the Congress elected the Central Committee and the Central Committee elected the Politburo. This suggested that the views of the people were carried to the highest level (democratic) while the 'centre' had contact with the people and passed decisions back down to them.

SED Communist Party

Congress

There were party congresses in 1946, 1947, 1950, 1963, 1967 and every five years from 1971. These were open to party delegates and provided a forum for the discussion of policies. They served to legitimise the party as a mass movement. Congress elected members to the Central Committee and approved the Central Committee's report.

City, provincial and local party organisations

Local party officials wielded much power and were carefully chosen by the secretaries to ensure support and control. For individuals, party membership brought advantages educationally and in jobs and housing. They elected delegates to the party Congress.

Cross-reference

More detail on Rudolf Herrnstadt and Wilhelm Zaisser is to be found later in this chapter, on page 76.

Cross-reference

The uprising of 1953 is covered later in this chapter, on pages 75–78.

The secret police, or Stasi, is discussed in more detail in Chapter 8, pages 128–130.

The political differences between Ulbricht, Wilhelm Zaisser and Rudolf Herrnstadt were only resolved, in favour of Ulbricht, after a failed uprising in 1953, the same year as Stalin's death; further 'factionalism' was promptly dealt with in 1956 and 1957–58.

By the end of the 1950s, Ulbricht's position seemed far more secure, in part because of the apparently loyal backing of his young protégé, Erich Honecker. Central control as a whole had also been tightened. This included the political bias of the judiciary, the extension of the standing police force (*Kasernierte Volkspolizei* or 'barracks' police) to 50,000 in 1951 and the setting up of the Ministry of State Security (February 1950) with an elaborate country-wide apparatus of security and surveillance.

Key profile

Erich Honecker, (1912–94)

Honecker had been an active communist in his youth and imprisoned in a concentration camp between 1935–45. After liberation, he became chairman of the Free German Youth in the Soviet zone. He rose in office and joined the GDR Politburo in 1956. In 1961, as Secretary for State Security, he arranged the building of the Berlin Wall. He initiated the overthrow of Ulbricht and replaced him as leader from 1971, becoming Head of State in 1976. In 1989 he lost office and fled to the USSR in 1990. He was returned for trial in Germany, but was spared due to ill health.

Party and State were fused into one with the disappearance of the five Länder in 1952. The leaders of the 14 new districts were responsible for all administrative matters as well as acting as the local party chiefs.

By the 1960s, and with the coming of the 1961 Berlin Wall, the greater security of Ulbricht's personal position led him to widen the scope of the Central Committee and allow more consultation with experts on specific policy areas. Younger and more qualified 'technical experts' were brought into the party machine and yet the centralisation of power continued and the final decision-making remained in Ulbricht's hands as the 'supreme father-figure'. However, from the mid-1960s, as Ulbricht suffered from ill health, Honecker began to assert himself, gradually undermining Ulbricht's position until he was finally able to outmanoeuvre the long-standing leader in 1971.

Cross-reference

The building of the Berlin Wall is the subject of Chapter 6, pages 89–102.

Key terms

Apparatchik: a loyal member of the Communist Party establishment, employed by the party and entrenched in the system.

Throughout his 22 years in power Ulbricht enjoyed immense power, although he lacked any personal charisma. He was the arch-bureaucrat or '**apparatchik**' and was sustained in his position because it was in the interests of the USSR to keep him there during this period of Cold War. He was surrounded by a few key decision-makers such as the Minister for State Security or Stasi chief, Erich Mielke, who held his position from 1957 to 1989, and Günter Mittag, Head of the Office for Industry and Construction from 1963. Mittag who was closely associated with Ulbricht's later reform programme and was ultimately to become Secretary for the Economy under Honecker.

The 'ruling class' which determined how the country was run was really very small. Although there were a large number of political functionaries (officials) involved in the running of the state, the majority of them possessed very little real power and enjoyed few privileges. Mary Fulbrook has even suggested (in *The People's State*, 2008) that these functionaries were worse off than their fellow citizens because they had no personal control over their careers, suffered acute pressures and stress and could not improve their lifestyles through (illegal) Western contact.

Ulbricht and the small East German power elite enjoyed a distinctive lifestyle. Between 1945 and 1960, they lived in secluded, well-guarded and spacious old villas, with pleasant gardens and a nearby park in the northern suburbs of Berlin, close to the USSR military headquarters. However, problems of security meant that in 1960 the top echelons of the SED leadership were moved out to a walled-in residential settlement 2 km from the small town of Wandlitz, in the woods north of Berlin, where conditions, although far short of the most opulent Western standards, were, according to Fulbrook, *'the height of hypocritical luxury'*.

Cross-reference

For more detail on Wandlitz, look ahead to Chapter 8, page 132.

While membership of the privileged elite brought benefits in terms of lifestyle, it also meant submission to party discipline. There was no personal life for a high-ranking party official. The key members of the Politburo and Central Committee spent their days working long hours in their offices. Most were in a dull grey building in central Berlin that had formerly housed the Nazi Reichsbank, although Mielke did not even have the dubious pleasure of meeting his fellow officials over lunch in the SED headquarters canteen, as the Stasi had a separate headquarters building. It was in these heavily guarded centres that the real work of running the GDR took place, by apparatchiks living in almost total isolation from the 'people'.

The riots of June 1953

Fig. 4 *The outbreak of riots in the Potsdamer Platz*

On 17 June 1953 the gradual consolidation of SED rule was shattered by an outbreak of strikes and demonstrations by workers which quickly spread from East Berlin to almost every part of the GDR. Ulbricht's leadership within the SED looked uncertain for a time and yet he proved able to ride the crisis.

The troubles were the product of a number of interrelated factors, both economic and political. The short-term cause was Ulbricht's May directive in which he increased the work norms (quotas) for workers by

Cross-reference

To understand the causes of the riots of 1953 fully, you should first read the section on economic development in the GDR, on page 79.

Fig. 5 *Workers' hopes were crushed by the arrival of Soviet tanks*

Exploring the detail

Rudolf Herrnstadt and Wilhelm Zaisser

Rudolf Herrnstadt (1903–66) and Wilhelm Zaisser (1893–1958) were SED members who opposed Ulbricht's methods of bringing socialism in the 1950s. Both had been active members of the Communist Party during and before the war, and both had spent time in Moscow. Returning to the GDR, Herrnstadt became chief editor of *Neues Deutschland* while Wilhelm Zaisser was appointed Minister of the Interior in 1948 and Minister of State Security, member of the Politburo and Central Committee of the SED in 1950–53. Zaisser was one of the most powerful men in the country and, using his vast knowledge of intelligence work, built the Stasi into a powerful organisation. On Stalin's death in March 1953, Moscow considered Zaisser as a replacement for Ulbricht but after the June uprising Ulbricht was able to consolidate his power and removed Herrnstadt and Zaisser. They were accused of being hostile to the party and removed from their positions.

Cross-reference

To recap on Beria's proposal to 'sell' the GDR to the West in 1953, look back to Chapter 4, page 61 (Exploring the detail box).

Key terms

Collectivisation: farming the land as a joint, or 'collective', group. Targets for production would be laid down and workers paid wages for fulfilling their allocated work.

10 per cent, but behind this there were underlying longer-term concerns affecting many groups within society:

- Enforced socialism had led to a mass exodus of the population (447,000 between January 1951 and April 1953), depressing the economy further and leading the bishops of the Evangelical Church, in February 1953, to warn the government to take notice of the distress.
- Workers resented low wages, high taxation (which was used to pay for the new armed border guards) and rising food prices.
- Farmers resented the low prices they were receiving for their crops and the fines handed out when they were late with deliveries.
- Independent businessmen and artisans feared their businesses would be nationalised by the state.

Politically, Ulbricht was under pressure to modify his policies. After Stalin's death in March 1953, he became more vulnerable, particularly since the new leadership in Moscow favoured détente with the West. Within governmental circles there was unrest following the arrest of the leading CDU politician Georg Dertinger (Foreign Minister) and LDP Karl Hammam (the Minister for Trade). Even leading SED members, Rudolf Herrnstadt, editor of the daily newspaper *Neues Deutschland*, and Wilhelm Zaisser, Minister for State Security, challenged the direction of Ulbricht's personal leadership and, for a while, they had the support of the Russian secret police chief, Lavrentii Beria, for some time considered the likely new leader in Moscow.

In early June the SED leaders were summoned to Moscow and told that they should halt moves towards **collectivisation**, give encouragement to independent businessmen and stop the persecution of the Churches. However, they did not force Ulbricht to cancel his new work norms. The resulting strikes and protests took the GDR leadership by surprise and shocked the USSR. In revealing the depth and breadth of social discontent, they shook the confidence of the SED elite and especially the authority placed in Walter Ulbricht.

From East Berlin, riots spread to more than 400 cities, towns and villages throughout East Germany and embraced a broad cross-section of society. Furthermore, as they spread they became more political in character and in addition to the abolition of quotas, demonstrators began to demand more fundamental changes such as free elections. There were chants calling for 'death to communism' and even some shouts of 'long live Eisenhower'!

Key profile

Dwight David Eisenhower, (1890–1969)

The US General Eisenhower had been the Supreme Allied Commander at the time of the defeat of Nazism in Europe and he led NATO from 1951–52. On retiring from the army, he served as President of the United States from 1953–61 and although this period is remembered for the anti-communist hysteria stirred up by McCarthy's 'witch-hunts', he ended US involvement in the Korean War and entered into negotiations with the Russians in 1959. However, the 1960 shooting down of an American U2 spy plane over the USSR and the 1961 construction of the Berlin Wall brought a deterioration in USSR/US relations in his last years of office.

A closer look

The riots of June 1953

On 16 June, building workers in the *Stalinallee* in East Berlin, where a massive construction programme was underway to transform the street into a Stalinist memorial, put down their tools and went to protest against the new work norms at the Trades Union (FDGB) headquarters. They were soon joined by others and in no time the affair turned into a general political protest. Since no senior SED figure appeared to speak to them at the central union building, they moved on to the *Haus der Ministerien* (the government building). Here, contradictory messages were received. Minister Selbman said the new work norms would be abandoned, but another Politburo message said that they would be 'reconsidered'. As the crowd became increasingly restless, they called for the resignation of the SED leaders, the lifting of the ban on the SPD, more consumer goods and the restoration of works councils. One worker announced a general strike for the next day – 17 June – and, indeed, on that day, a wave of uncoordinated strikes broke out in different locations in the GDR. It is estimated that approximately 300,000 to 372,000 workers went on strike, although this was only around 6 per cent of the total workforce. Workers gathered outside state and party offices and prisons, and there were even isolated attempts to replace the SED structure with local democratic governments. There was, however, very little participation in the upheaval from the middle classes, intelligentsia or peasants.

The end of the rising

Ulbricht had little choice but to back down on the work norms. However, the USSR was horrified by the escalating situation and reacted swiftly on 17 June by sending in tanks and Red Army troops, ordering them to

Casualties of the 1953 riots

The East tried to maintain the myth that the actions of the Red Army were responsible and restrained. Even today there is no consensus among historians regarding the numbers killed, but if to the doubtless under-estimated numbers of those killed in the streets are added those executed in the clamp-down which followed the crushing of the riots, there could have been in the region of 350 lives lost in this episode. There were, of course, also thousands injured or sentenced to gaol.

■ **Activities**

Thinking point

Could the riots of 1953 have succeeded in forcing change? Imagine you had been a participant. What would you have hoped to gain? Would you have expected more of your leaders?

Why was Ulbricht able to survive the 1953 crisis?

■ **Cross-reference**

East German foreign policy is discussed on pages 103–4.

open fire on the protestors. In total, around 20,000 Soviet soldiers and 8,000 *Kasernierte Volkspolizei* were deployed to crush the uprising. It is uncertain how many people died in this process but there was severe fighting in places, especially around the Potsdamer Platz, in Berlin. The official SED version put the deaths at 21, but other estimates have ranged as high as 125.

By 18 June order had mostly been restored, although there were still sporadic strikes and protests over the following few weeks.

The aftermath of the riots of June 1953

The crisis demonstrated that Soviet-style communism had not made any significant impression on East German political attitudes and Lavrentii Beria was arrested in the USSR on 29 June, partly because of his failure to bolster Ulbricht in East Germany. The USSR took the view that any thought of liberalising East Germany's internal policies had to be abandoned and rather than dismissing Ulbricht for provoking unrest by pushing the Stalinist line it gave him renewed support in order to hold back a further political and social crisis.

Following a trip to Moscow on 8–10 July, Ulbricht was able to gather sufficient support to take action against his political rivals. Zaisser, Herrnstadt and the Justice Minister, Max Fechner, who had defended the workers' right to strike, were removed from the Central Committee and expelled from the SED for factionalism in January 1954.

This left Ulbricht free to revert to his hardline policies and to carry through massive political repression. This included around 6,000 arrests and over the next few months the SED, national bloc parties and the national organisations were purged. Around 20,000 civil servants lost their jobs, as well as 50,000 lesser party members. Former Social Democrats featured strongly among those purged. At the Fourth Party Congress, Ulbricht was re-elected as First Secretary and, in the elections of October 1954, he again presented voters with a single list. Following these elections, which were hailed as an overwhelming endorsement for Ulbricht's leadership, 20 of the 28 ministries were given to members of the SED.

The Stasi was reformed, ordered to compile daily reports within each district and put under firmer party control. Under Soviet supervision, the police and paramilitary groups were re-equipped to make them more effective. Although the USSR insisted on some concessions – raising pensions, increasing the production of consumer goods and food prices lowered, any chance of radical change passed as Ulbricht became more entrenched than ever.

The crisis also confirmed the need for the USSR to build up the GDR diplomatically and economically as a separate entity from West Germany.

Further troubles in 1956

Although Ulbricht had survived the 1953 crisis, his position took another knock when the new Soviet leader, Khrushchev, gave his famous 'secret speech' in February 1956 announcing a policy of destalinisation at the 20th Party Congress in Moscow. Within the GDR there was considerable support for this approach and criticism of the SED had not disappeared. There was a rising in Posen in June and another series of strikes in August and September, while the Hungarian uprising at the end of October led to a further burst of industrial unrest and trouble in the East German universities in the autumn.

Ulbricht only just survived. There had been plans in Moscow to replace him with a more moderate figure; Karl Schirdewan had been selected and was being groomed for this post when the Hungarian uprising erupted. This distraction, coupled with Ulbricht's prompt action to prevent an escalation of troubles in the GDR by making political and economic concessions (including a cut in the working day, the release of 20,000 political prisoners and the use of factory defence forces) helped save his position. Khrushchev was anxious to avoid unrest in another satellite state by undermining its leadership and, in gratitude for his loyalty, Ulbricht was given another chance. He was thus able to defeat his reformist rivals (such as Wolfgang Harich who was arrested in early 1957), and by exploiting divisions among his opponents, he emerged dominant by the summer of 1958.

Key profile

Wolfgang Harich, (1923–95)

Harich was a journalist and Professor of Philosophy. He had been in communication with the SPD in the West and Polish reformists in 1956 in the wake of destalinisation in the USSR. He was pressing for liberalisation, democratisation and a change from SED to SPD government in order to facilitate reunification. Harich was arrested and sentenced to 10 years' imprisonment for establishing a 'conspiratorial counter-revolutionary group' – although he was released in 1964. His associates were given lesser sentences.

The economy and society

Ulbricht's approach to post-war reconstruction contrasted strongly with his Western contemporary Adenauer, since all policies in the GDR were shaped by communist ideology. The SED's main commitment was to build up a new workers' and peasants' state, so bringing about a radical transformation of East Germany, from a war-ravaged, traditionalist and largely agricultural area into a modern, classless, and industrial state. Through central direction, the old land-owning class; the bourgeoisie and the professional classes; the private businessmen and the factory owners; small independent tradesmen and farmers all needed to disappear in order to create this new-style Marxist-Leninist state.

Fig. 6 *Propagandist slogans abounded in East Germany. Here a shop reminds citizens to 'Be a friend of the Soviet Union'*

However, reviving and moulding the East German economy along these new lines proved a difficult task, particularly in the early years of the GDR. In comparison with the FRG, the state had some clear disadvantages and the SED's approach did not help matters:

■ Exploring the detail

The Marxist-Leninist approach

In order to achieve their vision of an egalitarian society, the SED pushed through policies regardless of the will of the people. This was in accordance with the Leninist view that it was necessary to be undemocratic in order to achieve what was in the people's own best long-term interests. The SED claimed to act on behalf of the 'oppressed classes', whether they liked it or not. They felt that the end justified the means.

■ Key terms

VEB: this stands for *Volkseigener Betrieb* or people-owned enterprise. This was the official form of industrial enterprise in the GDR. VEBs were publicly owned and were often combined in groups called *Kombinate*.

COMECON: Council for Mutual Economic Aid – set up in Moscow in 1949 in response to the Marshall Plan.

■ Exploring the detail

The expellees

By a law of September 1950 the expellees received some financial assistance to buy tools and household furniture and they were promised priority in housing. Thus their basic needs were met, but little more than this.

■ Cross-reference

For the uprising of 1953, look back to page 77.

■ After the initial dismantling of more than a thousand industrial plants, the USSR continued to demand heavy reparations – 25 per cent of all industrial goods – until 1950. Even after this, the SED could only determine the course of the economy with reference to the USSR (and from 1950, COMECON).

■ The GDR was cut off from supplies of coal and steel from the Ruhr on which its industry had depended and it had limited natural resources of its own.

■ The loss of labour, particularly skilled labour, to the West proved a drain which continued and grew as change spread.

■ State planning, involving changes in the management of factories, the splitting up of large farms and the introduction of collectivisation, led to dislocations and difficulties.

Industry

Initially, 213 *Sowjetische Aktiengesellschaften* (SAGs) were set up to produce goods for the USSR as part of East Germany's reparations. These included some of the most important factories in the chemical, mechanical engineering, electronics, precision tool manufacture and optical industries.

Most other plants were turned into **VEBs** which were deemed 'people's enterprises'. These nationalised industries accounted for approximately 76 per cent of total industrial production and these developed into large combines by the 1970s. Banking and insurance were also taken into the state's hands, while *Hos* – state trade organisations which ran a range of shops – were established to curb the independent retailers who were gradually undermined by punitive taxes.

Five Year Plans were launched on the Soviet model and ambitious production targets were set and constantly revised, to give the impression of progress.

In 1950, the first Five Year Plan promised to double the output of 1936. Its emphasis was on heavy industry and the demands of remilitarisation. This meant that metallurgy and machine-building were paramount. The same year, the GDR joined **COMECON** and by 1951, 76 per cent of its trade was hence directed to the Soviet bloc.

Starting from such a low initial base the plan was soon heralded as achieving striking success, most notably in iron, steel and chemicals. Of course, accurate figures are hard to find, but it would seem that the steel industry, at least, fulfilled its target and the economy was able to absorb and profit from 3.25 million expellees into the East German workforce, even if on less generous terms than in the West.

In 1952 at its annual conference the SED declared that the GDR was now ready for the 'Building of Socialism' and announced that it would accelerate its plans to overcome the last vestiges of capitalism. However, attempts to raise the level of productivity led to the uprising of 17 June 1953 and after Stalin's death more attention was given to the growth of the consumer goods industry.

In 1956, a second Five Year Plan introduced more regional specialisation so as to allow the GDR to fulfil its position in relation to the less developed countries of COMECON, but it proved a failure. In 1959, it was quietly abandoned and a new Seven Year Plan introduced with ambitious targets, particularly in the production of energy, chemicals and the development of engineering. Ulbricht announced that production was to be increased to such a level that by the end of 1961, the socialist economy would overtake that of the FRG with a higher per capita consumption of foodstuffs and most consumer goods. Although the plan brought some initial success, its targets were totally unrealistic and with another downturn in the 1960s the plan was abandoned in 1962. So, although the GDR economy was growing at about 3 per cent per year by the 1960s, this seemed poor compared with the 8 per cent averaged by West Germany in the 1950s.

Despite the propaganda and public announcements, the East German economy was beset by innumerable problems. Little heed was paid to supply and demand. Plans were often out of date before they were implemented, or managers met targets by lowering standards and not investing in equipment. By fixing prices for goods and emphasising quantity rather than quality or even demand, the state encouraged shoddy workmanship, dislocations in supply and targets which could only be met by neglecting the consumer industries and keeping wages at a permanently low level.

Growing numbers of East Germans fled to the West for economic rather than political reasons and by 1961, Ulbricht had been forced to build the Berlin Wall to stop the haemorrhage. This gave the GDR renewed self-confidence and in June 1963, the *neues Ökonomisches System* (New Economic System), which introduced a more flexible approach to economic planning, was launched. This permitted some decentralisation. Profit incentives and greater decision-making powers were granted to middle-level managers and a move away from the emphasis on quantity ensured that the profitability of goods (governed by demand) was taken into account in industrial planning. However, the system proved incompatible with the continuation of centrally-fixed prices and in the wake of the 'Prague Spring' in Czechoslovakia in 1968, the system was abandoned in favour of increased centralisation.

Agriculture

Here the move was towards the collectivisation of farms. The land reforms introduced at the end of 1945 had broken up large land-holdings and there followed two waves of collectivisation – in 1952 and 1960. The move towards the establishment of cooperatives began in 1952 and former independent farmers and farm labourers were forced to become members of collectives, borrowing equipment from government-owned tractor and machine stations. By 1959, 45 per cent of agriculture fell into this category.

After a second wave of collectivisation in 1960, 85 per cent of agriculture was collectivised. Changes were also introduced so that collectives had their own livestock and machinery, held 'in common'.

The change in established patterns of farming was initially detrimental to production. The lack of food supplies contributed to the troubles of 1953 and between 1959 and 1960 many farmers and hungry townsfolk fled to the West. Agriculture was beset by a lack of fertilisers reducing yields and a shortage of livestock reducing the country's supply of milk, cheese and meat. The situation was so bad that rationing of meat, sugar and butter had to be reintroduced in 1961 and through the 1950s, fat consumption was only 50 per cent of what it had been between 1934–38. However, the situation improved in the 1970s, by which time East Germany was largely self-sufficient, although its citizens had a rather restricted choice in their diet.

Cross-reference

The building of the Berlin Wall is the subject of Chapter 6, pages 89–102.

The 'Prague Spring' is outlined in Chapter 8, page 135.

Did you know?

The border between East and West Germany was closed in 1952 (see Chapter 6, page 90), but there was still a relatively easy 'escape route' for East Germans wanting to escape to the West. If they travelled to East Berlin, they could cross into West Berlin. From here they could journey to the FRG. In the years from the formation of the state to 1961, approximately 3.5 million people left the GDR this way (around 500,000 came the other way). The escape route was closed by the building of the Berlin Wall (see Chapter 6).

Activity

Thinking and analysis

Make a two-column chart. On one side list the main economic policies and developments in the FRG and on the other those of the GDR. (You may need to look back at Chapter 3 to help you with this.)

Use your chart to explain any similarities and differences.

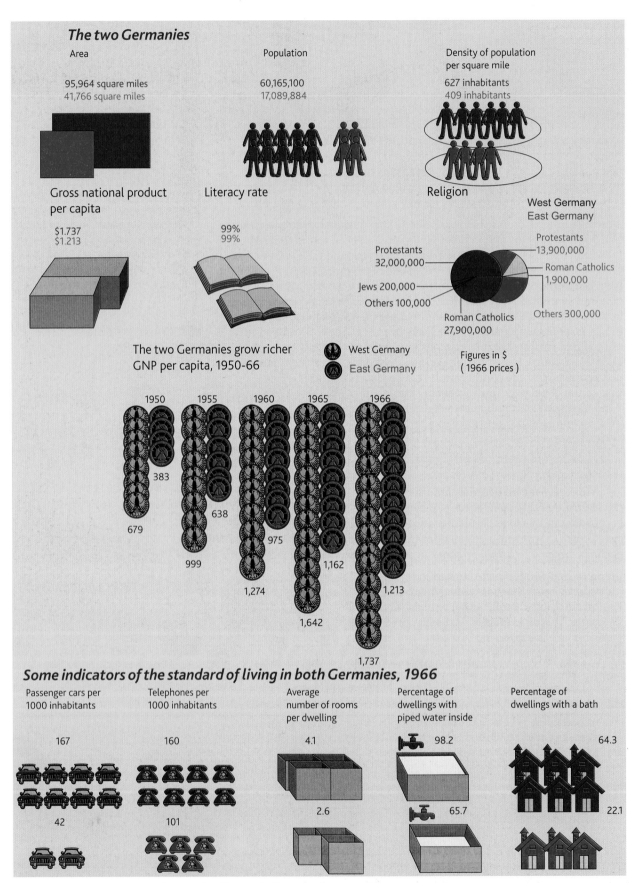

The two Germanies

Area

95,964 square miles
41,766 square miles

Population

60,165,100
17,089,884

Density of population per square mile

627 inhabitants
409 inhabitants

Gross national product per capita

$1.737
$1.213

Literacy rate

99%
99%

Religion

West Germany
East Germany

Protestants
32,000,000

Jews 200,000

Others 100,000

Roman Catholics
27,900,000

Protestants
13,900,000

Roman Catholics
1,900,000

Others 300,000

West Germany
East Germany

Figures in $
(1966 prices)

The two Germanies grow richer GNP per capita, 1950-66

1950 — 679 / 383
1955 — 999 / 638
1960 — 1,274 / 975
1965 — 1,642 / 1,162
1966 — 1,737 / 1,213

Some indicators of the standard of living in both Germanies, 1966

Passenger cars per 1000 inhabitants

167
42

Telephones per 1000 inhabitants

160
101

Average number of rooms per dwelling

4.1
2.6

Percentage of dwellings with piped water inside

98.2
65.7

Percentage of dwellings with a bath

64.3
22.1

Fig. 7 *The economic position and standards of living in both Germanies, 1966–67*

The attempt to impose State Socialism

The GDR had promised a 'workers' paradise' and it did offer its workers a reasonable degree of security in employment, housing and other welfare services. Basic foodstuffs were substantially subsidised, as were housing and transport, and everyone was entitled to benefit from the educational opportunities provided by the state. So-called 'workers' and 'peasants' faculties were set up to provide those from disadvantaged backgrounds with the opportunity to enter further and higher education. Efforts were also made to help women enter or remain in the labour force.

However, such benefits came at the expense of personal freedom. All workers were compelled to belong to a national trade union organisation – the League of Free German Trade Unions (FDGB). This gave workers some protection by arbitrating in disputes and also providing organised holidays and other workers' benefits. However, it acted as the mouthpiece of the SED, reporting on any 'subversive' activity and ensuring government decrees (for example work norms) were carried out.

Furthermore, although there were no 'classes' in the pure sense, there were still salary differentials and while top doctors, engineers, scientists and communist officials and generals might command comparatively high salaries and privileges, for the masses, wages remained low (at least in comparison with the West).

Fig. 8 *Monotonous rows of flats and office blocks filled East German towns and cities*

Everyone in the GDR had a job. Not working was considered asocial and punishable. Schoolchildren were introduced to the world of work with a weekly school day at a production plant to learn about the planned economy, while factories were like second homes, with flats for workers and their families. Some factories had hospitals, day nurseries and other facilities. Large factories had a 'wall of fame' with photos of workers who had met or surpassed the desired production levels and fast work was rewarded with bonuses, decorations or titles. The 'activist movement' encouraged effort and commitment and copied the Stakhanovite movement in the USSR. In the GDR, a 51-year-old miner, Adolf Hennecke from Zwickau, was carefully groomed to exceed his norm in one shift by 250 per cent, and actually achieved 387 per cent. Those who failed to meet norms, on the other hand, could be punished.

Promotion and access to professional positions was also reliant on the state and could only be achieved through the appropriate education and training, available only to political conformists. Under Ulbricht,

◼ **Did you know?**

The activist movement was modelled on the Stakhanovite movement in Russia, named after a miner who exceeded his production norms.

Summary exercise

Adopting the viewpoint of the ruling SED party, describe:

1 the ideal GDR citizen

2 the characteristics of a typical 'class enemy'.

there were positive measures to advance children from peasant and working class families, at the expense of middle class children. This state preference for those from the lower social bracket was partially relaxed in the 1960s, as scientific/technological changes placed a higher premium on education, skills and talent.

Thus, while communism brought upward social mobility for some, for others – most particularly those labelled as 'class enemies' because of their family's wealth or land – the discriminatory practices proved onerous or even unbearable. It is therefore little surprise that one in six East Germans fled to the West in the 1950s.

Youth and education

From the outset, youth activities were strictly controlled and monitored by SED party officials. Only officially sanctioned youth organisations were permitted and of these, the most important was the Free German Youth, (FDJ). This was established in 1946 as a vehicle for educating young people in the principles of the state.

Fig. 9 *Young Pioneers in the 1960s*

Membership was open to all between the ages of 14 and 25 but although membership was voluntary, it became essential for anyone who wanted to advance themselves educationally or in seeking jobs. A good deal of pressure was exerted through schools, but there was no doubt the organisation's control over recreational and sports' facilities, resort areas and entertainment, as well as university entrance and scholarships, persuaded the young that membership was worthwhile.

A further organisation, the Ernst Thälmann Pioneers, or JP – *Junge Pioniere* (Young Pioneers) was set up to cater for children of 6 to 14 years and by the 1960s nearly all children of that age group were members. They enjoyed its educational, cultural, and sports programmes for the young.

Among the other youth-oriented organisations was the GST – *Gesellschaft für Sport und Technik* (Society for Sport and Technology) which was established in 1952 and provided paramilitary training through sports activities such as parachuting, marksmanship and other skills-oriented programmes. The GST also held *Wehrspartakiade* (military sports games). The *Deutscher Turn-und Sportbund der DDR* (German Gymnastics and Sports Federation) was yet another youth organisation responsible for training athletes for sporting competition.

Complementing these youth organisations was a vast educational programme, whereby, from their earliest years, East German school children were indoctrinated in Marxist-Leninism in order to provide them with a new 'socialist' identity. The crèche and kindergarten were followed by a system of schooling designed to create the 'socialist personality'. Private schools were abolished and religious instruction had already disappeared in 1946. From 1954, a secular state ceremony, the *Jugendweihe*, was introduced as an alternative to religious confirmation.

In 1959 a system of comprehensive schools and a national curriculum were established. Marxist-Leninism was a compulsory subject at all levels (even higher education). An emphasis was also placed on practical work experience in addition to academic learning, and science and technical subjects were given a high priority. At every level achievement targets were set and teaching staff were subject to close supervision.

There were various routes into higher and further education, including a type of Sixth Form College – the *Erweiterte Oberschule* – for the more academic. There was a also a range of elite schools established for those identified as having special talent – be it in sport, music or as children of the political elite.

Schools and universities were viewed as vehicles for producing a supply of skilled workers, technicians and managers for industry and agriculture. Educational opportunity depended in large measure on political conformity. A university education or the opportunity to enter a profession was completely blocked to anyone displaying dissident behaviour or who came from a family of dissidents. Even the children of outspoken Christians could find their career paths blocked.

There were occasional youth protests in the universities and some 'deviant' youth behaviour. Symbols of Americanism, such as blue jeans and rock 'n' roll could land young people in trouble. Western influence was labelled 'agitation hostile to the state' and high spirits and the unguarded voicing of opinions was dangerous. A Stasi report for late November 1959 recorded:

> On 27.11.59 at 21.45 o' clock a horde of youngsters, around 80 individuals, came roaring down the Alaunstrasse in the direction of the Luisenstrasse and cried, 'We want our old Kaiser Wilhelm, We don't want Pieck, Grotewohl and Ulbricht, we want Rock 'n' Roll'. At the moment 15 people are in custody.

1

Exploring the detail
The Young Pioneers
This organisation was named after a former Communist Party leader who was murdered by the Nazis in Buchenwald Concentration Camp.

Cross-reference
Chapter 8 opens with an account of the experiences of one young female athlete (page 125).

That such behaviour was deemed worthy of an official report, says something about how the GDR checked up on its citizens. However, overall youth policy appears to have been quite successful before the 1980s. Membership rates of youth organisations were high, even if there was not a universal take-up, and most who failed to join did so for religious reasons. Petty incidents aside, young people were, on the whole, far less likely to cause trouble to the authorities in the GDR than their counterparts in the West.

A closer look

A defiant pupil – Rainer Penzel

Occasionally, despite the party's attempts to channel the energies of young people, some would rebel. Such was 17-year-old Rainer Penzel, who, until 21 September 1969, had been both a model pupil and a leader within the Free German youth. His crime was to organise a protest with some fellow sixth-form students against the erection of the Berlin Wall and a new law introducing compulsory military service, which, their headmaster informed them, was essential if they wished to go to university. They decided to wear black jumpers to school by way of protest – and refused to sing a pioneer song at the morning flag ceremony. Their activities were recorded and sent to the Politburo. Both Ulbricht and Honecker received personal copies of the report. Rainer was charged with treason and sentenced to five years in gaol. His parents were forced to undergo 'self-examination' and admit their errors in the political education of their children, some teachers were dismissed and the local FDJ criticised for their 'politically negative role'. Rainer later said, *'The prosecutor depicted our depravity in the darkest colours and tried to prove that we were dangerous. The others were sentenced to three and a half years. I was sentenced to five years because my actions had threatened the entire nation. We were dumbstruck. We weren't able to think any more.'* In prison, Rainer and his 'accomplices' were trained for menial jobs so that they could be integrated back into the working class when they were released.

Women

Equality of the sexes has always been seen as an important goal of communist societies and the GDR constitution of 1949 guaranteed women equality before the law. This included the right to work and receive equal pay. The revised constitution of 1968 went even further, proclaiming that work was not only a right but a duty. As a result it became the norm for women in East Germany to take jobs outside the home, and by 1977, 87 per cent of women between the ages of 16 and 69 worked in this way. Economic forces also encouraged women to work to augment the family income. However, although women entered the work place in huge numbers, the 'new socialist woman' was often burdened with traditional family duties too.

In 1965 a new Family Code called on men to shoulder their share of the household chores and the rearing of children, but the image of the working wife/mother was reinforced by social legislation that allowed them to take one 'housework day' off a month, have shorter working hours, longer leave and other benefits for childbirth. State nurseries, factory crèches and after-school provision helped women to cope and sometimes grocery stores and laundries were even provided in workplaces.

However, women never came to enjoy the equality that was promised and, whatever the official pronouncements might say, many found themselves forced to take the lower-paid, unskilled jobs or remain at the lower levels of all the professional hierarchies. Hardly any made the higher tiers of the political hierarchy and many had to shoulder the dual burden or work within and outside the home. While relatively high rates of divorce and children born outside marriage might indicate that women had opportunities for greater economic independence, there were also high rates of marriage and remarriage, which would suggest that many women felt the need for a partner on whom to rely for income.

 Summary question

With reference to either young people or women, explain how and why life in the GDR differed from that in the FRG.

Culture

As in the USSR, **socialist realism** was the main inspiration for the Arts and literature. Cultural activities were controlled by the state and measured according to their contribution to raising socialist awareness and moulding the socialist personality. Jazz, Western literature and modern art were dismissed as decadent and irrelevant.

All East German culture was subject to censorship and writers who felt unable to support the regime left for the West. Any type of literature, from a current affairs journal to a fictional love story, had a political agenda and only Church publications escaped the full rigour of the censor's scrutiny. Newspapers and magazines were either produced directly by the SED (and its puppet parties and the mass organisations) or were subject to political interference and censorship.

In 1959, after a conference at Bitterfeld, there was an attempt to forge a closer relationship between the manual workers and the Arts. Workers were urged to 'take up their pens' while writers were encouraged to seek experience of manual work.

Culture thus became subsumed into the state and was often little more than propaganda. Paintings, banners and slogans proclaimed the socialist message: love and friendship with the USSR, the glorification of the worker and the wisdom of political leaders.

The Church

The attempt to impose state socialism was hindered by one major institution – the Church. Catholics remained a quiet minority but the Protestant Churches, consisting of eight loosely connected regional Churches, provided a potential forum for opposition which it was hard for the SED to ignore. Ulbricht tried to weaken the Churches in the 1950s, removing Church influence in education, making the *Junge Gemeinde* – Young Christian organisation – illegal, introducing the *Jugendweihe* and promoting secularism. This all had limited effect, however, since the Churches continued to run old people's homes, childcare facilities, hospitals and other essential services on which the state relied. During this period, some East German Churches maintained their links with the West, but as the Cold War intensified these were broken.

This provided an opportunity for a truce between Church and State in July 1958. An agreement was made whereby the Church was allowed to continue as a separate body, respecting the 'development towards socialism' but the state had to accept that every citizen was entitled to freedom of belief and conscience.

Key terms

Socialist realism: this was the name given to art which expressed socialist values. Socialist art was meant to help the state fulfil its ideological purpose.

Cross-reference

The *Jugendweihe* is explained on pages 84–86.

The relationship between Churches and state remained uneasy throughout the 1960s but in 1969, German Protestants decided to form their own separate East German Church and work 'within' (rather than against or alongside) the state. This paved the way for better relations, but while the Church learnt to accommodate itself with socialist rule, individual Christians were left to their own consciences. Many kept their thoughts private. Those who spoke out, such as Otto Dibelius, Bishop of Berlin, found themselves subjected to repeated harassment.

■ **Key profile**

Otto Dibelius

Otto Dibelius (1880–1967) was a German bishop who became Chairman of the Council of the Evangelical Church in Berlin-Brandenburg in 1949. He had been a forceful opponent of the Nazis, but he was equally opposed to communism. Consequently, after the foundation of the GDR in 1949 he used his influence to condemn communist repression. Dibelius was forced to remain in West Berlin from 1961 after the building of the wall – the GDR refused to allow him to enter East Berlin or East Germany itself. He was President of the World Council of Churches from 1954 until his death in January 1967.

The impact of economic and social change

By 1955, the GDR could claim to be the wealthiest country in the Soviet bloc, but even Ulbricht knew that this wasn't enough. His attempts to catch up with, and even surpass, the capitalist West failed miserably, and he was never able to bask in the superiority of the socialist system which he so often spoke of.

The exodus of citizens spoke for itself and in 1952, the inner German border had to be fortified with wire fences and armed guards to keep the population on the Eastern side of the border – even that had proved insufficient; in 1961, a wall was to be built in Berlin.

This is not to say that there weren't those who accepted, and maybe benefited from, the economic and social change the SED brought. Certainly some of those formerly at the bottom of the social hierarchy saw a rapid rise in their fortunes. However, for those higher up, or for those for whom dislocation outweighed the social benefits, or to whom personal freedom was a value prized above all others, it was a different story.

It is difficult to measure the degree of resentment felt against these enforced social changes. For the vast majority of East German citizens, there was no escape from the political ideology of the state. The German writer J. Kocka has referred to the GDR as a *'politically drenched society'*, with its citizens, according to Fulbrook, *'institutionally incorporated into the social organisations of their state'*. For the majority of young people growing up in the GDR, this was perceived as 'normal'. However, for those who could remember a time before Hitler, this enforced control over every aspect of life must have been hard.

■ Cross-reference

The closing of the border in 1952 is covered in Chapter 6, page 90, and the building of the Berlin Wall in Chapters 4 and 6.

■ Summary question

'In the years 1949 to 1971, the GDR came nowhere near to creating the "workers' and peasants" paradise which it had promised'. Assess the validity of this view.

6 East–West Division in Berlin and in Europe

Key terms

S-Bahn: Berlin's above-ground railway network.

Did you know?

Vopo (short for *Volkspolizei*) was actually a West German nickname. In the East, the *Volkspolizei* were more commonly known as the '*VP*', '*Bullen*' and '*die Grünen*' (from the colour of their uniforms).

The night of 12 August 1961 began like any other for the duty police at the West Berlin Police Headquarters. It was only shortly after 1.00am on the morning of Sunday 13 August that strange news began to reach the station. At the Friedrichstrasse Station, the last stop for Eastern **S-Bahn** trains before they entered West Berlin, the conductors had shouted for everyone to get off. At 1.54am reports came in from Spandau that the S-Bahn from Staaken to Berlin was being turned back into the Soviet zone and passengers were being asked to leave the train. Reports from Wedding that the S-Bahn service at the Gesundbrunnen station had been disrupted soon followed. More ominous reports came at 2.20am: *'Fifteen military trucks with Vopos* (the people's police) *on board at the Oberbaum Bridge; armoured scout cars at Sonnenallee; Vopos and border guards with machine guns at the Brandenburg Gate'*.

Key chronology

13 August 1961	The border between East and West Berlin is closed, barriers are erected.
14 August 1961	Brandenburg Gate is closed.
26 August 1961	All crossing points are closed for West Berlin citizens.
26 June 1963	President John F. Kennedy visits Berlin and says: '*Ich bin ein Berliner.*' ('I am a Berliner.')
17 December 1963	West Berlin citizens may visit East Berlin for the first time for more than two years.
3 September 1971	Four Power agreement over Berlin; visiting becomes easier for West Berliners.

The Berlin Wall

The reasons for the building of the Berlin Wall

Until 1961, Berliners were still able to move freely through the entire city. Around 12,000 West Berliners worked in the eastern sector, while 53,000 East Berliners worked in the western sector. However, this freedom of movement encouraged obvious comparisons to be made. While living standards in the Eastern sector were tolerable, just a few hundred metres away in the West were opulent modern office blocks, town buildings and glittering shops full of a huge variety of desirable Western goods. Here West Berliners enjoyed an open lifestyle and political freedoms unheard of in the East. The temptation was obvious. The West had deliberately poured massive sums of money into West Berlin to put capitalism on full display and this, coupled with the picture of Western life seen on the West German TV channels, watched nightly with a mixture of curiosity and envy by many East Germans, had its effect.

The freedom of movement in Berlin offered an ideal 'escape' route for dissatisfied East German citizens who were otherwise unable to travel to the West, after the 1,381 km inner-German border had been sealed in 1952. They had only to walk or take a train across the open border into West Berlin and declare their intentions and from there, they could be flown or transported by road to the FRG.

■ Did you know?

Sealing the border, 1952

Between 1949 and 1952 the inner German FRG/GDR border had remained largely unfortified. However, Stalin was anxious that border defences be strengthened and when the Western allies decided to abolish the largely meaningless western zonal boundaries, the GDR ordered the construction of inner-German defences to keep out 'spies, terrorists and smugglers'. A 10 m (30 ft) strip was ploughed along the entire length of the inner border, with an adjoining 500 m (1,500 ft) wide zone (known as the *Schutzstreifen*) and a further 5 km (3 mile) wide zone (the *Sperrzone*) in which only those holding a special permit could live or work. Trees, vegetation and even houses were destroyed to enable border guards to keep watch over the border and the farming of fields along the border was only permissible in daylight hours and under the watch of armed border guards.

Fig. 1 *On the west of the wall, Berlin prospered and its citizens enjoyed high living standards*

Between 1949 and 1961, 2.5 million people had left the GDR (from a total population of approximately 17 million); approximately 1.6 million of these had departed the socialist state, through Berlin. This represented nearly a sixth of the East German population. Most of them were young, well-qualified and trained. In fact the SED had accused the West of deliberately wooing professional and skilled workers from the GDR to sap its strength. In reality, the move westwards was driven by the poor food provisions of the 1950s contrasting with the economic miracle in the West, and the expropriation and political suppression felt in the East. Nevertheless, this drain of manpower proved insufferable to Ulbricht. It was both economically and psychologically damaging his country and he was determined to halt the flow.

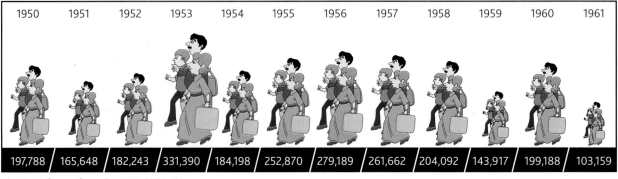

1950	1951	1952	1953	1954	1955	1956	1957	1958	1959	1960	1961
197,788	165,648	182,243	331,390	184,198	252,870	279,189	261,662	204,092	143,917	199,188	103,159

Fig. 2 *Refugees from the GDR, 1950–61*

■ Activity

Summary chart

In chart form summarise the arguments that might have been used by the SED to justify the building of a wall in Berlin and beside each, give the West's likely response to that argument.

Berlin had also become of symbolic importance in the Cold War battles between the USSR and America and its position – 110 miles into East German territory – had made it a useful base for espionage. Having Western capitalism on its doorstep had always antagonised the SED and it was particularly galling to find well-off Westerners raiding the East Berlin shops for cheap state-subsidised goods. The Soviet leader, Khrushchev, would ideally have liked to push the West out altogether and create a neutral Berlin. It was only when it became obvious that the West would not agree to such a demand that he bowed to Ulbricht's pressure and agreed to the closure of the border.

Fig. 3 *Adenauer visiting the Marienfelde Refugee Centre, which overflowed with East Germans seeking asylum in the West*

The Berlin Crisis, 1958–61

On 27 November 1958, Khrushchev issued an ultimatum giving the Western powers six months to agree to withdraw from Berlin and make it a free, demilitarised city. At the end of that period, Khrushchev declared, the Soviet Union would relinquish its own Berlin rights, which included complete control of all lines of communication with West Berlin (as guaranteed by the USSR under the terms of the allied occupation statute) to the GDR. This would mean that Western powers would only have access to West Berlin with the permission of the East German government – and this would, of course, also force them to recognise the GDR, whose legitimacy they had refused to accept. America, Britain and France rejected the ultimatum. They wished to neither lose face nor to abandon an important propaganda and intelligence base even though the stakes were high and the risk of war loomed. Consequently, they asserted their determination to remain in West Berlin and to maintain their legal right of free access to that city.

An international crisis was averted in 1959, when the Soviet Union withdrew its deadline. However, Khrushchev had succeeded in persuading the Western allies that the issue needed to be looked at again and a meeting of Foreign Ministers was arranged in Geneva in the summer of 1959. Although the three months of negotiations on the issue of German unity and the future of Berlin failed to reach any important agreements, they at least showed a desire to reach a compromise and led

Cross-reference

For the refusal of the Western powers to recognise the GDR, look back to Chapter 4, page 63.

Chapter 4 also discusses in detail the issue of East–West relations, including the Berlin Crisis of 1958–61, from the perspective of the West.

Activity

Thinking point

Why do you think Khrushchev was prepared to precipitate a crisis by issuing this ultimatum?

Khrushchev to visit the US in September 1959. At the end of his visit, Khrushchev and President Eisenhower issued a joint statement in favour of disarmament and said that the problem of Berlin and *'all outstanding international questions should be settled, not by the application of force, but by peaceful means through negotiations.'*

A follow-up summit, to be held in Paris in May 1960, was, however, called off at the last moment following the shooting down of an American U2 spy plane over the USSR. Ulbricht grew increasingly frustrated at Khrushchev's failure to stem the tide of border-crossers. He wanted this issue dealt with immediately and for it to be removed from the context of a broader peace settlement with the West, about which agreement seemed no nearer. He stepped up the GDR's own propaganda as the protracted negotiations had set off a mass panic in the East among those who feared the last door to the West would soon be permanently closed. In 1959 about 144,000 people fled the country; in 1960 the figure rose to 199,000; and between January and August 1961, an astonishing 181,007 people left. Of these emigrants, 48.2 per cent were under the age of 25.

Ulbricht was convinced that the only way to stop the exodus was to use force, but this presented a problem for the USSR because the Four Power status of Berlin specified free travel between zones and specifically forbade the presence of German troops in Berlin. Khrushchev retained hopes that the new, young and inexperienced US President John F. Kennedy, who took over in 1960, would prove easier to manipulate.

It is not known who made the actual decision to erect the Berlin Wall, but the impetus undoubtedly came from Ulbricht, Honecker (the minister in charge of state security) and the SED, rather than the USSR. During the spring of 1961 the East German regime built up supplies of building materials for the erection of a wall. Kennedy met Khrushchev at the Vienna summit of June 1961 and, in one last attempt to win the battle by diplomacy, Khrushchev renewed his ultimatum. However, Kennedy was determined to show that he could be tough and not only refused any revision of the existing Four Power agreements, he also showed he meant business by increasing the strength of the US military, requesting funds from Congress for a civil defence programme and the construction of fall-out shelters in case of nuclear attack. Ironically, it was also in June 1961 that Ulbricht declared, *'No one intends to erect a wall'*; a sure sign that he was already thinking of such a solution.

By the early summer, Khrushchev was therefore persuaded that he would have to agree to Ulbricht's request for support to build a wall to plug the border gap, and so at least deal with the immediate problem worrying East Germany. On 12 August, 40,000 refugees fled to the West. They were to be the last mass exodus before the wall's erection.

The building of the wall

The S-Bahn had been placed under the control of the GDR under agreements made between the allies at the beginning of the occupation. When news reached the Berlin police headquarters early in the morning of Sunday 13 August, of disruption to services at the East–West Berlin border stations, this was not their specific concern – although they were naturally anxious about what it meant. The situation in the West was made all the worse since the police were unable to contact the Mayor of West Berlin, Willi Brandt, who was at that moment on an overnight train travelling to Nuremberg to continue his campaign trail for the forthcoming West German elections.

■ **Cross-reference**

The events of Sunday 13 August are described at the beginning of this chapter, on page 89.

All 13,000 West German police officers were summoned from their beds to confront what rapidly turned into a crisis as uniformed men from the Soviet sector were seen advancing to the border line and stringing barbed wire and erecting barriers. By 3.37am, the Associated Press was relaying the news to the world that the Brandenburg Gate had been closed off and at 3.53am the German press agency confirmed, *'Vopo putting up barbed wire'*.

Meanwhile, in East Berlin, the 'Melodies at Night' programme had been interrupted at 1.10am, to inform listeners:

> The government of the Warsaw Pact States approached the People's Chamber and the government of the GDR with the suggestion that measures be taken at the border to effectively remove the subversive activities directed against the countries of the socialist bloc and to secure reliable surveillance of the entire territory of West Berlin.

1

To prevent any interference from East Berliners, armoured personnel carriers and tanks had appeared in the main avenues and 10,500 Vopo and Border guards were reinforced by military forces, who took up positions along the borderline.

Brandt was finally contacted at 4.30am and immediately flew back from Nuremberg. He later recalled: *'We drove to Potsdamer Platz and to the Brandenburg Gate. We saw the same picture everywhere: construction workers, barriers, concrete posts, barbed wire, GDR military'*.

By Sunday morning, 13 August 1961, the border with West Berlin was closed. The underground and overground train network, as well as the streets that had connected East and West Berlin, were cut in two.

That same Sunday, Miriam Flotow, who had until four days earlier been living in East Berlin but had moved back to her home district in the West after separating from her husband, heard the news on the radio and drove across with friends to Bernauerstrasse to see this wall for herself:

> The atmosphere was oppressive. There were many people there, standing dumbfounded, looking at the barrier of barbed wire and soldiers. Many people were crying, waving to relatives. I, too, had an Aunt in the East. It never crossed my mind I wouldn't see her again for years. We were all very emotional on this evening. But we were still certain that the whole commotion would be over soon. Even now with the city divided in two, no one thought that the division would last almost three decades.

2

A closer look

Bernauerstrasse

Nowhere in Berlin were the drastic consequences of the divided city presented more clearly than in Bernauerstrasse. Before 13 August it was a normal residential street in a densely populated Berlin neighbourhood. On both sides of the street were tenement houses and while one side of the street and the street itself belonged to the district of Wedding in West Berlin, the houses on the south side were part of the East German district of Mitte. There were border signs, but no one took much notice of them. However, all this changed. When the border barrier went up, residents of the buildings on the south, numbered 1–50 found themselves on the border line. No longer could anyone cross the street or meet friends or relatives on the other side. However, although the doors of these buildings were immediately sealed, the windows looked straight into the West and were thus regarded as a tempting proposition for those desperate enough to make the jump for freedom. Hundreds of people managed to find entry to these buildings and jumped through the windows in those first few days. There were dramatic scenes and even deaths. On 19 August Rudolf Urban attempted to slide from a window, fell, injured himself and died from his injuries several days later. On 22 August, 59-year-old Ida Siekmann jumped from a third floor window and missed the mattress that had been put down to catch her fall. She also suffered fatal injuries. On 24 September the police and Stasi attempted to pull 77-year-old Frieda Schulze, who had climbed out of her window, back into the building as the West Berlin fire department arrived with a safety net for refugees to jump into. However, the potential escape route did not last long. GDR guards walled up the windows and at the end of September the 2,000 residents on the East Berlin side of the street were forced to leave their apartments. These buildings were later torn down.

Fig. 4 *Desperate attempts at escape – Frieda Schulze makes a bid for freedom*

In just 24 hours, East German troops and workers had begun to tear up streets running alongside the border to make them impassable to vehicles and to install fences along the 156 km (97 miles) around the three western sectors in addition to the 43 km (27 miles) which actually divided West and East Berlin. Barricades of paving stones augmented the barbed wire, tanks were gathered at crucial places and all public transport and communications were disrupted. On 14 August the Brandenburg Gate was symbolically closed. Friedrichstrasse railway station alone remained open and here West Germans who had found themselves in the East of the city and on the wrong side of the new barrier said farewell to those they were forced to leave behind. Such were partings that took place there, it became known as the Palace of Tears.

The consequences of the building of the Berlin Wall

The end of the 'Berlin Crisis'

Fig. 5 *Tanks massed at Checkpoint Charlie in a frightening standoff in October 1961*

The erection of the wall left the West unsure how to react. In October 1961, US diplomats and troops deliberately crossed into East Berlin to test their right of access to the eastern zone in keeping with the original Four Power agreement and the Soviets reluctantly conceded the point. However, on 27 October, the 'Berlin Crisis' unleashed by Khrushchev's ultimatum of 1958, to which the Western allies had refused to agree, came to a head. American and Soviet tanks faced each other in a tense 'stand-off' at Checkpoint Charlie, one of the border crossings, and only after 18 hours was this tense situation defused as both lines withdrew. It was an admission that the GDR would be allowed to keep its wall and any lingering hopes of reunification were driven even further away.

Both East and West were forced to come to terms with what had happened and on the part of the superpowers there was a desire not to push matters any further. Both wanted stability in central Europe and were tired of the demands put on them by their respective Germanies. According to Tony Judt:

> The first decade of the Cold War had given German politicians on either side of the divide unparalleled leverage over their patrons in Washington and Moscow. Afraid of losing credibility with 'their' Germans, the Great Powers had allowed Adenauer and Ulbricht to blackmail them into 'hanging tough'.

3

Khrushchev went back on his promise to Ulbricht and did not sign a separate peace treaty with the GDR which would have given East Germany control over the access routes to Berlin. Futhermore, Khrushchev ordered Ulbricht to avoid any actions that would increase the tension.

In the West, some were secretly relieved that the wall had ended the threat of another confrontation over Berlin, like that of 1948. President Kennedy resigned himself with the comment, *'It's not a very nice solution but a wall is a hell of a lot better than a war'*, while his Secretary of State, Dean Rusk, observed that the wall had its uses, *'the probability is that in realistic terms it would make a Berlin settlement easier'*.

Fig. 6 *President John F. Kennedy made his famous 'Ich bin ein Berliner' speech in West Berlin to underline his support for West Germany almost two years after the building of the wall*

In the summer of 1962, Kennedy recalled the military reinforcements he had sent to West Germany but to appease West German anxiety, this was accompanied by promises that America would never leave their zone and this was reinforced by Kennedy's *'Ich bin ein Berliner'* speech in June 1963. The wall thus remained and between 1961 and 1989 it stood as a powerful symbol of the division between East and West, almost making Churchill's 'Iron Curtain' speech a reality.

Consequences for the GDR and for Berliners

Ulbricht may not have got all he had hoped for, but he had his wall and the knowledge that the USSR had not 'sold out' to the West proved a huge relief. Soviet assistance in shoring up his regime had again proved vital and the closed border in Berlin meant that he could consolidate his rule in the GDR. The SED justified the building of the wall as a defensive measure against 'Western imperialism' and it was referred to as the 'anti-fascist protective wall'.

With the building of the wall, free movement between the two sectors of the city came to an abrupt halt and GDR citizens effectively became prisoners within their own state. There were eight border crossings of which Checkpoint Charlie became the most famous, but these were for outsiders. East Berliners were ineligible for permits and West Berliners were equally unable to visit the East until 1963.

Cross-reference

An extract from Churchill's 'Iron Curtain' speech can be found at the beginning of Chapter 2, page 28.

Western reactions to the building of the Berlin Wall are the subject of Chapter 4, pages 65–66.

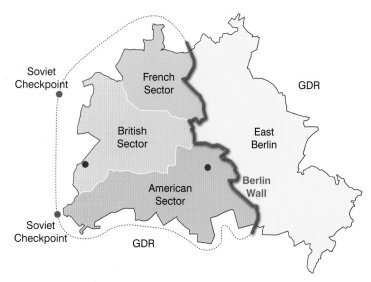

Fig. 7 *The divided Berlin*

The initial chaos was enormous, since families were divided and Berliners were unable to get to their jobs on the other side of the city. However, after the initial shock subsided, Berliners on both sides of the wall accepted that there was little to be gained by protesting and they learned to reorientate themselves within their own sector.

West Berlin survived on the enormous subsidies poured into it by the FRG. Fearing that its own citizens, and in particular young people of working age, would leave once half the former urban area had disappeared, the FRG offered *Zittergeld* (literally tremble-money) to families and individuals prepared to stay in the capital or come and settle there. However, this did not stop an exodus and by the 1970s almost a quarter of all West Berliners were over the age of 65 – twice the proportion in West Germany itself. Similarly only 15 per cent of children were under 15 years of age compared with 23 per cent in the rest of the FRG.

Nevertheless, in a determination to win the propaganda war, West Berlin was given generous grants and low business taxation so that it became the scene of impressive new town and office buildings, dazzling arrays of shops and international restaurants, including Italian, Chinese and Turkish. Some production facilities and administrative offices of federal government departments were relocated there and it also became popular among those looking for alternative lifestyles, with cheap rents, abundant night-life and no conscription into the Bundeswehr (which was forbidden under the allied occupation law). The walled-in half-city was thus kept alive.

It was a different story on the other side of the wall. There were no alternative lifestyles there, for the Stasi rounded up non-conformist youth and kept a tight watch on decadent 'Western' behaviour. A good deal of building took place – but much remained drab by Western standards – with identical tenement blocks, poorly surfaced roads and increasing pollution as growing economic pressures forced the ruling SED to cut corners.

In 1987, the East Berliner Lutz Rathenow produced a book simply entitled *Ost-Berlin* (East Berlin). He had to get it published in West Germany and it was banned in the GDR but in it he caught the atmosphere of the eastern half of the city all too clearly and his work went on to achieve cult status in 1989–90.

> An industrial city. Daily it hoists its smoke. A layer of filth settles over things. Everyone smells the same odour and soon nothing else at all. But the moaning bores you. The nose, unaccustomed to pleasant scents, needs the stench. You feel good in smog. Walks in the woods cause headaches. Like a friend who, to toughen up, smokes two packs a day of the cigarettes with the highest nicotine level. His maxim: fight poison with poison. I've never known a Berlin other than the one that exists today, except for my experiences as a child in the West section. Whoever lives here for years is reminded of the losses which new buildings cannot make up for. Destructive redevelopment at its worst. This ruthless destruction of evolved social structures was part of the plan to turn Berlin into a 'socialist city'. It's all conceived on the basis of statistically measurable humanity, the individual degraded to a thing that can be ignored.

4

Westerners were certainly aware of the different lifestyle of their Eastern cousins. The priority of Western politicians led by Brandt (Mayor of West Berlin between 1957 and 1966) was to make the best of a difficult situation by pressing for agreements that would lessen the impact of the wall on the personal level of individuals and their families. The first success was at Christmas 1963, when West Berliners were allowed to visit the eastern part of the city under special arrangements for a period of under three weeks (18 December 1963–January 1964). Each entry permit was valid for just one day from 6.00am to midnight and each visitor had to exchange 10 West German marks into East German marks at a rate of 1:1. Obtaining permits involved long queues of sometimes more than 12 hours in icy weather and not all were successful, but for those who made it there was finally the opportunity for a family reunion.

Cross-reference

For more on Willi Brandt, see Chapter 7, pages 113–17, and Chapter 8, pages 135–38.

From September 1964, pensioners from the GDR were allowed to visit relatives in the Federal Republic and West Berlin and, at the end of January 1971, telephone communication was restored between the two halves of the city. However, it was not until the Four Power agreement of 1971 that conditions markedly improved. Following this accord, new negotiations took place to increase travelling rights, allowing West Berliners to travel to the east for 30 days a year. This helped normalise relations between the two halves of the divided city.

Cross-reference

For the Four Power agreement of 1971, look ahead to Chapter 8, page 137.

Wall escapes and victims

Fig. 8 *A young East German soldier makes a leap for freedom*

Only 48 hours after the wall went up, Conrad Schumann, a young 19-year-old soldier of the GDR's National People's Army, was marching up and down beside the low barbed wire barrier, carrying his gun and fulfilling the orders he had received to stop the people on Bernauerstrasse from entering the West. As he did so, he could hear the taunts of the Westerners and they proved enough. He jumped over the fence, threw down his weapon and ran to a West German police van. On the western side, a photographer caught the moment and the picture was flashed all over the world. It was a wonderful piece of propaganda for the West, but also a sign of what was to come. In the first six weeks after the border was closed 85 border guards fled to the West.

Initially, the border guards were ordered not to fire real bullets to prevent escapes, but on 22 August the Politburo, tiring of the endless escapes, issued the order, *'that any violation of the border to our German Democratic Republic, will be answered with the call of firearms'*. On 24 August, 24-year-old Günter Liftin was the first to die in this way. He had attempted to escape by swimming across the Humboldt Harbour which was on border territory. A guard had fired two warning shots, which he ignored; the guard then aimed. The third shot killed him.

Fleeing from the GDR became a very dangerous undertaking. On 29 August, Roland Hoff was shot while attempting to swim across the Teltow Canal and by the end of October, 15 people had lost their lives, despite international protests. During the 28 years of the wall's existence, over 100 were shot trying to escape. A further 3,200 people were also caught trying to escape; they were arrested and given prison sentences of many years.

There were other deaths too. In June 1962, Reinhold Huhn, a border guard, was shot by a West German 'escape-agent'. Within the GDR his death was celebrated as that of a martyr in the fight against the West and the incident became a pretext for the strengthening of the border defences.

> ### Did you know?
> The last person to be shot while attempting to flee was killed in February 1989, although one more would-be escapist in May of that year took to the skies in a self-made hot-air balloon which crashed and killed her.

It is, perhaps, surprising that more than 5,000 people actually succeeded in escaping (574 were members of the armed forces). Some of these attempts involved elaborate schemes and months of careful planning and operations were often aided by 'escape-helpers' living in the West who acted from political motives – or in the hope of monetary gain. Tunnels were dug between East and West and cars were equipped with hiding places and false foreign passports acquired. One intrepid group cut the top off a car and deflated the tyres to a point where the car could still move and pass beneath low road blocks.

In December 1961, a passenger train en route from Hamburg to Berlin with a steam engine and 32 passengers on board succeeded in ramming through the barrier to carry its passengers into Western territory unharmed. In June 1962 a group of refugees on a passenger steamer escaped across the Landwehr canal. In 1964, nine people successfully escaped in hidden compartments in a BMW while in 1966, two East Berliners managed to tear down a piece of the wall with a bulldozer.

■ Exploring the detail

In August 1962, Peter Fechter, an 18-year-old East Berliner, and a friend dodged the border guards to make an escape attempt to the West. His friend successfully scaled the final wall and made it to freedom, but Peter was not so lucky. As he tried to climb the final barrier he was shot and slid back into No Man's Land. The West Berlin police arrived but did not dare approach, so Fechter lay wounded for around an hour and may already have died by the time the East German police removed him under the cover of a smokescreen. He was pronounced dead at the East German police hospital. Fechter's death provoked violent demonstrations in West Berlin. He became a martyr representing the ruthlessness of the East German regime.

Fig. 9 *Adenauer lays a wreath at the Peter Fechter memorial*

■ A closer look

The refugee escape-helper

Joachim Rudolph was an East Berlin refugee who had managed to crawl and swim his way to safety in the West in September 1961. Once there, he joined with others who were anxious to help relatives escape from East Berlin and they conceived the idea of a tunnel which would cross beneath Bernauerstrasse (where the southern buildings sat on the boundary) and on to the next street. Using only spades and pick axes, they set to work in the spring of 1962, from the cellar of an old factory at the corner of Bernauerstrasse (on the western side). At first they only dug at night, but progress was slow, so they brought in more friends and operated round-the-clock shifts, thus digging between 1 and 3 metres each day. Work was temporarily suspended when water seeped in and had to be pumped out and they eventually surfaced after 120 feet. Rudolph and two of the other tunnel builders cautiously emerged into the cellar of a building on the eastern side and Rudolph gingerly pushed his way out into the street where he could see the border guards patrolling. That evening, 29 refugees made their way into the narrow escape tunnel. There were young people and pensioners and even a four-month-old baby among them. But, as the first refugees were embraced in the West, there was another water leakage and the last refugees had to crawl on hands and knees through the mud. The tunnel could not be reused. 14 days later the tunnel entrance caved in on the eastern side and the tunnel was discovered. The border guards had never believed such a feat possible.

The extension of the wall

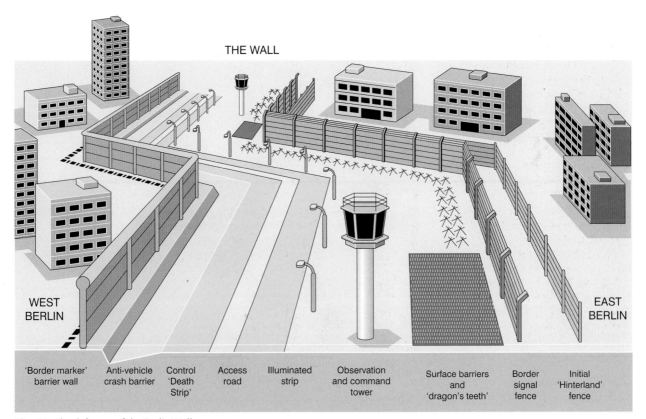

Fig. 10 *The defences of the Berlin Wall*

Over time, the wall was built up to become an increasingly effective defence. On 15 August – the same day that Schumann made his dramatic escape in a single leap – soldiers had already begun removing the temporary barrier and replacing it with a concrete wall topped with barbed wire. By November 1961, metre-wide concrete plates were piled on top of one another, for example in front of the Brandenburg Gate where the ground level was slightly lower than elsewhere. East German border units were also set up as a subsection of the GDR army from September 1961, with special training for the increasingly complex task of border defence.

The wall became ever more monstrous. In June 1962, a second, parallel fence some 100 metres farther into East German territory was built and buildings that stood in the border area were pulled down. Even graveyards were flattened and the underground canal system was barricaded. The empty area between the fences was known as 'No Man's Land' or the 'Death Strip' and was 6–15 metres wide. The No Man's Land was covered with raked gravel, to show up footprints and offered no cover. It had clear fields of fire for the wall guards and was also patrolled by guard dogs.

In 1966, watchtowers were erected and other elaborate defences appeared. There were anti-vehicle ditches dug to stop motorised escapes, five metre-high lamp masts to illuminate the area, a control path for patrol cars, a sensor and signal fence which set off an alarm when touched and watchtowers, bunkers, tripwire, shooting sites and dog-runs. This 'death strip' was also patrolled by border guards who were stationed at regular intervals. The 'third-generation' wall of 1968 also had a pipe-shaped topping to make any attempt to scale it with a ladder virtually impossible, and in 1971 a further fence of close-knit barbed wire was added.

■ Exploring the detail

Final attempts to extend and reinforce the wall began in 1976 when the square blocks and concrete girders on the west were replaced by a 3.6 metre-high wall made of prefabricated concrete plates. This was referred to as the 'fourth-generation wall' and remained until 1989. The individual concrete segments were 3.6 metres high, 1.20 metres wide and 15 centimetres thick. A new asbestos and concrete pipe 40 centimetres in diameter was also placed on top of the wall and a 2.10 metre projecting 'foot' abutment made the wall stable, so that not even a heavy truck could break through it. It is estimated that 45,000 concrete segments, costing 359 DM each, were erected around West Berlin.

Fig. 11 *Concrete soon replaced barbed wire to provide a more effective barrier*

■ Activity

Creative thinking

Create a poster display on the Berlin Wall and its impact. Different members of the group might like to concentrate on different aspects linking to both the wall and its defences, and the attempted escapes through, under and over it.

■ The influence of the USSR and the Warsaw Pact: relations with the West

Fig. 12 *As the position of Berlin again appeared uncertain, John F. Kennedy met with Nikita Khruschev in Vienna in June 1961*

Influences on the GDR

The GDR's relations with foreign powers were characterised by two massive constraints. Firstly, the GDR was firmly planted within the Soviet bloc and owed its very existence to the ambitions of the USSR. This meant that its freedom of action was limited by the USSR. It was almost impossible for Ulbricht to act without the full backing of 'Mother Russia' – even in domestic affairs, he was constantly reminded of the GDR's dependency on the USSR. This is highlighted in the appeal for Russian tanks to crush the workers' uprising in June 1953, or in the need for Soviet backing for the building of the Berlin Wall in 1961.

The other constraint was the attitude of the West and, in particular, that of the FRG. Through the Hallstein Doctrine, the FRG refused to have diplomatic relations with any country (other than the USSR) which recognised the GDR as an independent state. The West claimed to speak for the East Germans in all matters, in the absence of any democratic right for the East German people to voice their own opinions. This meant that any country wishing to benefit from the possibilities of trade with the FRG was effectively barred from having anything to do with the GDR, leaving the latter isolated.

The GDR thus found itself a victim of the Cold War between the USSR and the US-dominated West. While the Cold War raged, Berlin remained divided and the FRG turned its back on the GDR, preferring the comfort of Western integration to a desire for German reunification. The West took heart that Adenauer's 'magnet theory' appeared to be working and until the coming of the wall in 1961, the numbers of refugees fleeing the West had heartened the FRG, while leaving the GDR struggling to preserve its own national identity.

■ Activity

Discussion point and summary essay

In pairs, consider the following question: 'Why was Berlin a centre of Cold War tension between 1945 and 1961?'

To answer this, you will probably want to refer back to Chapters 2 and 4. Share your thoughts with your class and write an essay answer to the question.

■ Cross-reference

The FRG's foreign policy, including the Hallstein Doctrine, is discussed in Chapter 4.

Cross-reference

For the issue of the Polish–German border and the agreements reached at the Potsdam Conference, refer back to Chapter 1, pages 17–18.

Did you know?

The only time the Warsaw Pact countries acted as a joint force was in the invasion of Czechoslovakia in 1968 to crush a rebellion that was threatening communist dominance.

The GDR looked eastwards, of necessity. An early move was to recognise its frontier with Poland, a fellow Soviet state. In the Goerlitz (or Zgorzelec in Polish) Treaty of July 1950, the GDR accepted the Polish–German frontier, along the Oder–Neisse Line, as agreed at Potsdam. However, although the treaty bound Poland and the GDR, apparently settling the long-standing dispute over Germany's eastern frontier, it was not regarded as legitimate by the West. Since the member states of NATO refused to recognise the GDR's legitimacy to make international treaties, this left the Poles uncertain as to whether there would be a further revision.

The Warsaw Pact

When West Germany was admitted to NATO in 1955, it confirmed the USSR's fears of the dangers of the return of an armed Germany on its borders. Consequently, the USSR set about creating the Warsaw Pact in May 1955 to bring the states of eastern Europe together under a single military command. In order for the GDR to be accepted into this defence alliance, the USSR had to recognise its sovereign status. As a result, admittance into the Warsaw Pact helped to strengthen the position of the GDR.

The treaty provided for friendship, cooperation and mutual assistance between the eight communist states of eastern Europe: Poland (where the treaty was signed), Czechoslovakia, Hungary, Romania, Albania, Bulgaria the GDR and, of course, the USSR. Each state provided a promise of mutual defence if any of its members was attacked, but they also made a pledge not to interfere in the internal affairs of other member countries and to respect each country's national sovereignty and political independence.

Membership of the Warsaw Pact demanded that the GDR have its own army; the *Nationale Volksarmee* (National People's Army or NVA) was set up in 1956. At first, around a quarter of the officer corps was made up of former officers of the Nazi Wehrmacht and their military knowledge and combat experience combined with that of USSR-trained officers helped to build an effective fighting force. As the World War II veterans gradually retired, political allegiance became the most important criterion for promotion. The proportion of SED members in the officer corps reached almost 95 per cent by the later 1960s and the SED ensured control by organising intensive political education for all ranks.

In its first six years, the NVA was an all-volunteer force in the lower ranks but conscription was introduced in 1962, and the NVA's strength was increased to about 170,000 troops. The NVA described itself as 'the instrument of power of the working class'. The motto, inscribed on its flag, was 'For the Protection of the Workers' and Farmers' Power', and it claimed to protect peace and secure the achievements of socialism. However, since East Germany was at the frontline of the Cold War, the Volksarmee was heavily funded by the USSR and its chief purpose was to be in a state of readiness, in case of a conflict with NATO. Indeed, such was the degree of USSR commitment that the army became the best-trained and equipped in the Warsaw Pact, with the exception of the USSR's own forces.

The coming of the Warsaw Pact had a downside for Germany as a whole, however, in that it hardened the division of the country. Although the eastern states and the USSR had recognised the GDR, the FRG still refused to do so, and in the later 1950s, the GDR was in quite an isolated position. It made treaties with China and Mongolia as well as improving its relations with Poland, but its non-recognition put it in an unfavourable position, even with regard to developing countries.

The GDR welcomed the Berlin Crisis of 1958–59, since they regarded the presence of the Western powers in Berlin as an affront to their national sovereignty in the East. The SED had wanted a much tougher stance than Khrushchev was prepared to offer though. Ulbricht had hoped to banish the West and take full sovereignty over Berlin for the GDR, but for the USSR, Berlin was simply a pawn in the Cold War. Ulbricht initially pressed for military action, but when it became clear that this would not happen, he gave support to Khrushchev's ultimatum of 1958, which demanded the signing of a peace treaty with the two Germanies and a neutral West Berlin. With the failure of the ultimatum, Ulbricht tried to assert himself. He demanded that the USSR sign a separate treaty on Berlin with the GDR, and hand over Soviet control. Ulbricht even sent an official delegation to Peking in January 1961, at a time when Soviet relations with China were deteriorating, in order to put pressure on Khrushchev to comply. It is an indication of the GDR's limited powers to manoeuvre that Krushchev did not respond. However, as the flood of refugees from East Berlin threatened the state with economic collapse, the USSR did (reluctantly) agree to the building of the Berlin Wall in August 1961.

It was not until the late 1960s that the GDR's relations with the West took a turn for the better and the reasons were, once again, out of the hands of its SED rulers. As the US and the USSR adopted a policy of détente, in the wake of the Cuban Missile Crisis, so the possibility of an East–West German rapprochement became more likely. Under the 'grand coalition' of CDU/SPD in the West, which replaced the CDU government in November 1966, the Hallstein Doctrine was gradually abandoned and diplomatic relations were established with eastern European countries such as Romania (1967) and Yugoslavia (1968). Gradually, the FRG came to accept the reality of the Soviet bloc and the GDR and, under a new West German Chancellor, Willi Brandt, relations were revolutionised from 1969 through the policy known as ***Ostpolitik***.

Learning outcomes

In this section you have examined the way the GDR was moulded by Ulbricht and the SED. You have considered its political, economic and social development and have been invited to reflect on the impact of those developments. You have also seen how a combination of economic and political problems forced the country to close its borders and erect the Berlin Wall, effectively 'imprisoning' its population. A study of the GDR's relationship with the USSR and the West has also enabled you to appreciate the constraints under which the GDR functioned. How some of those constraints were broken down will be seen in the next section.

■ Cross-reference

To recap on the Berlin Crisis of 1958–61, review pages 91–92 and also Chapter 4, pages 63–64.

Foreign police in the GDR after 1961 is covered in Chapter 8.

■ Key terms

Ostpolitik: a new eastern policy intended to reduce tensions between East and West and to enable West Germany to work with eastern bloc states (including the GDR) for their mutual benefit. Ostpolitik is covered in detail in Chapter 8.

Practice question

'Ulbricht was a very skilful and successful leader of the GDR between 1949 and 1971.' Assess the validity of this view.

(45 marks)

Study tip Before answering the question, you need to reflect on the most suitable plan. At A2 it will not always be possible to simply balance points which agree with a quotation against those that do not, since views, such as this one, may have more than one point on which agreement and disagreement might take place. Being skilful is not the same as being successful and both need to be assessed. It might therefore be better to consider a thematic approach here. You could, for example, think of politics, the economy, society, foreign relations and for each make a note of the times when you feel Ulbricht was skilful, and others where he was not, as well as times when he was successful and others where he failed, at least in part. Before you begin to write you need to decide whether on balance you think he was skilful and successful – or was only one of these – or whether he failed on both counts. Try to make some independent judgement and uphold this in your answer as you debate the various areas he dealt with.

The Two Germanies, 1961–1989

Internal Developments in the West

On 2 June 1967, the Shah of Iran was on a state visit to West Berlin. As he drove in procession for his evening's entertainment at the Opera House, thousands of students lined up behind police barricades to protest against the Shah's brutally repressive regime. A few lobbed paint-filled balloons, but none came close to the Shah, who disappeared into the Opera House without even noticing the protest. However, as the protestors began to disperse, the police swooped, using a new technique known as the 'Liver-Sausage Method'. This was so called because the crowd of demonstrators was 'stuffed' long and tight on the pavement between the barricades and buildings – like a stuffed liver sausage. As policemen rushed into the middle of the 'sausage', the demonstrators pushed sideways (causing the sausage to explode at both ends) whereupon hundreds of police were waiting with their truncheons at the ready. In the pandemonium, a protester whom the police took to be a ringleader was seized and a gun pointed at his head. Probably accidentally, that gun went off and Benno Ohnesorg, who had never before attended a protest demonstration, was left dead. Another protestor, Gudrun Ensslin, screamed '*This fascist state means to kill us all! We must organise resistance. Violence is the only way to answer violence. This is the Auschwitz Generation, and there's no arguing with them!*'

Key chronology

October 1963	Erhard becomes Chancellor
December 1966	Kiesinger forms the Grand Coalition
April 1968	Rudi Dutschke is shot
May 1968	Emergency law is passed by the Bundestag
October 1969	Brandt becomes Chancellor
November 1972	Brandt is re-elected
November 1973	Rise in oil prices
May 1974	Resignation of Brandt; Schmidt becomes Chancellor
October 1976	SPD/FDP coalition under Schmidt just manages to retain power
October 1977	Mogadishu Incident
1980	Formation of the Green Party
October 1982	Kohl becomes Chancellor
January 1987	FDP/CDU/CSU coalition under Kohl retains power with a reduced majority

Cross-reference

The various political parties are summarised in Chapter 3, page 46, along with the election results for 1949–61. The NDP was founded in 1964 and replaced the DRP. The Green Party was founded in West Germany in 1979 to campaign on environmental issues.

Political and economic developments in the West, 1963–1989

Erhard's chancellorship, 1963–66

When Erhard replaced Adenauer as the Chancellor at the head of a CDU/CSU-led coalition government in October 1963, it looked as though little was going to change. Indeed, Erhard's first speech

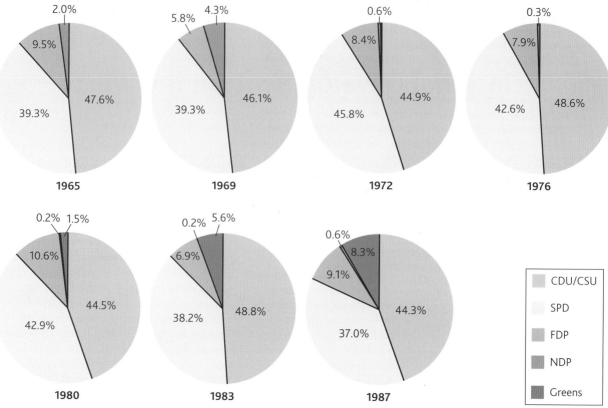

Fig. 1 *FRG election results, 1965–87, showing percentage of votes for the major parties*

■ **Cross-reference**

Ludwig Erhard is profiled in Chapter 3, page 53.

■ **Exploring the detail**

Adenauer's later years

Adenauer remained as party chairman at Erhard's bidding until 1966, but he was to prove a constant thorn in Erhard's side. Although the latter tried to consult him and telephoned him frequently, Adenauer persistently refused to talk to him and frequently criticised him in public, thus helping to undermine his position.

■ **Key terms**

Economic recession: this is a slow-down in economic activity, usually characterised by falling levels of investment and a decline in business profits, bringing lower levels of public spending and growing unemployment.

as Chancellor confirmed such an expectation. While he spoke of continuing developments in economic and social policy, for which his reputation went before him, he had nothing new to say on issues such as reunification, Berlin, European integration, defence or NATO.

However, Erhard soon found his leadership tested by an unexpected economic downturn. In 1964, economic growth had remained good with overall production up 8 per cent, wages up 8.5 per cent and the rise in the cost of living only 2.5 per cent. There was no unemployment and 850,000 unfilled jobs. The feeling of confidence which such statistics brought ensured that the CDU/CSU gained 47.6 per cent of the vote in the election of 19 September 1965, even though the SPD took 202 seats to the CDU/CSU's 246. The FDP gained 49 and continued as an alliance partner.

Erhard felt well able to launch a new social and economic programme – the *'formierte Gesellschaft'*, literally, building cooperation within a social market economy, but an **economic recession** hit the Federal Republic in 1965 which came as a shock to the German people. The crisis was first felt in the Ruhr coal industry, but it soon spread to the whole of the country. Its cause was primarily excessive public spending which had left the government's expenditure outstripping its income.

Helmut Schmidt, the SPD leader, complained that the government had overspent modernising the railways and had paid more than it should have done for military equipment from the US. Erhard's 'green plan' which subsidised agriculture was also proving extremely costly and with wages rising faster than production the result was high inflation.

Helmut Schmidt, (born 1918)

Schmidt was the son of a schoolteacher from Hamburg and was still a student when the Second World War broke out. He served in an armoured division on the eastern front and then returned to Hamburg after the war to complete his studies in economics. He joined the SPD and worked in city administration between 1949 and 1953. He was elected to the Bundestag in 1953 and served as Minister of Defence from 1969–72 and Minister of Finance from 1972–74. He was elected Chancellor in 1974. During his second term he lost the support of the left wing of his party, and the emerging Green Party, and was succeeded as Chancellor by Kohl in 1982.

Inflation was running at 4 per cent per annum by 1966, and Erhard was forced to cut his spending plans by 10 per cent and order economies. He even suggested everyone might work an extra hour per week – a proposal which was rapidly shouted down by unions that were trying to negotiate higher pay and a shorter working week. He also raised interest rates to reduce demand and try to get prices down, but this only plunged Germany further into recession.

The neo-Nazi National Democratic Party (NPD) founded in 1964 enjoyed unexpected success as a result of the downturn. It decried the 'weak and ineffectual' government of the FRG and although it did not poll enough votes to gain a seat in the 1965 Federal elections, it won eight seats in the Land elections in Hesse and 15 in Bavaria in November. Commentators began to express the fear that the FRG would (like the Weimar Republic) be unable to stand up to the economic crisis.

In July 1966, the CDU/CSU coalition lost the Land election in Rhineland-Westphalia, which was a sign of its failing strength. There were disputes within the coalition over how to deal with the recession and while the CDU/CSU wanted to raise taxes, the FDP saw spending cuts as the way out of the crisis. To make matters worse, Erhard failed to persuade the Americans to accept cuts in the FRG's contribution to the stationing of American troops in West Germany, and the FDP resigned from the coalition. Consequently Erhard was forced to resign in November 1966 and was replaced as CDU/CSU leader, and Chancellor by Kurt Georg Kiesinger. Willi Brandt became Deputy and Foreign Minister.

Cross-reference

Willi Brandt is profiled on page 113.

Question

The Erhard administration of 1963 to 1966 is generally written off as a failure. Is this fair?

Kurt Georg Kiesinger, (1904–88)

Kiesinger came from Tübingen and was educated there and in Berlin, where he worked as a lawyer. He joined the Nazi Party but refused to become a member of the Guild of National Socialist Lawyers in 1938. During the Second World War he worked in radio propaganda. In 1945, he was interned by US troops, but cleared by a denazification court. He entered politics as a founding member of the CDU and served in the Bundestag between 1949 and 1958. He then became Minister-President (prime minister) of Baden-Württemberg between 1958 and 1963. He replaced Erhard as Chancellor in 1966, but having lost the support of the SPD in the Bundestag in 1969, he was succeeded by their leader, Willi Brandt.

The grand coalition of 1966–69

Fig. 2 *Negotiations for the Grand Coalition, 1966. Front (l–r) CDU – Barzel and Kiesinger; Back (l–r) SPD – Brandt, Schiller and Schmidt*

The problems facing the state were considered so serious that a temporary alliance between the CDU/CSU and the SPD was forged and a 'grand coalition' under Kiesinger formed in December 1966. It had its advantages for both sides of the partnership. The SPD finally had their chance to show their ability in government, while the CDU/CSU escaped from the demands of the FDP. Most Germans welcomed this development, in the face of economic difficulties, but there were also those on the left who felt that forming a government with such an overwhelming majority was tantamount to turning the FRG into a one-party state. There were also some criticisms of Kiesinger himself, particularly from left-wing writers such as Günter Grass, since the new Chancellor had once been a member of the Nazi Party. It could be claimed that it was his work – as a lawyer – that had forced Nazi Party membership, but the charge never went away and Kiesinger was acutely embarrassed by it.

Criticisms increased when, in May 1968, the coalition added an amendment to the constitution, to permit an elected committee to take emergency measures in the event of civil unrest or war. Formerly, only the 'occupying powers' had possessed such a right, but under this amendment, an elected committee of 22 members of the Bundestag, together with one representative from each Land (state) in the Bundesrat, was to have the power to issue decrees if two-thirds of the committee agreed. Again, left-wing journalists, writers and intellectuals joined students in an outcry of protest, in which concerns about the future of parliamentary democracy in Germany were voiced. The SPD Students' Federation set up the APO (Extra-Parliamentary Opposition) while a group which styled itself the 'Emergency of Democracy' fiercely campaigned against the constitutional amendment, fearing it might become another Article 48.

The grand coalition faced opposition from the extreme right as well as the left with the extremist NPD gaining in strength. The right-wing NPD gained 48 seats in six different Länder parliaments in 1967 and did even better in 1968, winning 12 seats in Kiesinger's own Land – Baden-Württemberg. Its very existence contributed to a sense of political agitation which contrasted with the prevailing political apathy of the 1950s. There was even discussion about changing the proportional representation system to a direct, first-past-the-post system, as in Britain, so as to make it virtually impossible for such an extremist party to win a seat. However, a public survey in January 1968 revealed that such a system would perpetuate the rule of the CDU/CSU, to the detriment of the SPD, and consequently support for change waned.

Despite the political tensions, the coalition allowed an official West German Communist Party (DKP) to be formed in September 1968. Although the Communist Party had been banned in 1956, it had continued as an underground movement and at a time when a number of young people were rejecting the established parties in Germany, it was felt that a legitimate party would be less dangerous than a 'secret' network.

To counter the economic crisis, Economics Minister Karl Schiller (SPD) and Finance Minister Franz-Josef Strauss (CDU) worked together to devise a range of policies which went some way towards restoring confidence.

- In June 1967 the 'Law for promoting stability and growth in the economy' (the Stabilisation Law) increased Federal government involvement in economic matters – giving it powers to raise loans, alter taxes and build reserve funds for investment in times of economic slump.
- Article 109 of the constitution (the 1949 Basic Law) was changed to allow for greater central government control over the spending and taxation policies of the individual states of Germany – the Länder.
- Changes were made to increase co-operation between the central and state government in expanding higher education, agriculture and health as well as developing the economic infrastructure, improving motorways and developing rail networks. (This altered the relationship between the central government and the Länder and was an essential step towards greater economic growth.)
- Co-operation between workers, employees and the state towards effective economic planning was encouraged by an initiative known as 'Concerted Action'.
- Public spending (which had been increasing faster than government revenue since 1961) was drastically cut. Taxation was raised, many tax concessions removed, and VAT, increased from 10 per cent to 12 per cent.

In 1967, the budget was made to balance and by 1968, unemployment was down and industrial growth had been increased to 6 per cent. In 1969 inflation fell to 1.5 per cent.

However, despite the economic improvements, the coalition was beset by inner tensions which grew worse in 1969. The SPD members felt the CDU/CSU were holding back welfare reforms and there was also disagreement over foreign policy, as the SPD accused their partners of reluctance to pursue détente. Furthermore, in March 1969 the SPD candidate, Gustav Heinemann, defeated the CDU/CSU Gerhard Schröder in the presidential elections after a long battle to win the votes of the FDP.

The Bundestag elections in September 1969 saw a hard-fought campaign, in which the SPD set out to win over the disgruntled left-wing journalists and their followers who had opposed the grand coalition. The elections produced a slender majority for the SPD and FDP which took 48.5 per cent of the vote (the FDP contributing just 5.8 per cent); Willi Brandt (SPD) and Walter Scheel (FDP) agreed to create a social-liberal coalition government, breaking the hold of the CDU/CSU (which gained 46.1 per cent) for the first time.

Cross-reference

A number of student protests took place in 1968; these are described on pages 112–13.

Franz-Josef Strauss is profiled in Chapter 4, page 62.

Cross-reference

For the discussions over the policy of détente, look to pages 135–38.

Question

Can you explain why the formation of the SPD–FDP coalition might have been deemed a victory for the forces of democracy in Germany?

1968

1968 saw a wave of student unrest in France, America, Italy, Britain, communist eastern Europe and elsewhere. Some protests were political, some concerned opposition to the Vietnam War and some had local causes. The most extreme riots – in Paris – involved over a million students and workers who fought in street battles with the police. Tanks were even brought to the Parisian outskirts and the situation appeared quite revolutionary. In America students expressed their disillusionment with capitalist democracy, while in Czechoslovakia they sought to embrace it. Everywhere, it seemed, youth was making its presence felt.

Cross-reference

The death of Benno Ohnesorg is outlined at the start of this chapter, on page 107.

Fig. 3 *'Red' Rudi stirs up student revolt*

On 21 October, Brandt was elected as Federal Chancellor by a narrow majority of 251 to 249 in the Bundestag. He was the first SPD Chancellor since 1930. For those who had doubted the FRG's ability to evolve into a successful parliamentary democracy, this change of government seemed to allay fears.

The student protests of 1968

Germany was not alone in experiencing a wave of student protests in 1968, but they were to assume a character of their own, possibly because there was a wider generation gap in Germany than anywhere else in Europe. German students at university in the 1960s were the first generation of the post-Hitler era and 'democracy' had a special meaning for them. Young people nursed a conviction that their parents' generation had been to blame for Nazism and all its horrors. A feminist, Barbara Köster, later recalled:

> For a long time I had severe altercations with my parents and fought against the fascist heritage they forced on me. At first I rejected their authoritarian and puritanical conception of child-rearing (white Sunday gloves and the way one had to hide the fingernails behind the back if they weren't above reproach), but soon we came into conflict over a more serious topic: the persecution of the Jews. I identified with the Jews, because I felt myself to be persecuted by my family.

1

It didn't matter whether those adults had been supporters, or had simply failed to oppose Nazism; either way they were seen as responsible for Germany's past. The trial in 1963–65 of 17 former Auschwitz guards renewed the debate about the Nazi past and led students to demand that the older generation confront this. Some, encouraged by left-wing intellectuals, even saw the emergency laws and formation of the grand coalition as a move back to the old ways of ruling and believed it was incumbent on youth to stop this drift. The fact that there were former Nazis in positions of power (including the Chancellor, Kiesinger) led to accusations of hypocrisy.

Added to this, there was a growing anti-American revulsion as the Vietnam War took its toll. America had been extolled as the leader of the 'free world', and the overseer of West Germany's post-war growth. However, its behaviour in Cuba and Vietnam caused young Germans to question its leadership. Among the radical youth there was an uncomfortable feeling that their lives were the product of American wealth and their high standard of living, maintained at others' expense.

In addition to all this came grievances against Germany's overcrowded and outdated universities with their authoritarian ways, which dated back to pre-1945. Berlin, in particular, had a large student population (partly due to the fact that students were exempt from military service) and it was here that the nucleus of the student protest movement lay.

The death of Benno Ohnesorg in June 1967 provided a martyr for a student-dominated left-wing protest movement. The writer Günter Grass referred to this as *'the first political murder in the Federal Republic'*. The incident resulted in the formation of the 2 June Movement with its members committed to avenging Ohnesorg's death. Although there had been student demonstrations before, this was the first student organisation to declare violence to be a legitimate means of action.

Another key date in the history of student revolt came in April 1968 when Rudi Dutschke – known as 'red Rudi' and one of the leaders of the 2 June Movement in West Berlin – was shot at by an opponent, provoking a round of student demonstrations. The Socialist Students' League played a major part in these and Kiesinger denounced the activities as 'planned political action of a revolutionary character'.

Key profile

Rudi Dutschke, (1940–79)

Rudi Dutschke had been brought up in East Germany but, dismayed by the shortcomings of Soviet socialism, had moved to West Berlin shortly before the wall was erected. However, he was similarly disappointed with the West, which he perceived to be authoritarian and full of contradictions. He studied sociology at the free university in Berlin and he decided it was the duty of the students to lead the masses to a better future. He wrote articles, gave interviews and led demonstrations. Although Dutschke survived the attempt on his life, he never fully recovered. His death ten years later was the result of an epileptic fit, brought on by the brain damage he had suffered, which caused him to drown in his bath.

The student revolt gathered momentum through 1968–69 with protests against the Vietnam War, the atom bomb and the government coalition – although the SPD was generally excused. Demonstrations were directed against 'bourgeois society' and united a variety of those on the 'left', save for the working class. Kiesinger condemned them: *'What is happening in Berlin and in various places in our universities, is the expression of the forces of anarchy'*, he said in 1968. However, this was a battle which, it seemed the government could not win. When the government tried to act firmly, it was condemned for allowing excessive police brutality and yet when the students got out of hand, provoking violence, it was accused of weakness.

Willi Brandt as Chancellor, 1969–74

Key profile

Willi Brandt, (1913–92)

Willi Brandt was born Herbert Ernst Karl Frahm and had been a social worker and keen member of the SPD in his home town of Lübeck until 1932 when he was forced to flee from the Gestapo. He took the name Willi Brandt and fled to Norway. In 1940 he moved to Sweden and joined the German resistance movement. He returned to Berlin in 1945 and became mayor (1957–66). During this time he resisted Soviet demands that Berlin become a demilitarised free city and survived the crisis over the building of the Berlin Wall in 1961. Between 1964–87 he was chairman of the SPD. He became Federal Chancellor in 1969 and is most remembered for his Ostpolitik towards eastern Europe After resigning in 1974, he accepted the chairmanship of an independent commission on international development issues and his 'Brandt report' was published in 1980.

Fig. 4 *Willi Brandt*

Cross-reference

Brandt's policy of Ostpolitik is discussed in Chapter 8, pages 135–38.

Brandt's election brought high hopes of social reform. He promised to 'dare more democracy' and to be the 'Chancellor of domestic reform'. Although much of his chancellorship was taken up with foreign policy, and his reputation has largely rested on his promotion of Ostpolitik with the GDR, he made considerable strides in extending social justice in order to create a fairer democratic society.

Social developments under Brandt

Welfare

- Pensions were raised by 5 per cent generally, and for the war-wounded and their widows by 16 per cent and 25 per cent respectively.
- Sickness benefits went up by 9.5 per cent and pensioners were made exempt from the 2 per cent health insurance contribution.
- Tax-free allowances for children were extended and a fund was set up to help handicapped children.
- The 1972 Pension Act made pension rights less dependent on financial contributions. Health and accident insurance were improved and family and unemployment allowances raised.
- A Town Planning Act introduced measures to protect the environment.

Education

- Expenditure on education and scientific research was raised by nearly 300 per cent between 1970 and 1974.
- The school leaving age was raised to 16 and more places created in schools.
- More money was allocated for school buildings.
- New scholarships were provided for graduates in 1970 and 1973.
- The 1971 Educational Support Law made grants available to allow students from poorer families to continue their education.
- Some Länder introduced comprehensive schools, although this caused controversy.

Employment

- Allowances for training and for refugees from the GDR were increased.
- There was spending on job creation schemes, especially in West Berlin and in undeveloped areas near the frontier.
- The social housing budget was increased by 36 per cent, railways by 14 per cent.
- A programme was launched to create new motorways and another to persuade goods traffic back on to the railways.
- There were increased grants for sport (in an attempt to match GDR successes).
- A factory management law in January 1972 gave workers more say in the running of their factories.
- Increased power was given to the workers' councils, although this did not become fully operational until 1979.

Cross-reference

To recap on Adenauer's establishment of workers' councils to help industry, look back to Chapter 3, page 50 and 54.

Liberalisation

- The voting age was lowered to 18 years old.
- Equality of the sexes was promoted and abortion became easier (although the divorce law was not reformed in favour of women until 1977).

- Censorship and laws against homosexuality were relaxed.
- Criminal law was reformed to become less harsh.

During the period in which Brandt was seeking to extend social reforms, Germany was suffering from growing inflation. This was not just a German phenomenon. Exchange mechanisms set up at Bretton Woods in 1944 were breaking down and the US had its own problems. Consequently, overseas speculators, tempted by a strong Deutschmark, sought to change their US dollars into German marks. This enabled the German banks to grant more loans to individuals and businesses on 'easy' terms and so putting more money into circulation. However, more money meant higher prices, which in turn led to workers demanding higher wages. Since the welfare reforms also drove up government spending, they exacerbated the already inflationary situation. This provoked arguments between the right and left wing within the coalition, the former wanting to curb government spending and the latter favouring it, because of its social benefits. In July 1971, the Bundestag had to be recalled to approve anti-inflationary measures since wages had risen by 145 per cent and the cost of living by over 4 per cent.

The Finance Minister Schiller (of the political right) resigned in June 1972 and Schmidt (of the left) took over, combining the Ministry of Finance and Economics. However, once in power, he drove through the cuts he had previously opposed!

Brandt was placed in a very difficult position. His government was plagued by a wave of terrorism, which swept through Germany between 1970 and 1972 and the stringent measures he was obliged to use to deal with it stirred up opposition from some of the younger members of the party – the **Jusos**. There were also heated controversies sparked off by Brandt's Ostpolitik and he only just survived a vote of no confidence in his Ostpolitik policy by two votes in April 1972. (It later emerged that these had only been obtained by bribery!) Nevertheless, Brandt's personal popularity remained strong. He had been awarded the freedom of the city of Berlin in 1970, the Nobel Peace Prize in 1971 and the freedom of Lübeck in 1972. When an election was called for in November 1972 as a referendum on Ostpolitik, SPD election posters exploited Brandt's sun-tanned photogenic image with the slogans, 'Willi must stay!' and 'Vote for Willi. Who else is there?'

Fortunately for Brandt, his Ostpolitik, which had allowed the first family reunions with those in the East and amnesties for political prisoners who were allowed to come to the FRG, proved immensely popular with the voting public. The SPD won the biggest victory in its history and its vote rose from 42.7 per cent to 45.8 per cent. For the first time in over 40 years it emerged as the strongest party in the Bundestag. The CDU/CSU vote correspondingly fell from 46.1 to 44.9 per cent, while the FDP vote rose from 5.8 per cent to 8.4 per cent. Brandt's coalition majority thus rose to 46 seats and he was re-elected as Chancellor.

Brandt's position appeared unassailable, although he himself had to go into hospital for a laryngitis operation, which meant that cabinet appointments were made in his absence by Schmidt and the deputy party chairman Herbert Wehner. This was unfortunate for Brandt as it weakened his political hold over the coalition. Rising inflation also continued to plague the government and it was made worse by the oil crisis which began in November 1973. Unemployment grew, unions demanded wage increases and there was a debilitating strike in January 1974. No wonder that Brandt, having suffered a setback in the local

Cross-reference

The terrorism which swept the FRG in the early 1970s is discussed on page 117.

Key terms

Jusos: this is an abbreviated form of *Junge Sozialisten* (young socialists) which was the youth movement of the SPD. Many young socialists were radical in outlook and attracted to the student movement. They forced intense debate within the party over its place and future. For example, in response to terrorism threats, Brandt increased surveillance of foreigners, tightened screening for applicants for jobs in government and permitted, where necessary, for mail to be opened and telephones tapped. Such measures were at odds with his political philosophies and much opposed by the radical Jusos.

Cross-reference

The impact of the oil crisis is described on pages 119–20.

Cross-reference

The election results for this period are presented on page 108.

elections in the traditionally strong left-wing town of Hamburg in March 1974, reflected:

> No serious investigation of causes [for his party's loss of support] could overlook my own mistakes and weaknesses. In many people's minds, expectations of success, had become an obsession with success, which no government, far less a coalition, could hope to satisfy in full. Exaggerated demands and verbal excesses contributed to this weakness, but the decisive factor was the economic pressure to which the Federal Republic had been increasingly exposed since the end of 1973.

2

Brandt might have ridden this storm, but his chancellorship floundered on quite a different matter. On his return from a visit to Cairo in April 1974, he learnt that one of his close advisers in the Federal Chancellery, Günter Guillaume, had been arrested as an East German spy. He had handled confidential documents and enjoyed Brandt's full confidence.

Fig. 5 *Unknown to Brandt, his close confidant Guillaume was secretly passing state secrets to the Soviets*

Key profile

Günter Guillaume, (1927–95)

Günter Guillaume was born in Berlin and had served as an officer in the East German army, a fact he did not reveal when he and his wife Christel emigrated to West Germany as apparent 'refugees' in 1956. He took work as a photographic salesman and joined the SPD in 1957, working his way up through the party and government, until receiving a job in the Chancellery in 1970. He passed crucial documents to East Berlin and even collected information while holidaying with Brandt in the summer of 1973. Guillaume was sentenced to 13 years in gaol for espionage, and his wife to eight years. He was released to East Germany in 1981 in exchange for Western spies, where he was treated as a hero, worked as a spy trainer and published his autobiography *Die Aussage* in 1988. After German reunification, Guillaume was granted immunity from further prosecution. The Brandt–Guillaume story is told in the play *Democracy* by Michael Frayn.

In 1974, the West German authorities discovered that Guillaume had been passing information on crucial policy matters to East Berlin, using courier, radio and 'dead-letter' boxes. His exposure provoked Brandt's resignation in favour of Helmut Schmidt in May 1974. Although it was later suggested that Brandt resigned because Guillaume had obtained information about his private life and was threatening to blackmail him, such a story was vehemently denied by Brandt who claimed that he resigned to maintain his personal integrity.

The student revolt and urban terrorism in the 1970s

The student protest movement of 1968 was to take a far more alarming form in the 1970s as some disaffected youth moved towards extreme violence. The most frightening of the violent youth organisations was the Baader-Meinhof Gang which resorted to arson, intimidation, kidnapping and assassination, and deliberately spread terror among ordinary citizens. One of its leaders, Georg von Rausch, said, *'We must, I must, quite simply, liquidate human feeling.'*

In 1972, Brandt was forced to tighten regulations relating to carrying arms, storing ammunition, peddling drugs and threatening politicians, in an attempt to deal with the terror – 150,000 police were employed in tracking the gang down.

The Palestine Liberation Organisation (PLO) posed another different, but associated, threat. Its members attacked an Israeli aircraft in Munich in 1970, killing one passenger and wounding 11 and in September 1972 they were responsible for the death of 11 Israeli athletes at the Munich Olympic games. The PLO also hijacked a German plane a month later, holding its passengers hostage until the remaining three Palestinians involved in the athletes' murder were released. It was the links that the Baader-Meinhof Gang made with the PLO that made this group particularly frightening to the authorities.

Did you know?

Dead-letter (or dead-drop) boxes are places where information is left to be picked up later by an agent. In this way there is no physical contact and information can be passed without alerting security forces.

Summary activity

List the domestic successes and failures of Willi Brandt with regard to domestic affairs. When you have studied his Ostpolitik in Chapter 8, you should refer to this list, to write your critical appraisal as given in the revision exercise on page 137.

Fig. 6 *The urban terrorists (l–r) Thorwald Proll, Horst Söhnlein, Andreas Baader and Gudrun Ensslin, awaiting trial after setting fire to two department stores in Frankfurt*

Cross-reference

Gudrun Ensslin is introduced at the start of this chapter, on page 107.

A closer look

The Baader-Meinhof Gang

In April 1968, Gudrun Ensslin and her boyfriend, Andreas Baader, left bombs in two Frankfurt department stores. As the flames leapt up, Ensslin phoned the German Press Agency, declaring *'This is a political act of revenge!'* In the same month, student leader Rudi Dutschke, was shot in Berlin, although he survived. This provoked a mass student demonstration attended by Ulrike Meinhof, a journalist. She gave shelter to Ensslin, who escaped from custody, and Baader, whom Meinhof helped to escape by posing as his co-writer. Thus was born the 'Baader-Meinhof Gang' or Red Army Faction (RAF).

The gang's activities included bank robberies and car-stealing – particularly the BMW nicknamed the 'Baader-Meinhof Wagen.' Gang members crossed Land boundaries to evade conviction and initially enjoyed a certain 'Robin Hood' - style sympathy from the general public. However, most German people took the side of the government as the terrorism grew more extreme throughout 1971. Gang members 'trained' with Palestinian terrorists in Jordan and there were murders and maimings, particularly of policemen, within the FRG.

The gang's leaders were rounded up in 1972. Police found a garage near Frankfurt am Main packed with explosives. They replaced the explosives with empty containers, installed a listening device and placed marksmen on nearby rooftops. When three men arrived, one was quickly captured but Andreas Baader and Holger Meins endured three hours in the garage, which was filled with tear gas, pushed in through holes drilled by the police. Eventually Meins gave himself up, and police stormed the garage and arrested Baader. The capture of his girlfriend, Gudrun Ensslin, followed when an observant shop assistant noticed a gun in her bulging jacket pocket.

Ulrike Meinhof was also tracked down and had to be forcibly anaesthetised and an X-ray of her head taken to prove her identity. (It was known that a clip had been inserted into her skull after an operation in 1962.)

However, the capture of the leaders was not the end of the gang's influence. The prisoners went on hunger strike, demanding to be treated as political prisoners, and Amnesty International lodged complaints. When the six-foot four-inch Holger Meins died in prison, weighing under 100 pounds after a hunger-strike, there was a retaliatory assassination of a judge, Günter von Drenkmann, the president of Germany's Superior Court of Justice.

For five years, gang followers, encouraged by the PLO, kidnapped and murdered, in an attempt to secure their leaders' release. A siege of the Saudi Arabian embassy in Khartoum in March 1972, for example, included a Palestinian guerilla demand for the freeing of the Baader-Meinhof Gang.

In 1975, the leaders were tried in a newly constructed prison courtroom – its roof covered with jagged razor wire to prevent helicopter landings, and steel nets to prevent bombs. There were a number of terrorist activities during the trial – followers kidnapped a politician and others held the staff of the German embassy in Stockholm hostage, while Ulrike Meinhof's suicide in prison in May 1976 brought demonstrations and a bomb at the American air base in Frankfurt.

The terrorist hijack of an Air France Airbus en route from Tel Aviv to Paris in June 1976 was accompanied by another demand for the prisoners' release and in 1977, a Palestinian hijack of a German plane was narrowly thwarted by German commandos in the Mogadishu Incident. As a result of this, Andreas Baader, Gudrun Ensslin and a third gang member, Jan-Carl Raspe, committed suicide.

The Red Army Faction continued bombing, maiming, and killing for almost another 20 years and in the early 1980s the RAF formed an association with the French terror group *Action Directe*. However, the fall of the Berlin Wall, and the collapse of communism, weakened the group's leverage and in April 1998 the RAF was officially disbanded and the last prisoner released.

Cross-reference

More on The Mogadishu Incident can be found below, on pages 121–22.

Activity

Thinking point

How would you account for the strength of feeling roused on both sides by the activities of the Baader-Meinhof Gang?

Economic developments and the impact of the oil crisis of 1973

Ever since the economic bubble burst in around 1965, the FRG had struggled to control inflation, and rising unemployment was a constant threat. West Germany was not, of course, alone in experiencing such problems. By the end of the 1960s, the post-war economic boom was over and western Europe as a whole was experiencing declining growth rates.

The situation was not helped when, in August 1971, US President Nixon announced that America was abandoning the system of fixed exchange rates and that the US dollar, which had formerly underpinned the international monetary system, was to be allowed to 'float' against other currencies. There were reasonably sound reasons for Nixon's decision, not least the dollar's over-valued rate, but its effect was to create a situation in which the 'liberalisation' of currency meant the easing of credit and further inflation.

Within the FRG there was mounting panic as the costs of imports rose. Between 1971 and 1973 the world price of non-oil commodities rose by 70 per cent and the price of food by 100 per cent. To add to this already unstable situation there followed a further shock. At the end of 1973, the Organisation of Petroleum Exporting Countries (OPEC) decided to double the price of crude oil. The shock this caused within the developed world was enormous. Oil prices had remained virtually unchanged since the 1950s – effectively leading to a reduction in the cost of oil during the boom years – and developed economies had come to rely on a ready supply of this comparatively cheap fuel.

The FRG was faced with paying 17 billion DM more for its imports; unemployment soared to over 400,000 and a temporary ban on Sunday driving had to be introduced. The country's balance of payments surplus of $9.481 million in 1973 fell within a year to a deficit of $692 million.

However, the unions, who had been used to bargaining from a position of strength in the growth years, continued to demand large wage increases. In January 1974, for example, the Union of Public Employees went on strike and forced the Länder to offer an 11 per cent pay increase. Economists predicted 8 per cent inflation and continuing high unemployment, which carried huge psychological implications for the German people.

Cross-reference

The economic downturn in the early 1960s is described earlier in this chapter, on pages 108–9.

Exploring the detail

OPEC and the Yom Kippur War

OPEC was first set up in 1960, and membership grew through the 1960s and early 1970s. On 6 October 1973 (Yom Kippur in the Jewish calendar), Egypt and Syria attacked Israel. Within 24 hours, the Arab oil-exporting states announced (through OPEC) plans to reduce oil production and 10 days later they announced an oil embargo against America (which supported Israel) and a 70 per cent rise in the price of petroleum. The Yom Kippur War ended with a ceasefire on 25 October, but Arab frustration at Western support for Israel led to a further price increase in December – doubling the cost of crude oil since the beginning of 1973.

Exploring the detail

Hyperinflation in Germany's past

The German people had suffered immensely from hyperinflation in 1923, when they were reduced to using barrows of money to pay for everyday items and again after 1929 when unemployment soared to 2 million after the American stock market crashed and loans were withdrawn from German businesses. The fear of any repetition of such horrors, which had helped bring Hitler to power in Germany, remained very strong.

Did you know?

During the boom years, West Germany had encouraged 'guest workers' to come from other countries to augment the work force (see Chapter 3, page 57). Many had taken low-paid unskilled jobs and it was these workers who were the first to feel the tide of rising unemployment in the 1970s. Four out of five BMW workers who lost their jobs in this decade, for example, were guest workers. In 1975, the FRG closed its recruiting offices in North Africa, Portugal, Spain and Yugoslavia. The same year 290,000 immigrant workers and their families left West Germany.

Summary question

For what reasons and in what ways did the oil crisis hit the FRG?

Schmidt initially reacted by creating more jobs and stimulating investment. There were tax reductions and increased child allowances together with bonuses for employers and workers who were prepared to relocate. By such means, the rate of inflation through 1974 was kept to 6 per cent (lower than any other industrialised country) and the economic growth rate reached 4 per cent.

However, such progress did not last and in 1975 unemployment reached 1 million and the GDP fell to 1.6 per cent. This prompted moderate expenditure cuts and reductions in tax concessions and measures such as a 2 per cent increase in VAT, angering the trade unions and those on the left of the party.

Schmidt also tried to work cooperatively within the EEC to control inflation. However, in 1978, as the West German economy seemed to be recovering, he proposed a more institutionalised arrangement – a European Monetary System (EMS) – at the Bonn Economic Summit. This would fix exchange rates within Europe, underwritten by the anti-inflationary policies of West Germany and the Bundesbank. This meant that the Deutschmark replaced the dollar as the currency of reference in setting exchange rates and it was adopted as the way forward in Europe (although the UK stayed out).

The crisis was not, however, over. In 1979, the overthrow of the Shah of Iran produced another panic among the oil-producing nations and a further 150 per cent price increase between December 1979 and May 1980 ended the decade on a note of uncertainty.

The depression of the 1970s actually seemed worse than it really was. In the event West Germany succeeded in keeping inflation to 4.7 per cent in the years 1973 to 1979 (compared with an average of 11.9 per cent for western Europe as a whole) and growth rates were still greater than they had been between 1913 and 1950. It was the contrast with the staggering growth rates of the immediate past that caused the government concern.

Fig. 7 *Turkish guest workers departing from Munich railway station in 1974*

Despite the various crises, the standard of living for most German people steadily increased throughout this period. Unemployment rates never got above 8 per cent of the labour force, despite the slump in demand for Germany's manufactured goods, although this was partly because most of the unemployed workers in Germany were not German at all, and were therefore not officially recorded as unemployed. For the majority, therefore, these were not unduly dismal times. Wages rose, more holidays were given and working hours declined.

Helmut Schmidt as Chancellor, 1974–82

Brandt had cultivated Schmidt as his likely successor and had given him considerable experience as Minister of Economics and Finance between 1972 and 1974. In this post he had gained a reputation for tough action and decisiveness, which contrasted strongly with Brandt's more reflective style of rule. He was a conservative Social Democrat with little sympathy for the left wing of his party or 'green' and pacifist issues. In this, his views were complemented by those of the new and rather more conservative leader of the FDP, Hans-Dietrich Genscher, who took office when Scheel became Federal President in July 1974. Complementing them was Hans Apel, a very able Minister of Finance, and the youngest cabinet in the history of the Federal Republic – with an average age of 49.

Although in the General Election of October 1976 the Schmidt-Genscher coalition (CDU/CSU and FDP) won only a two-vote majority, Schmidt soon showed his ability to deal with a number of crises, as well as pursuing his predecessor's popular policy of Ostpolitik; as a result, he remained at the top for four terms, until 1982.

The first crisis was economic, but this was soon followed by another crisis – the Mogadishu Incident of 1977 – when Schmidt showed his nerve and refused to give in to terrorists and the Red Army Faction (RAF).

Cross-reference

Helmut Schmidt is profiled on page 109.

Fig. 8 *Helmut Schmidt congratulates the commander of the GSG-9 commando team who helped liberate plane hostages in the Mogadishu Incident of October 1977*

A closer look

The Mogadishu Incident

After assassinating the federal attorney-general and the director of the Dresdner Bank, the RAF kidnapped Hans-Martin Schleyer, President of the Federal Association of German Industry. In return for his release a demand for the freeing of 11 terrorists associated with the Baader-Meinhof Gang was made. Schmidt refused. On 13 October 1977, a Lufthansa Boeing 737, flying from Mallorca to Frankfurt, and packed with German holiday-makers, was hijacked by Palestinians linked to the RAF shortly after take-off. The plane was diverted to Rome's Fiumicino Airport where, with

91 hostages, 'Captain Martyr Mohammed', the Palestinians' leader, announced, *'The group I represent demands the release of our comrades in German prisons. We are fighting against the imperialist organisations of the world.'* The hijacked plane flew on via Dubai to Aden, where it landed beside a runway dotted with armoured tanks put there to prevent it from landing. 'Martyr Mohammed' shot the pilot, Jürgen Schumann, and tossed the body unceremoniously on the tarmac before taking off for Mogadishu, Somalia. The hijackers threatened to blow up the Lufthansa plane if the prisoners were not released, but, with permission from the Somali government, on 17 October, Schmidt sent in a force of West German border guards (the GSG-9 commando team) which managed to land unnoticed, storm the plane, killing three of the four hijackers and seriously wounding the other, and rescue the passengers without injury. Although Schleyer was subsequently murdered, this was a defeat for the terrorists and led to the suicides of Baader and his accomplices.

Another crisis was a political one. There was opposition within his party to the policies of the FDP Economics Minister, Count Otto von Lamsdorff, who was restricting the circulation of money in an attempt to control inflation. Furthermore, there was division on the nuclear issue and in particular Schmidt's agreement to have US medium-range nuclear missiles stationed in Germany, which aroused considerable left-wing hostility.

The SPD also faced a challenge from the many pressure groups that had emerged in the 1970s, campaigning on environmental issues such as the building of airport runways or nuclear power stations. From these was born the Green Party in 1980 which attracted some of the left-wing SPD voters who had similar ecological and anti-nuclear interests.

By the autumn of 1982, SPD fortunes were in decline, while the CDU/CSU had reunited after its splits over Ostpolitik under Helmut Kohl. Consequently, Genscher pulled the FDP out of the coalition to form a new one with Kohl.

Summary question

Explain why the power of the SPD in government had been undermined by 1982.

The work of Helmut Kohl between 1982 and 1989

Key profile

Helmut Kohl, (born 1930)

Kohl was born in Ludwigshafen and studied in Frankfurt and Heidelberg where he became involved in student politics for the CDU. After working in industrial relations, he entered politics and was elected to the state parliament of the Rhineland-Palatinate in 1959 and was Chairman of the state's CDU between 1966 and 1976. In 1969 he was elected State Minister-President (prime minister) and served between 1969 and 76 when he challenged Schmidt for the chancellorship. He finally succeeded in 1982. He played a major part in the reunification of Germany and was subsequently re-elected as Chancellor in December 1990. He stepped down in September 1998.

Fig. 9 *Kohl's first government*

Kohl immediately announced a new economic programme, returning to the principles of the social market economy. He talked of the need for 'moral change' but, in practice, much continued as before.

An election was held to secure his position in March 1983 and he faced Hans-Jochen Vogel as the SPD Chancellor-candidate, replacing Schmidt. However, the party was too deeply divided to make a comeback and it was not prepared to consider a coalition with the Green Party, which might have provided it with a chance of continuing in power. These problems, plus Kohl's promise to continue with Ostpolitik, resulted in the worst SPD defeat since 1961. The CDU's share of the vote went up and the Green Party gained representation in the Bundestag for the first time.

Still, Kohl faced difficult circumstances, with unemployment still growing and pressure to do something about the 'underclass' of the socially deprived. He tried to restore the social market economy and abandoned the high spending policies of governments since 1966. He brought in tax cuts, phased over a seven-year period, and kept annual budget increases down to a maximum of 3 per cent. Nevertheless, he continued to subsidise farming, coal, steel and the aerospace industry and was obliged to keep a high level of spending on welfare.

Despite measures including early retirement schemes and retraining packages, unemployment was still over 2.2 million in 1987, but with a fall in oil prices in 1985 West German exports gradually recovered and inflation fell from 6.2 per cent in 1981 to 0.6 per cent in 1986. Consequently, West Germany was able to win back its economic power within the world once more and Kohl was able to claim some of the credit.

Kohl's leadership was not without challenge, however. There was in-fighting between his coalition partner Genscher (FDP) and Strauss (CDU/CSU), and in 1983, the CSU split when two of its members broke away to found a new right-wing republican party.

Sleaze also damaged Kohl. It was discovered that industry had been making secret and illegal donations to the coalition parties and in 1984 the FDP Finance Minister, Count Lambsdorff, had to resign because he

■ **Cross-reference**

Franz-Josef Strauss is profiled in Chapter 4, page 62.

■ Exploring the detail

The Bitburg Affair and the Nazi past

In the late 1970s and 1980s, Germany became less dependent on America and showed a new confidence in itself as a nation. This was partly engendered by the feeling that those then in power had not been part of the Nazi past. Kohl stated as much on a visit to Israel in January 1984, when he said that 'by grace of late birth' his generation was not directly guilty. In 1986–87 the topic became one of intense debate between intellectuals. Andreas Hillgruber compared Germany's own sufferings in 1944–45 with the sufferings of the Holocaust, while Ernst Nolte argued that the crime of the Holocaust was no worse than the Turks' massacre of the Armenians in 1915 or Stalin's of the kulaks in 1929. On the left wing, others, such as Jurgen Habermass and Rudolf Augstein (editor of *Der Spiegel*), argued that this was trivialising the Holocaust and part of a conservative counter-revolution.

■ Cross-reference

Election results for 1949–61 are provided in Chapter 3, page 46.

had exempted the Flick Corporation (one of the largest businesses in Germany) from tax payments, in return for contributions to the FDP. Although Kohl was not himself involved, he was nevertheless attacked for failing to spot and stop such practices.

The Bitburg affair also raised questions about Kohl's judgement. He had arranged a ceremony of reconciliation to mark the 40th anniversary of the ending of the Second World War at a small military cemetery at Bitburg. President Reagan, who was on a state visit to Germany, attended. Although it emerged that SS troops were buried there, Kohl continued regardless, despite Reagan's own uncertainty, and in media reports around the world his action was portrayed as distasteful and uncalled for.

By January 1987, the CDU/CSU vote had declined to its lowest point since 1949 (44.3 per cent) while the FDP vote had risen to 9.1 per cent and the Greens had also made gains. Although the SPD failed to unseat Kohl, who kept power with Genscher's backing, his coalition government looked unstable and as further support fell away over the next two years, it was widely predicted that Kohl would be forced to resign. However, what saved him was the collapse of the GDR.

■ Activity

Revision exercise

Copy the table. In the left-hand column, give the names and dates of the West German Chancellors between 1963 and 1989. In the second column list their successes, in the third, their failures and in the fourth provide an overall comment on their chancellorship. You might like to add pictures of each Chancellor and a further column with a brief summary of the career of each leader.

West German Chancellors	Successes	Failures	Comment

■ Summary question

How important were economic problems in undermining the stability of West German governments between 1965 and 1989?

8 Internal Developments in the East and the Impact of Ostpolitik

In this chapter you will learn about:

- life in the GDR under Erich Honecker
- economic change and political stagnation in the GDR
- the meaning of the 'niche society'
- Ostpolitik and its effects for both Germanies.

Andreas Krieger was a star GDR athlete who won a gold medal in the Stuttgart Olympics of 1986 with a shot put of 21.10 metres – only then, Andreas was called Heidi, and was a member of the female team. In 1979, at 14 years of age, Heidi had been selected to attend a prestigious sports club, where her coaches, realising her talent, prescribed a course of bright blue 'vitamin pills'. She was told that 'everybody' took them and they certainly enhanced her performance. Her body grew firmer and stronger, her muscles bulked out, her facial features changed and her voice deepened, By 18 she weighed 220 pounds (15 and a half stone). However, although she felt something of a misfit and experienced violent mood-swings, she recalled, *'I loved being a sporting champion for the GDR. I was proud of my country on that score and believed that we athletes strengthened the socialist republic with our achievements.'*

It was only after the collapse of the GDR and the end of her sporting career, that Heidi was actually able to discover that what she had been taking were androgenic, anabolic steroids – she was not the only one. During the GDR's history more than 10,000 East German athletes had been fed steroids and other substances. With bitterness, Krieger recalled in 2009, *'East Germany took my life away from me – the ability to make my own decisions. They made a laboratory out of me because they saw my potential. I wasn't allowed to decide for myself what I wanted to become.'*

Krieger eventually underwent a full sex-change operation to complete the process the GDR authorities had begun. Others suffered in different ways. Some former athletes developed cancer; some women found they could not conceive a child as their uterus had never developed; some had malformed children. Many struggled to cope in a post-communist world – yet in the GDR of Honecker, achievements like those of 'Heidi' in the 1986 European Championships instilled a sense of pride and achievement which helped make up for other problems in daily life.

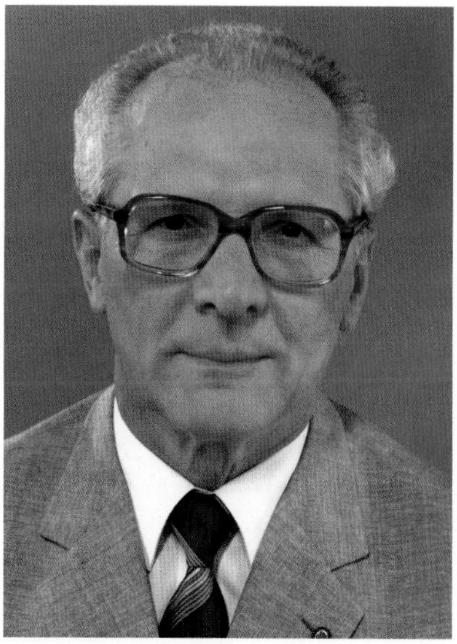

Fig. 1 *Erich Honecker*

Cross-reference

For Ulbricht's resignation and replacement by Honecker, look back to Chapter 5, page 74.

Honecker is profiled in Chapter 5, page 74.

Ostpolitik is discussed later in this chapter, on pages 135–38.

The GDR under Honecker

The closing of the border by means of the Berlin Wall of 1961 gave the GDR a new lease of life. It enabled Erich Honecker (who, with the support of the USSR, engineered Ulbricht's resignation 'on the grounds of ill health' on 3 May 1971) to enjoy what appeared to be a reasonably stable period of control, at least until the late 1970s. Ulbricht's ambitious reform attempts had failed, but border protection coupled with the FRG's new policy of Ostpolitik, which gave the GDR both much-needed cash and international recognition, imbued the East German state with a new-found confidence. It encouraged Honecker to press ahead, not only with a more generous package of welfare reforms, but also with an increase in consumer goods such as cars, fridges and televisions.

Honecker even announced a policy of 'no taboos' in cultural activities and in March 1978 came to an agreement with the Lutheran Church whereby it was allowed to permit discussion meetings on Church premises. The Church was the only organisation which fell outside the control of the state and Honecker felt that this concession would allow those with grievances the chance to air them in a controlled atmosphere, where they would do little harm.

Economic change

Honecker introduced a new policy, referred to as 'The Unity of Social and Economic Policy'. Its aim was to increase production sufficiently to make money to finance an ambitious home-building programme and further social reform. The initiative was designed to combine centralised planning, to ensure the overall direction of the economy, with a more flexible decision-making process at a local level, to prevent some of the problems that had beset the Ulbricht era.

Honecker nationalised the remaining independent firms in 1972, leaving only a very few craft activities in private hands, and he introduced a higher degree of specialisation in both agriculture and industry. The VEBs ('*Volkseigene Betriebe*') were replaced by combines which linked technological research, production and market research to make for more efficient production. In farming, different collectives concentrated on either crops or animals and 'cooperation councils' were established to coordinate the work of individual farms with their district administrators.

In industry, the GDR relied on imports of fuel and raw materials and by the 1970s, nearly a third of the GDR's trade was with the developed economies of western Europe. Thanks to the West German Ostpolitik policy, trade barriers between the two Germanies had been dismantled. This meant that the GDR effectively became an 'extra' member of the EEC. Furthermore, the GDR was able to obtain West German credit to cover trade deficits and if there was a bottleneck in supplies from eastern Europe, it could turn to the FRG instead. Altogether the GDR enjoyed a very favourable position. With loans from the FRG provided on easy terms, the GDR was far better able to cope with the economic problems of the 1970s and 1980s than its eastern European neighbours.

■ Cross-reference

The VEBs which existed under Ulbricht are outlined in Chapter 5, page 80.

Fig. 2 *Collective farming in East Germany in the 1970s*

Overall the GDR economy was relatively successful – at least in comparison with that of other eastern bloc countries. The numbers of tractors and combine harvesters used on the farms compared favourably with the horse-drawn ploughs in neighbouring Poland, and East Germany achieved a high degree of agricultural self-sufficiency, needing only to import grain and animal feed. Although the GDR continued to lag behind the West, the Honecker years saw considerable advances in consumer production and, in the 1980s, in microelectronics, electrical engineering and computer production. The chemical industry and vehicle manufacture also grew and there were attempts to develop nuclear energy. The East Germans enjoyed the highest standard of living in the eastern bloc and ownership of fridges, TVs and cars continued to grow.

However, it was not all rosy. The GDR's reliance on foreign trade made it particularly sensitive to the oil price rise in 1973 and, in the 1972–75 period, while import prices rose by 34 per cent, export values rose by only 17 per cent. The GDR was forced to import oil, coal and gas from the USSR at unfavourable rates and it still relied heavily on its own supplies of **lignite** for 70 per cent of its energy requirements in the mid-1980s. The costs of welfare provision also proved a drag on the economy. They amounted to twice the rise in the national income between 1971 and 1979.

By the early 1980s, the GDR's economy was almost totally dependent on loans from the FRG although Honecker refused to face up to reality. The GDR's growth rates halved between 1984 and 1988 and while the economic problems were well camouflaged, the GDR's debt to the FRG amounted to 38.5 million DM by November 1987. In later years, Markus Wolf, the East German spymaster, claimed that by the late 1970s, he was already aware that the GDR 'wouldn't work' – and economists elsewhere knew too.

Political stagnation

Since Ostpolitik had brought the GDR international recognition, there was no longer any need for the country to continue to regard itself as part of a larger German nation. Consequently, Honecker introduced a new constitution in September 1974 which instead emphasised '*Abgrenzung*' (separation). The idea was to give the GDR its own national identity. Although it also emphasised 'solidarity' and 'undying friendship' with the USSR, Article 1 stated:

> The German Democratic Republic is a socialist state of workers and farmers. It is the political organisation of the workers in the cities and in the countryside under the leadership of the working class and their Marxist-Leninist party.

1

The constitution, along with Honecker's relative tolerance of the Church and his proclamation of 'no taboos', might have suggested that the GDR was moving forward towards greater political freedom. However, many developments in the 1970s, and still more the 1980s, contradicted this and the old repressive atmosphere remained.

Wolf Biermann, a successful East German guitarist and singer, for example, was permitted to undertake a concert tour in the West, only to find himself refused re-entry to the GDR in 1976. When other artists and intellectuals protested, they too found themselves subject to repressive measures and in the late 1970s the government adopted the policy of deporting troublesome writers and artists to the West.

Activity

Research task

Try to find a picture and some information about the East German car – the Trabant. Make a one-page poster to show the advantages/disadvantages of this (or another) East German product.

Cross-reference

For the oil price rise of 1973, refer back to Chapter 7, pages 115 and 119–20.

Key terms

Lignite: this is a form of brown coal. It is deemed the lowest rank of coal and has a high moisture content which produces a particularly unpleasant smoke. This had adverse effects on the environment and public health.

Wolf Biermann, (born 1936)

Biermann was born in Hamburg where his father was a member of the communist resistance and was subsequently killed in Auschwitz. In 1961 Biermann formed the *Arbeiter und Studententheater* (Workers' and Students' Theatre) which produced *Berliner Brautgang*, a show about the building of the Berlin Wall. This was shut down by the authorities in 1963. Although a committed communist, Biermann's views alarmed the East German authorities and in 1963 he was refused membership of the SED. In 1965 he was denounced as a 'class traitor' and forbidden to publish or perform his music in public. He was allowed to undertake a tour in West Germany in 1976, but in his absence, the Politburo voted to strip him of his citizenship. Biermann continued his musical career in the West, criticising East Germany's policies. He was able to perform publicly again in East Germany in late 1989 and in 1998 received a German national prize.

The Berlin Wall continued to stand as proof of the GDR's political failure. The presence of border guards, Soviet troops, the people's police (Vopo), the workers' militia groups and the Stasi (state security police), which grew greatly in size during the 1970s and 1980s, made it clear that the state relied heavily on repression, even if political 'terror' was less evident than it had been in Ulbricht's day.

The Honecker era has been described as a period of political stagnation. The SED continued to dominate and whether through fear, political apathy or support, the mass of the populace consented in that rule. Admittedly, a tiny minority of political activists sought reform in the late 1970s and 1980s and began forming organised groups and networks, usually under the aegis of the Church, but it was only in the dramatically changed circumstances of 1989 that larger numbers found cause to speak out against the regime.

For the most part, the vast mass of the population were accommodated into the political and social structures and organisations of the state. This outward conformity bred self-confidence among the leadership so that, when Mikhail Gorbachev took over leadership of the USSR in 1985 and began spreading ideas of *perestroika* and *glasnost*, the GDR establishment showed no signs of following suit. There is no reason to doubt that Honecker really believed he could continue with the political system unchanged.

■ **Cross-reference**

The part played by the changing ideas in the USSR after 1985, including the concepts of *perestroika* and *glasnost*, is described in Chapter 9, page 143.

Fig. 3 *The feared Stasi symbol*

■ **A closer look**

'Fear' – the Stasi

The *Ministerium für Staatssicherheit* (Stasi) was the eyes and ears of the party; a political secret police, founded in 1950 as an ideological surveillance corps, their motto was the 'Shield and Sword of the Party'. In the 1970s and 1980s, the number of agents grew and by 1989, they had more than 93,000 full-time employees and 173,000 unofficial collaborators working for them. They infiltrated virtually all spheres of life, using undercover agents and informers who spied on neighbours, colleagues and even relatives or spouses and reported their findings to liaison officers who used an

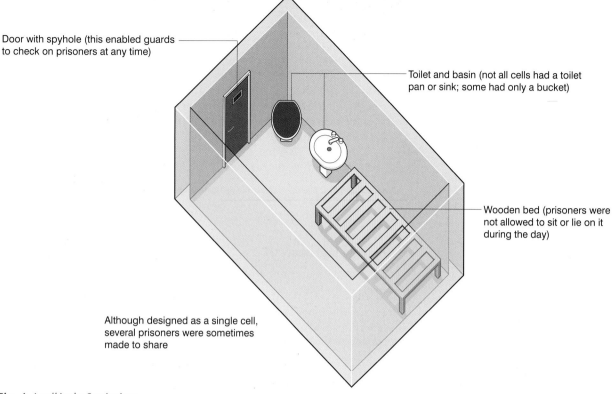

Door with spyhole (this enabled guards to check on prisoners at any time)

Toilet and basin (not all cells had a toilet pan or sink; some had only a bucket)

Wooden bed (prisoners were not allowed to sit or lie on it during the day)

Although designed as a single cell, several prisoners were sometimes made to share

Fig. 4 *A cell in the Stasi prison*

assumed name. They not only rooted out non-conformity, they also stopped it ever developing in the first place by instilling fear into the minds of the GDR citizens. Furthermore, the Stasi were used to coerce individuals and groups into loyalty and spread propagandist messages. Even the Churches, which were the only organisations permitted to exist outside SED control, were infiltrated by Stasi agents.

Anyone in the GDR could expect their mail to be checked, their phone and flat to be bugged and their personal details to be kept on file. The Stasi had unrestricted access to all files, including bank statements and medical records. They could undermine the career or even the family life of anyone who came to their attention. They had their own military units, holding prisons, safe houses and other properties as well as their own supply facilities, recreation areas and medical services. They also had special communication systems. The extent of their activities only came to light after the collapse of the GDR when the huge files – often filled with the most trite of findings – were discovered, along with their collection of 'smell jars' in which were placed scraps of upholstery from the chairs on which suspects had sat for interrogation and which were kept for future identification.

After the collapse of the Berlin Wall in 1989, angry citizens stormed its offices and many officials were rounded up, but not before they had shredded hundreds of thousands of incriminating documents. Since then, thousands of archivists have painstakingly worked to try to recreate these documents and discover the truth about their activities. By 2000, 3.4 million citizens had asked to see their files; many uncomfortable and disturbing facts have been brought to light, including

Activity

Research task

Undertake a personal investigation into the work of the Stasi. In particular, try to find some Stasi reports. The film *The Life of Others* and Anna Fund's book *Stasiland* would be especially interesting to see and read.

Activity

Thinking point

Before reading the next section, reflect on which you feel was the most important reason for the survival of the Honecker regime – fear, political apathy or support.

 Exploring the detail

'actually existing socialism'

This was the term used by Honecker to describe the stage the GDR had reached in its journey to Marxist-Leninism. Since the full revolution seemed still far distant, the country was to enjoy its 'actually existing socialism'.

Activity

Stretch and challenge

What difficulties face historians studying life in the GDR?

180,000 people identified as informers, although the real figure is believed to have been much higher. Once such case concerns Vera Lengsfield who discovered that her own husband and father to her two children had been spying on her for much of her married life. Every political conversation she had had with him and every dinner party she had given had been faithfully reported to the Stasi. Admittedly, he had tried to warn her not to attend a peace rally in 1988, but it led to her arrest and, after a humiliating interrogation, including sitting on a piece of fabric to provide a 'smell' sample and a month in an airless cell, 7 paces long and 5 wide, she was expelled from the country – largely thanks to her husband's reports.

 Activity

Thinking and analysis

Compare and contrast Walter Ulbricht and Erich Honecker (before 1989) as leaders of the GDR.

You may wish to do this orally or you could write an essay answer. Try to think of themes to address, e.g. political position/policies, economic position/policies and social position/policies.

The niche society

One rather odd phenomenon of this undoubtedly repressed society was that few citizens challenged it and many more seemed to accept or even support it. According to Mary Fulbrook:

> That a lot of people did not like the GDR is certainly true. But this alone is not sufficient to explain either its apparent stability over forty years or its sudden and unexpected downfall within a matter of weeks. In short, there is more to the inner history of the GDR than the Cold War division of Europe and the presence of Soviet Tanks. However illegitimate its origins, however repressive in practice, 'actually existing socialism' actually existed. People lived in the GDR and in different ways they came to terms with it. They participated in the youth and trade organisations, the women's and cultural leagues, the work brigades; they played the system to further their aspirations.

2

There were, of course, some who failed to conform. Some chose to leave – either legitimately or by subterfuge. Others stayed but made their protest. The Stasi diligently recorded examples of anti-SED graffiti, swastikas and oppositional leaflets. However, such explicit comment was relatively rare and while there were increasing protests against travel restrictions in the 1980s, there was little outcry against the broader issue of restrictions on personal and political freedom. Protest tended to be individual, focusing on a specific issue, rather than a collective one. It was often as much the product of youthful hot-headedness as of true political feeling. Indeed the state could hardly have survived at all if the majority of its citizens had continually and actively opposed it.

Fig. 5 *The Young Pioneers were brought up to love and support Honecker and the GDR*

For the greater part of its time, the GDR appeared to produce a conformist society. Socialist organisations flourished – be they sports clubs, art and leisure centres, women's groups or youth movements. Citizens enjoyed 'socialist' holidays; they joined socialist trade unions and they took part in parades on national days. They met their work norms and obeyed the law. To all outward appearances they readily accepted 'actually existing socialism'.

Undoubtedly there were among them sincere adherents of socialism who remained optimistic that the GDR could build a socialist society and that the future lay with communist societies. Such criticised the Americanisation of the FRG and remained convinced that capitalism only undermined social welfare provision and opened the way to fascism. Many in government service in particular felt this way.

However historians such as Mary Fulbrook, who have examined the 'anatomy' of the GDR regime believe that the SED never succeeded in winning the mass of the population over to its socialist ideas, despite its control of education and monopoly of propaganda. Although socialist organisations enjoyed high membership rates, it must be remembered that similar organisations were popular everywhere. The people had little choice. If they wanted to play sport or enjoy a youth camp, they had to join. If they wanted to reach university or advance in their career, they had to conform. It was as simple as that. Membership did not necessarily imply ideological commitment.

Certainly, the passage of time made a difference. In 1953 there had been a workers' rebellion but once it became clear that the state was there to stay and a new generation grew up knowing of nothing else, it became easier for

Exploring the detail

For more on this dip into Mary Fulbrook's *Anatomy of a Dictatorship*. Details are provided in the Bibliography.

The life of the elite

At the top of German society were the party bosses, many of whom lived in an exclusive compound at Wandlitz, to the north of Berlin. Locals renamed it 'Volvograd' because of the constant procession of chauffeur-driven Volvo cars that purred along to the comfortable residences there. Life at Wandlitz was a far cry from that of the ordinary German citizen. There were supermarkets stocked with all kinds of food, including the almost impossible-to-get bananas, and leisure and sports facilities of a type unseen elsewhere. Such eminent party members could shop in special department stores and some also possessed hunting lodges and country retreats. Honecker even had his own forest stocked with game for shooting parties.

citizens to take the GDR for granted and accept its demands. For millions of people the GDR was their life. They grew up there, went to school, served in its armed forces, went to work, furnished a flat and raised a family there. It was possible to lead a happy family life in the GDR and sometimes it was quite easy to forget about politics and ideology. When that happy family life was threatened by political issues, the East Germans learnt to behave in the way that would cause them the least personal inconvenience. They learnt strategies for keeping out of trouble and for getting around the most irksome of demands to obtain the maximum personal benefit. They learnt to 'play the system', to withdraw into themselves and keep their thoughts private.

Life was, of course, often far from idyllic, given the frequent shortages of food and other goods caused by the ill-adjusted economy. People spent time hunting down scarce goods – but they learnt to live with it. They bartered, worked after hours and participated in illegal trading, but this was a way of life.

Fig. 6 *A sample of food products available in the GDR*

Shortages in the GDR

There was a saying in the GDR 'everything is available – just not at all times or in all places'. The shops and suppliers of East Germany suffered from the vagaries of the planned economy whereby the distribution of goods was uneven and inefficient. Goods were allocated to vendors by the government, but products could arrive in the wrong place, at the wrong time or fail to arrive at all. Since goods were often scarce, housewives tended to buy goods, whether they wanted them or not, whenever they arrived at a store. The careful housewife would not, for example, miss the opportunity to buy a large quantity of envelopes or invest in several pairs of shoes of the correct size when they were in stock because it might be several months before any more reappeared. Fresh and cold meats might be snapped up on a Thursday ready for the weekend, in case no more arrived. Fruit and vegetables were frequently hard to come by – even homegrown German products; the German with allotment produce could usually barter for other necessary items. Prices were set by the government so electricity, gas, water and some basic foods were very cheap but desirable items, like a Trabant car, required both money and patience. There was up to a 16-year waiting list and once the prize was obtained, a new quest began – for spare parts. In the final years of the GDR hardly any product was available 'at all times and in all places'. Sellers rationed goods and to obtain babies' nappies or children's clothes it became necessary to produce ID or preferably take the children along as proof of their existence!

By the 1980s there were over 2 million party members, but it is likely that most were only there for career reasons or outward appearances. For the majority, life in the GDR, centred on the family and the workplace. Most citizens enjoyed regular employment, an apartment and a high level of welfare provision. They were consequently ready to overlook their loss of freedom and the constant surveillance. Sociological surveys of workers in the 1980s show that a sense of security was rated highly by workers and while living standards were tolerable – and they were certainly better than those in other eastern bloc countries – most accepted their lot. The GDR population are thus said to have lived in a 'niche society' – a term used by the FRG's first representative in the GDR, Günter Gaus. They came to terms with the regime and got on with life as best they could.

There were even times when citizens displayed intense patriotism such as when then they applauded their athletes' Olympic success in 1976, 1980 and 1988. They also celebrated their soccer team, especially when they triumphed 1–0 over West Germany in the 1974 World Cup. However, this should not be confused with a belief in SED values. Indeed, outward displays of socialist fervour were rare. For all the talk about the creation of a 'workers' paradise', by the 1980s Western television almost undoubtedly had a far greater influence over East German behaviour than the socialist diatribes.

Even Honecker came to accept that complete control was not possible and pressure to display constant socialist commitment diminished during the period of his leadership. Indeed, despite the public conformity and outward show, even some SED members harboured a private indifference.

Fig. 7 *Margitta Gummel, winner of the gold medal for shot put at the 1968 Olympic Games in Mexico City, where she set a new world record*

A closer look

A participatory dictatorship

Although the GDR was not a democracy in the Western sense of the word, after the failure of Ulbricht's early attempt to bring about the total ideological indoctrination of the population, some degree of questioning and debate was permitted. There was a sense of paternalism within the SED government, whereby the party was concerned to know and respond to the interests of its people. One of its slogans was '*Alles zum Wohle des Volkes*' ('Everything for the benefit of the people') and there was certainly some attempt to ascertain and respond to the citizens' concerns. In practical terms this meant that party members could express their opinions through appropriately phrased representations to the deputies, while ordinary GDR citizens were allowed, and even encouraged, to draft *Eingaben* (letters of complaint) to the various state bodies and express their grievances about matters such as the allocation of resources. Indeed the Eingaben gave them a vehicle by which they might attempt to influence the direction of state policy so long as they did not challenge the ideological basis of SED rule and since authorities were obliged, by law, to reply within a certain time, those complaints that could be remedied, often were.

Obviously complaints had to remain within certain bounds and there was no channel for 'collective grievance' since strikes, for example, were forbidden. Nevertheless, the very existence of the Eingaben, coupled with the toleration given to the Church suggests that the GDR was a more responsive state than is sometimes assumed. There was clearly a space in which the individual might express his concerns within the GDR, and this has led Mary Fulbrook to refer to it as a 'participatory dictatorship' rather than a totalitarian state.

Cross-reference

Look back to page 125. Little did the people know the lengths to which the state was prepared to go to cultivate its young athletes and swimmers!

The political stagnation of the East German regime served to perpetuate political passivity. It is well known that when there are changes of policy and upheavals at the centre of government, people are inclined to question and to challenge, while when political leadership remains stable and a government runs smoothly, it will produce unthinking conformity. This is exactly what happened in the GDR during the long years under the rule of Ulbricht and Honecker. It would seem that there was always cynicism and dissatisfaction beneath the surface. The many applications for exit visas (even though such applications were not viewed favourably by the regime) suggest that dissatisfaction was there. Perestroika in the USSR and the gradual division within the SED leadership in the late 1980s offered the realistic possibility of political change in East Germany. However, the degree of public dissatisfaction was slow to materialise even then. After 40 years, the system was so ingrained that in 1989 many of its opponents looked to reform it rather than overthrow it.

The rapid collapse of the mass organisations and decline in party membership in 1989–90 (when 90 per cent of members left) suggests that there was never much real commitment to SED socialism. Furthermore, the huge votes for Western political parties in March 1990 would further support the view that all the years of propaganda had little impact on the East German citizens.

The situation is well summarised by Mark Allinson, who has also sought to explain why, in recent years, a sense of nostalgia for the old GDR has been felt in East Germany:

> While German unification or the end of SED rule seemed impossible, most people were prepared to live and work within the framework, and a significant proportion were dedicated to preserving it. Over 40 years a common identity developed; many citizens experienced pride in their country's achievements without necessarily supporting the SED. The dichotomy between GDR identity and rejection of the SED found expression after 1989 in GDR 'nostalgia' alongside the majority's clear desire to abandon 'real socialism'. This sense of community, fostered in adversity, must principally explain the GDR's enduring stability within the context of divided Europe, despite the distance between the SED and many of its subjects.

3

Activity

Thinking point

Why was there so little open opposition to the GDR regime?

Activity

Research exercise

Try to find out more about life in the GDR and prepare class presentations. Topics you might like to explore are:

- schools, education, the youth
- work and the workplace
- the activities of the Stasi and Stasi prisons
- housing, furnishings and GDR products
- the media and fashion
- holidays and leisure
- travel – both public and private.

A closer look

Socialist sex

East Germany developed its own sexual culture in which socialism was claimed to bring 'better love'. According to one unidentified East German woman interviewed in the 1990s, *'East German women had more fun, everybody knows that. After all, it was a proletarian society. None of this bourgeois concern with chastity until their wedding night.'* SED propaganda made much of the fact that prostitution and pornography were banned in the GDR and, thanks to state support, women were able to commit themselves to a long-lasting relationship. Sex before marriage was positively encouraged and the introduction of the contraceptive pill, together with abortions on demand in 1972, spread liberal attitudes. By 1989 one in three East German children was born outside marriage. Nudity (or 'free body culture') was also seen as healthy and normal. From the mid-1960s, nude bathing grew in popularity and by the 1970s full nudity was the norm on beaches and in holiday areas. Nudity was also perceived as normal within the home. As Kurt Starke, a leading East German sexologist, said, *'on nudist beaches it didn't matter if you were a party secretary or a cleaner.'* Although nudity itself was not regarded as erotic, these attitudes encouraged the spread of erotic dancing and striptease, nude photography and soft-porn movies. Such developments now seem strangely at odds with the traditional view of the GDR as a backward-looking regime, yet by the mid-1980s, such activities were growing fast.

Détente, Ostpolitik and mutual recognition

During the 1960s, Cold War tensions began to relax and from about 1968 to 1980 the world entered a period known as 'détente'. There were various reasons for this, perhaps the most compelling being the aftershock resulting from near nuclear confrontation in the Cuban Missile Crisis of 1962. The futility of the USSR/US arms race, in which a nuclear parity had been reached, also became more obvious as both the superpowers faced economic problems at home.

In Europe, events in 1968 showed political instability in both the West and East, with student riots and a Soviet invasion of Czechoslovakia ending the reforms of the '**Prague Spring**'. The new West German Chancellor, Willi Brandt, was firmly convinced that not only West Germany, but the whole of Europe would benefit from a reduction of tensions and greater links between West and East and he developed a policy known as Ostpolitik. Brandt wanted to 'normalise' relations between the two Germanies and believed the Hallstein Doctrine had become outdated. There seemed little doubt that the GDR would remain, particularly after the building of the Berlin Wall; it seemed only common sense to try to encourage the opening of channels between the two Germanies and to make the relationship between the two states as beneficial as possible to both sides.

From the Soviet side, there was also the impetus for improved relations. There had never been a formal peace treaty after World War II and the USSR was anxious to secure one and win the West's acceptance of the division of Germany and the territorial situation in eastern Europe.

As Mayor of Berlin at the time of the building of the Berlin Wall, Brandt had direct experience of the miseries of division and he aimed to relieve some of the personal suffering by negotiating with the City Council of East Berlin in an attempt to improve visiting rights for West Berliners.

■ Key terms

Prague Spring: This was an attempt to introduce liberal reform in Czechoslovakia.

■ Cross-reference

For the Hallstein Doctrine, namely the FRG's non-recognition of the GDR and refusal to have diplomatic relations with states which recognised East Germany, look back to Chapter 4, page 63.

There were, of course, those who saw matters differently. Such argued that negotiation with an 'illegitimate' state only served to perpetuate it. Negotiation with an illegitimate state was, so some conservatives said, breaking the Basic Law which had established the constitution of the FRG and which contained an explicit commitment to work for German reunification. Any concessions made, they argued, would strengthen division and be to the detriment of the West. Nevertheless, Brandt pushed ahead with his policy and it proved popular with the electorate.

An early success came at Christmas 1963, when Brandt agreed to refer to East Berlin as the capital of the GDR in return for a concession that allowed West Berliners to visit relatives on the other side of the wall over an 18-day period. Brandt furthered this policy from December 1966, when he was made Foreign Minister in Kiesinger's Great Coalition Government and again, on his appointment as Chancellor in September 1969. In fact, Brandt's first policy statement went as far as to say that the government was willing to consider the recognition of the GDR as a separate state.

Amid much acclaim from the East German people, Brandt met the East German Prime Minister, Willi Stoph, in Erfurt (GDR) in March 1970 and again at Kassel in West Germany in May. While these negotiations were in process, Brezhnev of the USSR met Honecker (on behalf of the ageing Ulbricht) in July and stressed the advantages of détente and Ostpolitik. It was Egon Bahr, Brandt's closest policy adviser, who finally managed to negotiate a treaty with the USSR. This was signed in August and followed by others with the eastern European satellite states.

Fig. 8 *The signing of the Moscow Treaty, with Brandt on the left and Kosygin for the USSR on the right; Brezhnev stands between them*

The Moscow Treaty, 12 August 1970

- The FRG accepted the eastern European borders, for example that between the GDR and Poland.
- The FRG no longer claimed to represent the whole of Germany.
- It was agreed that the GDR should join the UN.

The Warsaw Treaty, December 1970

- Both the FRG and Poland recognised the Oder–Neisse border.
- The remaining ethnic Germans in Poland were to be allowed to emigrate to the FRG.

■ The FRG promised Poland trade and financial aid.

The Prague Treaty, December 1973 (Negotiations between the FRG and Czechoslovakia began in October 1970, although they were not finalised until 1973)

■ The 1938 Munich Treaty which had incorporated the Sudetenland into Germany was declared null and void.

■ Czechoslovakia's post-1945 frontiers were recognised.

■ The remaining ethnic Germans in Czechoslovakia were to be allowed to emigrate to the FRG.

The Four Power Berlin Agreement, September 1971

■ The USSR and GDR recognised West Berlin's ties with the FRG and the right of West Berliners to visit the FRG. (This led to further agreements on transit traffic, postal services and visiting rights.)

This opened the way for a treaty to settle relations between the two Germanies. However, Brandt had first to fight an election on the issue in the face of considerable parliamentary opposition. For the German electorate, it seemed that the advantages to be gained from better East–West relations far outweighed any consideration of future reunification and Brandt received overwhelming support – an exceedingly high turnout which gave Brandt's SPD more votes than the CDU/CSU for the first time. In recognition of his efforts to improve the European situation he was awarded the Nobel Peace Prize in 1971.

The Basic Treaty, June 1973

■ The FRG recognised the GDR as an equal and independent (but not foreign) state.

■ GDR citizens were still to be regarded as 'German' citizens, who were automatically entitled to FRG citizenship if they came to the West.

■ An exchange of 'representatives' rather than ambassadors was arranged.

■ The West German commitment to work for reunification was repeated but there was also an emphasis on working for better human contact and communications between the two states, recognising 'two German states in one German nation', and emphasising a sense of shared national identity.

■ A visa was introduced whereby West Berliners could stay in East Berlin for one full day.

The results of the Ostpolitik policy

Ostpolitik, culminating in the Basic Treaty, certainly brought the two German states closer together. Communications between them improved and, at a personal level, the division caused less suffering.

However, at an international level, Ostpolitik drove the two states further apart. Their separate existence was acknowledged and, as a result, the GDR took the opportunity to declare itself a separate socialist nation in its new constitution of September 1974, and in 1975 signed a 25-year treaty of friendship with USSR.

Ostpolitik did not encourage Honecker to become any more liberal in outlook – rather the reverse. With a new found confidence, he urged the USSR to crush the Solidarity reform movement in Poland in 1980–81 and ignored the growing swell of dissent in his own country from 1985. However, the GDR gained a good deal from Ostpolitik. By 1984 it was recognised by 132 states; it joined the UN; it participated in the

Cross-reference

The FRG election results for this period can be found in Chapter 7, page 108.

Activity

Revision exercise

How successful was Willi Brandt during his time as German Chancellor? You will need to look back at the list of points you made in Chapter 7. You should use these together with what you have learnt about Ostpolitik policy to write a critical appraisal of Brandt as Chancellor.

Cross-reference

The new constitution of 1974 is outlined on page 127.

Fig. 9 *One aspect of the improving relations resulting from Ostpolitik was the exchange of political prisoners and spies between East and West*

international Helsinki Conference in 1975 and it received large loans from the FRG.

The West, for its part, exchanged ambassadors with the Soviet Union, Poland, Czechoslovakia and Hungary, bought the freedom of 34,000 political prisoners up to 1989, and ensured that there were more opportunities for personal telephone calls and visits between East and West. However, not all believed the price worth paying. According to the historian Hans Klein, writing in 1996:

> The apparent successes of the Brandt government's Ostpolitik did not, of course, silence the opposition. Franz-Josef Strauss called Brandt the 'Chancellor of the sell-out' and spoke of the 'Finlandisation' of Germany, that is, of neutrality with Moscow's blessing. The policies of the new government stirred controversy among the public as well. This came to a peak with Brandt's visit to Warsaw to sign the treaty normalising relations between the FRG and Poland on 7 December 1970 (when Brandt knelt at the memorial for the victims of the Warsaw ghetto). Brandt said, 'those who wanted to understand me could understand me, and many in Germany and elsewhere did understand me'. But there weren't all that many in Germany who did. A poll taken by *Der Spiegel* magazine reported that 48 per cent considered Brandt's gesture to be excessive and only 41 per cent thought it appropriate.

4

Although some felt that Brandt had surrendered a principle and got little in return, it should be remembered that Ostpolitik made the GDR dependent on the FRG. Ostpolitik served to prop up the weak economy of East Germany, enabling it to continue without reforms, but in so doing it laid the seeds for the GDR's destruction. It may not have worked as originally intended, but, by 1989, the GDR could no longer survive without the West.

Activity

Thinking and analysis

Imagine you were one of the following:

1 a member of the GDR government

2 a member of Brandt's cabinet

3 a member of the USSR government.

Would you have supported Ostpolitik? Give your reasons why.

Activity

Discussion point

Did the FRG pursue a 'sensible' policy in its dealings with the GDR?

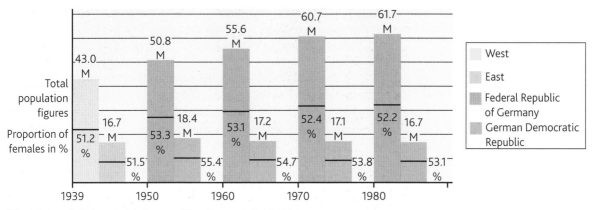

Fig. 10 *Population growth in East and West Germany 1939–80*

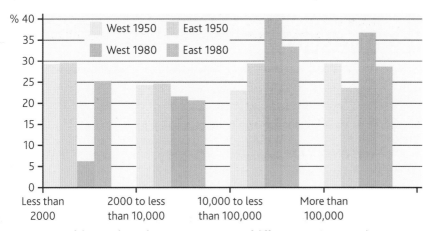

Fig. 11 *Percentage of the population living in communities of different sizes in East and West Germany*

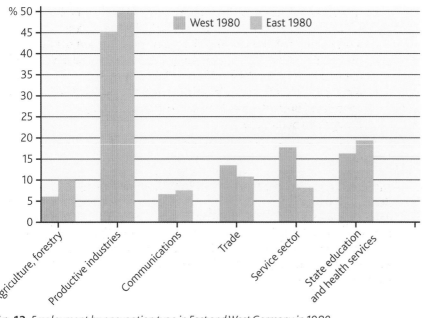

Fig. 12 *Employment by occupation type in East and West Germany in 1980*

Learning outcomes

In this section you have examined the development of the two Germanies from the building of the Berlin Wall in 1961 to the eve of the break-up of the GDR in 1989. Throughout this period, the reunification of Germany would still have appeared a distant and unlikely prospect, due to the fact that the West was wrapped up in political in-fighting under Erhard, Brandt, Schmidt and Kohl, and its energies were sapped by the economic problems and urban terrorism of the 1970s. You have also noted how the GDR under Honecker evolved into a mature 'niche society', which gave scant thought to the future as it battled with daily shortages and resigned itself to political stagnation. Finally, you will be aware that the policy of détente and Ostpolitik had served, at least in part, to harden the East–West division through acceptance. You will discover in the next section what happened to change all this within the space of a year.

Practice question

To what extent did the people of East Germany form a 'niche society' in the years 1949 to 1989?

(45 marks)

Study tip Obviously you will need to explain what you understand by a 'niche society' at the beginning of your answer and you will then need to provide material to support the idea of a 'niche society' and counter it with evidence to the contrary. In favour, you might refer to state welfare provision, employment, socialist societies and organisations, as well as the indoctrination and repression (to explain why people withdrew into themselves). To balance this you might cite examples of discontent and the levels of emigration, and refer to the events of 1989 – about which you will read more in the next section.

9 # Events Leading to the Opening of the Berlin Wall

In this chapter you will learn about:

■ the growth of political activism in the GDR

■ the influence of Gorbachev and the impact of changes in the eastern bloc

■ the freedom protests and silent marches

■ the part of Honecker in the internal collapse and opening of the Berlin Wall

■ the final attempts to reform and preserve the East German regime.

■ **Key terms**

Trabi: this was a nickname for the East German Trabant car. West Germans tended to look down on these inferior cars, which had none of the style or power of the popular West German models. The body of the car was made from a material comprising cotton fleece and plastic and was therefore easily damaged!

On the evening of 9 November 1989, a young doctor was working late at his desk in West Berlin, listening at the same time to the radio:

> Escalation of events. With every new hour there is new information. […] Berlin is suddenly at the centre of the world. […] Questions, questions, rumours; the border is open? […] Every hour, every half hour, news. And then it really happens; they're coming over!
>
> It is about 11.00pm. I go over to my housemate, Mark. We want to go to the border.
>
> What a moment! Everywhere along the way West Berliners are greeting East Berliners. […] To the border-crossing! Cars parked illegally all over the place. […] A cluster of people fills the concrete narrow passageway between East and West. Spotlights. Cheers. People really are coming from over there. Small colorful **Trabis** are sprayed with champagne. They look out. […] They hold back their tears. They wave, shake hands and start from the constant banging on the roof of their Trabis. They are uncertain whether the car can stand it. […] The crowd on the west side is now also pushing forward. […] 'The Wall must go!' We spur each other on. Every Trabi is a catalyst for more cheers.

1

■ Internal problems in the GDR
The growth of political activism in the GDR

According to Mary Fulbrook:

> The East German regime never succeeded in quelling dissent, discontent or opposition. What was new about the 1980s was not the growth of opposition – nor even the growth of discontent, but rather a combination of other factors. These include the changing forms and orientations of a growing minority of political activists who were seeking, not to overthrow the regime, nor even to escape from the GDR, but rather to improve it from within; the changing domestic political context of their actions, including both the growth of opportunity to act and the changing responses of the state to what were deemed 'hostile-negative forces' and, finally, changing aspects of the international context.

2

The mass protests witnessed in the GDR in the autumn of 1989 had long tapering roots which can be traced back to the agreement Honecker

Cross-reference

Honecker's agreement with the Church leaders is outlined in Chapter 8, page 125.

Exploring the detail

The emergence of Reform Groups in the mid-1980s

Typical of the new types of reform initiatives were:

- the Women's Peace Movement, bringing together peace groups from all over the GDR (from 1984)
- the IFM (Freedom and Civil Rights Movement) founded in January 1986 as the first truly independent political group outside the Church
- the regional peace workshops of the mid-1980s, which went beyond 'peace' to a discussion of human rights
- the emergence of Reform Groups in the mid-1980s socialist democracy, and ecological questions which had been made topical by the Chernobyl disaster, when a Soviet nuclear reactor blew up in 1986.

This era also saw the birth of other environmental groups, such as the UB (Environmental Library) of 1986.

Exploring the detail

Rosa Luxemburg and Karl Liebknecht

Rosa Luxemburg and Karl Liebknecht were communists who had been killed during the period of the Weimar Republic in the Spartacist rising of January 1919.

made with the Church leaders in March 1978 to allow controlled freedom of discussion under Church leadership. Honecker had, at a stroke, given dissidents a space for debate and while his intention had been to limit their influence under a compliant Church leadership, this was to provide the seed from which the reform movement of the late 1980s would emerge.

Initially, the agreement seemed to work in the government's favour and the Church had adopted a conciliatory role. Manfred Stolpe, who from 1962–89 was the lay head of the Protestant Churches of the GDR, was also a Stasi agent. There were occasional demonstrations, as for example on the anniversary of the Hiroshima bombing in August 1983, but the Stasi ensured that such activities were either suppressed before they could begin or tightly controlled by the state. On this occasion, according to Stasi records:

> Measures were introduced in all the affected districts and areas to investigate these plans further and, in conjunction with the relevant state organs, either to prevent the planned activities or to exert influence in such a manner as to ensure that the course of events unfolded without any disturbance, or to reduce them to purely religious activities.

Key profile

Manfred Stolpe, (born 1936)

Manfred Stolpe was a lawyer who became active in the Protestant Evangelical Church in the GDR. He was head of the Secretariat of the Evangelical Churches between 1962–81 and sat on the governing body of the Churches as President of the Eastern Region between 1982–90. In 1990 he joined the SPD and became the Premier of the state of Brandenburg (1990–2002) and subsequently the Federal Minister of Transport between 2002 and 2005.

However, from the mid-1980s, the climate began to change with the arrival of the reformist Mikhail Gorbachev as First Secretary of the USSR. More specialised reform groups focusing on particular issues began to grow, publications appeared and new networks crossing local and regional boundaries were established. Such organisations became increasingly irritated with the conservative Church leadership, which lost the limited control it had exerted over dissident movements. As movements grew bolder, the only way to control the developing pressure for reform was by the use of the Stasi. This in turn brought further political activism (which even spread to some of the lower-level members of the political elite). There also seemed to be some indications of greater tolerance on the part of the state. Despite an initial attempt to prevent this, the Olof Palme Peace March from Ravensbrück to Sachsenhausen saw unofficial placards carried alongside the official banners of the state organisations for the first time in September 1987.

However, in the winter of 1987–88, there was a further clampdown. The traditional Luxemburg–Liebknecht parade of January 1988 was used as an excuse for a demonstration in favour of greater freedom in the GDR and the banner quoting Rosa Luxemburg, '*Freedom is always the freedom to think differently'* was displayed. Large numbers were arrested, the most prominent leader sent into exile and other held, for considerable periods without charge. This only encouraged more to join the incipient 'civic movement' and organised, non-violent demonstrations of sympathy and solidarity took place all over the GDR. There were candlelit meetings, concerts, church vigils and, in Leipzig, Monday prayer services became an important regular event. The relations between Church and State had broken down and Stolpe could no longer control other Church leaders who added their voices to those of the dissidents.

Honecker's mistake was to resist any dialogue. Pretending that all was well, the regime relied on repression – even to the extent of censoring Soviet anti-Stalinist films and the German edition of *Sputnik* which had 180,000 East German subscribers. The Soviet magazine contained support for the reformist policies being introduced by Gorbachev in 1988. However, the activism could not be totally repressed and as changes began to take place in the other communist states of eastern Europe, the political opposition movement in Germany entered a new phase.

The influence of Mikhail Gorbachev

Fig. 1 *Despite their apparent cordiality, Honecker (left) and Gorbachev (right) had very different views on the future of communism. They are shown with their wives Margot Honecker and Raisa Gorbachev*

In March 1985, Mikhail Gorbachev became leader of the Soviet Union. He took control of a state whose economy had been disastrously weakened by impossibly high defence-spending demands, and his answer was *perestroika* (reconstruction) and *glasnost* (openness). He wanted to steer the USSR along a new course.

His reforms fostered an expectation of change in eastern Europe – in the GDR it was widely assumed that Honecker, and the elderly ruling elite, would step down in favour of younger men, who would bring in greater democratisation and domestic restructuring.

In the later 1980s, as the economic, social and political difficulties of the USSR grew, Soviet strategists began to hint that the USSR was no longer in a position to prop up the communist states of eastern Europe. Gorbachev's renunciation of the 'Brezhnev Doctrine', which had confirmed the USSR's right to interfere in the internal affairs of its satellite states, made sense to the Soviets, but was to have disastrous implications for the leadership of the GDR. For the USSR, the cost of maintaining a military presence had come to outweigh the benefits and it was even alleged that such a presence reduced, rather than enhanced, Soviet security.

The shifts in policy under Gorbachev had the effect of breathing new life into the incipient reform movements of the eastern bloc countries and the so-called 'Sinatra Doctrine' (a phrase taken from the Frank Sinatra song lyrics, 'let them do it their way'), meant that the USSR kept its distance as reformist ideas brought changes in Poland and Hungary. However, Gorbachev grew increasingly irritated with Honecker, whose refusal to consider reform in the GDR went against all he was trying to do. It is perhaps not surprising, therefore, that even as Gorbachev travelled to the GDR to join in the GDR's 40th anniversary celebrations on 7–8 October 1989, the Moscow leadership began to explore ways of removing him from power. In Berlin, Gorbachev made his message clear. The GDR had to take responsibility for its own future and change was unavoidable. While voices from the swelling masses at the reform demonstrations might shout for 'Gorbi', Honecker remained unmoved. As events turned out, the USSR did not need to involve themselves further. Just days later, it was the East Germans themselves who forced Honecker's resignation, although it was Gorbachev who had provided the indirect stimulation and the direct impetus to change the leadership.

The impact of changes in communist eastern Europe on the GDR

There is no doubt that the changes in both Poland and Hungary in 1989 acted as catalysts for change in the GDR. The communist Polish government collapsed on 16 August 1989, and was replaced by a coalition led by the reform movement Solidarity, while in Hungary, the summer saw its communist government begin to reform itself with moves towards a multi-party democracy.

When the Hungarian government issued the momentous orders for their frontier guards to dismantle the border fence with Austria (an event which took place in full view of the world's TV cameras), the first breach in the iron curtain was, quite literally, accomplished. For those that wanted to take advantage of the opportunity, it became relatively easy to move from East to West across this border in the summer of 1989.

Hungary had always been a popular holiday destination for East Germans, whose travel was restricted to the communist bloc countries. It is not surprising, therefore, that some of those holidaying on the shores of Lake Balaton in the early summer of 1989 seized the opportunity to drive into Austria and then on to the FRG where they could receive a West German passport and a small cash sum. By August 1989, the trickle of emigrants turned into a flood and camps close

Fig. 2 *The emergence of 'Solidarity' in Poland heralded the collapse of communism in eastern Europe*

to the border were packed with East Germans preparing to travel west. Although the GDR government tried to halt this by prohibiting travel to Hungary, many, particularly young East Germans, simply defied the order. In the West, Red Cross reception camps had to be hastily set up to cope with the swelling numbers.

Heading directly for Hungary was not the only 'escape-route'. Some East Germans travelled to Prague in Czechoslovakia, where they climbed over the fence into the West German Embassy, while the Czech government, anxious to keep on good terms with the FRG, ordered their own police to stand aside. Trains were subsequently permitted to carry these 'embassy refugees' to the FRG and this encouraged other East Germans to try the same method. Soon, hopeful East Germans crowded the West German embassies across communist eastern Europe. Prague, Warsaw, Budapest and even the embassy in East Berlin itself was flooded with hopeful travellers, anxious to secure a rapid escape to the West.

By the end of August, the situation was growing out of control and to relieve the pressure, on 11 September the Hungarians opened their border fully so that East Germans could pass as they pleased. After this the heavily defended East–West German border seemed virtually redundant. For weeks, trains made their way westwards laden with fleeing East Germans.

However, there came word in October that the government was planning to close the Czechoslovak-Hungarian border to halt the extraordinary exodus. More than 5,000 would-be escapees set up camp in the grounds of the West German embassy in Prague, forcing diplomats to turn their offices into dormitories. Since the GDR was about to celebrate its 40th anniversary and dignitaries from across the Soviet bloc were due to visit, the SED government was forced to give ground and allow those in Prague to travel westwards, provided the trains returned through East Germany – the idea being that the opportunity to travel could be interpreted as a sign of the generosity of the East German government.

A closer look

The freedom trains and escape to the West

Prague was flooded with hundreds of East Germans in September 1989 seeking asylum in the West German embassy. They climbed over the fence and when rooms and corridors were full, camped in the extensive garden. The situation worsened daily, until an agreement was reached between representatives of Czechoslovakia, East Germany, West Germany and the USSR that the refugees would be allowed to travel to the West. Within hours of the announcement on 30 September, East German 'freedom trains' set off from Prague, taking the asylum seekers through East Germany to West Germany.

Although these trains were supposed to be a 'one-off' concession, several hundred more East Germans arrived the next day. By 3 October, around 5,000 people occupied the embassy and more crowds surrounded the hopelessly over-crowded building. More special trains were consequently sent to the West on 4 October.

In a bid to prevent further departures, the GDR considered introducing a visa for travel to Czechoslovakia, but it produced such an outcry that it had to be cancelled on 1 November. By the 3 November, another 5,000 East Germans had entered the embassy premises.

Did you know?

Since the FRG had always maintained that East Germans were citizens of the FRG, the right to a passport for GDR citizens was automatic. In the euphoric atmosphere which the new chink in the iron curtain had created, many travelling west in mid-1989 were greeted by ecstatic West Germans who handed out balloons, clothes, toys, leaflets and cards from employment agencies.

Altogether approximately 15,000 refugees passed through the embassy in Prague before 9 November. Most of the 23 freedom trains went through the East German towns of Dresden, Freiberg, Karl-Marx-Stadt (now Chemnitz) and Plauen, where they encountered demonstrating crowds of East Germans, some of whom tried to board the trains and had to be restrained by East German police dogs. Lenin had once joked that if German revolutionaries stormed a railway station, they would queue up to buy a platform ticket – but he was proved wrong on 3 October 1989 when a crowd of East Germans stampeded into Dresden. A local historian, Hans Klopfleisch, commented, *'We hadn't seen anything like this since the worker riots of 1953. Word spread that the regime was closing the East German-Czech border. The people here felt they had been completely cut off from the world. They thronged into the station, onto the rail tracks, blocking the trains. There was this feeling that East Germany had briefly opened up and was about to close down again.'* On this occasion, when the police and National People's Army moved in, demonstrators responded with a hail of cobblestones and broken bottles; police cars were set on fire and there was an unprecedented orgy of pent-up anger.

German protest groups and the silent marches

The civic movement

In the summer and autumn of 1989, a number of new movements for reform and democratisation emerged in the GDR. These were largely the preserve of the educated urban professionals and so became known as the 'civic movement'. Some organisations were specifically political, others acted as debating forums, but they are all significant as they brought discussion out into the open and away from the confines of the Church.

Following a human rights seminar in August, for example, a new East German Social Democratic Party was born. This was officially founded on 7 October. It was not connected to the Western SPD but was committed to pursuing its own programme of socialist democracy in the East. It declared its intention to end the SED's monopoly of power and promote open debate on the future of the country. Within a few weeks it had more than a thousand members. Another socialist grouping, the 'United Left', was also founded in September, although this enjoyed rather less success.

'Democracy Now' was another new organisation and although not a political party as such, it published a manifesto for reform on 12 September. Its founders encouraged people to involve themselves in their own problems. They wanted a free market economy and were committed to fighting for the human rights of free speech, movement and assembly, and for controls over the media, education, unions and other organisations to be lifted. 'Democratic Awakening' was set up with similar aims by a group of protestant clergymen on 1 October. It declared that it would work for a 'socialist society on a democratic basis'.

A closer look

Rainer Eppelmann – a founder of 'Democratic Awakening'

East Berliner Rainer Eppelmann had never been a conformist. He had been neither a member of the Young Pioneers nor taken part in the Jugendweihe. Consequently, he had not been able to take East German school examinations. His parents had sent him to school in West Berlin before the wall was built, but after that he was 'caged' and when called to serve his turn in the National People's Army, refused to take the soldier's oath and was sentenced to eight months in gaol. On release, he trained to become a pastor and eventually became well known, from the late 1970s until 1984, for organising church masses featuring blues music which attracted young people. At its peak, several thousand teenagers attended his blues masses, revelling in the chance to meet like-minded people and discuss environmentalism, human rights and 'peace'. He knew he was spied upon by the Stasi, but it was not until after he published the 'Berlin Appeal', asking for the removal of all occupation troops from Germany, in 1982, that he experienced a number of 'unreal' events: a mysterious 'accident' at a traffic light when another car cut in on him and when a wheel that came loose on his car after he had collected it from a garage. Little wonder that Eppelmann wanted to do something more than simply hold candlelight vigils in his church in the 1980s. Instead he became a co-founder of 'Democratic Awakening'.

One particularly influential new body was *Neues Forum* (New Forum) – an organisation committed to free and open discussion outside the confines of the Church, which was founded on 10 September. Its founding document declared:

> The disrupted relationship between state and society cripples the creative potential of our society and hinders the solution of pressing local and global tasks. We fritter ourselves away in a bad-tempered passivity and yet we have so many more important things that we could be doing for our life, our country and humanity.

4

Neues Forum tried to register with the authorities as a legal body, but was refused permission because, according to the government, *'there is no social need for the association'*. However, the group soon disproved this by collecting 25,000 signatures within its first month. Consequently, although strictly illegal, it continued to thrive and demonstrated the desire of people such as writers, musicians, lawyers, doctors, students, clergymen and other intellectuals to participate in open debate.

Other new political groups included women's groups intent on 'real' equality and environmental groups such as 'List 2', which eventually came together as the Green Party on 5 November 1989. However, in the summer and early autumn of 1989, the civic movement remained limited in scope and hindered by the lack of clear leadership. It was fragmented into so many different groups that each was vulnerable to Stasi infiltration and repression.

Nevertheless, there was some cooperation, such as when the Social Democrats, Democratic Awakening, Democracy Now, Neues Forum and other pacifist groups met in Berlin on 4 October to address an audience of 2,000. They issued a joint declaration, *'We are united in our will to transform the state and society democratically'*, and speeches called on all GDR citizens to work for a democratic renewal, human rights, pacifism, ecological improvements, intellectual freedom and social solidarity.

As the weeks passed, the reform movement in the GDR was able to marshal ever-larger numbers of the formerly passive GDR citizens to its cause. Protest also became more open and daring, and the long-suppressed private grumbles began to be shared and spread.

The centre of the freedom protests was Leipzig. The regular Monday prayer service in Leipzig's Nikolaikirche had already become a focus for peaceful change and greater personal liberty and youthful peace protestors took to the streets after the service waving banners demanding *'an open country with free people'*. The Stasi took action to break up this and a further demonstration after the service the following week. However, the Stasi interference simply led the protestors to adopt a different approach. On 18 September, they emerged from their service, candles in hand and marched silently, moving in different directions, offering no threat and presenting no easy target to the Stasi, who were unsure how to react.

Fig. 3 *Freedom march in Leipzig, 1989*

There followed regular 'silent marches', which grew in size with the passing weeks. On 25 September, 5,000 marchers took to the streets, their silence interrupted by shouts of *'we are staying here'*, *'Gorbi, Gorbi'*, and the singing of *'We shall overcome'*. On 2 October, 20,000 citizens turned up to protest peacefully, but the Stasi still tried to break up the march, using clubs and dogs. On 7 October, during the celebration of the GDR's 40th anniversary, the protest in Leipzig was met with even more extreme force. Water cannons were used and 210 protestors were arrested.

The situation had reached a crucial juncture and rumours began to circulate that the next Monday would see a massive crackdown, rather like that witnessed in Tiananmen Square in Beijing during June. Nevertheless, the usual Monday night service was held on 9 October and a march planned. Nikolaikirche itself was, in fact, so packed (since 400 SED members had been ordered to attend) that other churches had to be used to manage the overflow, while 70,000 people waited outside.

There were police, militia and combat troops all on the alert around the church and the Stasi had a vast presence inside as well as outside the building. However, at the end of the service, the procession set off silently as usual at around 6.00pm. It was thanks to the desperate appeals to the central authorities of three local SED officials, who were alarmed by the potential for bloodshed – together with the Pastor Peter Zimmerman and Kurt Masur, the conductor of the Leipzig Gewandhaus Orchestra, who had rather incongruously been conducting Richard Strauss's playful *Till Eulenspiegel* that evening – that sometime between 7.00 and 8.00pm, the armed forces, police and Stasi all miraculously disappeared, while the traffic police stopped the traffic to allow the procession to pass peacefully. The silence was broken as the marchers shouted, *'We are the people!'*

A closer look

Siegbert Schefke was a dissident East Berliner. His flat was kept under constant surveillance by the Stasi because he had made a number of environmental films and they had given him the codename 'Satan'. Siegbert was aware of the forthcoming Leipzig protest movement march on 9 October despite the usual news blackout about what was going on, and reckoned it would be a crucial moment. Consequently, on 8 October, he arranged timers on his lights and radio, climbed through a skylight and made his way via the roof to join a friend in a waiting Trabant. They drove to Leipzig, changing cars twice on the way, to fool any watching Stasi and, growing more apprehensive, they passed tanks and military convoys, all heading for the city. Schefke persuaded a priest, Hans-Jürgen Sievers, to allow him to hide in the church tower to film the demonstrations. The priest was willing but, as a precaution, withdrew cash to give his children, in case he was caught and imprisoned. The atmosphere was tense. According to Sievers, as young people flocked to the churches, they said farewell to their parents *'as if they were going to war and did not expect to come back alive'*. In the side streets, the armed police massed in full riot gear and hospitals were on the alert with extra supplies of blood flown in. As Schefke filmed he could see the Stasi watching from another high building opposite and had to cover the red light of his camera with chewing gum to avoid being spotted. The film, which mercifully did not show violence, but was a witness to the strength of public feeling, was handed over to a contact whom Schefke met in a 'revolving door' of a Leipzig hotel. Concealed in underwear, it was smuggled to the West where it was shown on West German TV the next day. Millions of East Germans thus saw how their own regime had lost its nerve and were themselves inspired to demonstrate. Schefke himself returned to Berlin, re-entered his flat the way he had left and was amused to find himself dutifully followed by the watchful Stasi on a trip to the bakery the next morning. They had no idea that this was the man whose TV pictures helped bring about the collapse of the GDR. The priest was also able to chuckle over the moment when he had cooperated with 'Satan' to help destroy the regime.

Did you know?

It later emerged that frantic negotiations among local SED officials and phone calls to national Party Headquarters had resulted in the decision around 7.30pm to give the order for the withdrawal of the security forces. This was a turning point in the development of the protest movement and opened up possibilities for further peaceful protest and debate.

This success breathed yet more life into the Reform movement. The following week over 100,000 marchers appeared in Leipzig; on 23 October, there were more than 250,000; on 30 October, 350,000.

The pattern was repeated elsewhere. In East Berlin, the Gethsemane church was used for peaceful candlelit vigils in support of reform. The candles, guarded by children, were symbolically kept burning in the hope of peaceful change and some started fasting and remained in the church for days on end without food. Halle, Plauen, Dresden, Chemnitz, Erfurt and Potsdam and other towns all over East Germany saw civil disobedience and peaceful reform demonstrations, although Stasi action could sometimes lead to confrontation.

When 7,000 demonstrated in Berlin on the GDR anniversary day of 7 October, they met heavy-handed policing. According to a contemporary opposition sympathiser:

> Civilians in leather coats and uniformed police clubbed, pushed and grabbed about a thousand demonstrators, herding them into waiting trucks. After a bumpy ride through dark streets, those arrested were dumped in gaols. Many were beaten and mercilessly interrogated about imagined treasonous conspiracies. They were kept standing for hours, denied food, water and sleep and could use the bathroom only with a guard. After signing incriminating confessions, first time dissidents were usually warned and let go after a day or two. Repeat protestors were fined and presumptive ringleaders remained jailed, cut off from legal recourse or friends. Instead of cowing the crowds, this brutal repression only spurred them on.

5

Since Gorbachev had made it clear that the Red Army would not intervene to quell unrest, the government struggled to maintain the upper hand and after backing down in both Leipzig and Dresden on 9 October, the Stasi were held in check and the government tried to combat dissent politically instead.

Activity

The following are all slogans used by protest groups in 1989. Explain the meaning of each in relation to the grievances and hopes of the protestors.

We are the people (*Wir sind das Volk*)	No violence
The rule of law is the best state security	Germany, fatherland
Now or never – freedom and democracy	Let the people lead
Legal recognition for the Neues Forum	Freedom of the press
The cart is stuck in the mud – old drivers must go!	The Wall must go!
As we demonstrate today, so we shall live tomorrow	We are staying here!

Gorbi, Gorbi

And some which rhyme in their original German form`:

SED – that hurts (*SED – das tut weh!*)

Visa free as far as Hawaii (*Visa-frei nach Hawaii!*)

Cycle round Europe – but not as a grandfather
(*Mit dem Fahrrad durch Europa, aber nicht als alter Opa!*)

Erich Honecker and internal collapse

Erich Honecker seemed to be caught entirely unawares by the surge of opposition that welled up 'from below' in the summer and autumn of 1989. Perhaps blinded by the impact of Ostpolitik, Honecker had grown more, rather than less distant and assured during the 1980s and when Soviet perestroika had roused reformist hopes and brought changes to the communist governments in Poland and Hungary, the 76-year-old leader and his elderly SED government adamantly refused to follow the Russian lead, repeating only unrealistic slogans about victorious socialism. When the Hungarian border was opened and a crisis threatened as embassies filled with East German refugees, Honecker was not well and he underwent a gall-bladder operation on 18 August, shortly before his 77th birthday.

After an absence of six weeks, during which the SED leadership seemed powerless without him, Honecker returned and sought to regain control by banning visa-free travel to Czechoslovakia on 3 October. Honecker was determined that nothing should mar the 40th anniversary celebrations of the GDR on 7 October, which he regarded as his personal triumph.

Did you know?

The government floundered without direction for six weeks, seemingly paralysed without its leader. There was, of course, considerable speculation as to who might replace him. The old-school hardliners backed Egon Krenz while the reform-minded pro-Gorbachev communists favoured the moderate Dresden party chief, Modrow, who was not even a member of the Politburo.

Fig. 4 *The 40th anniversary celebrations in the GDR*

A closer look

Celebrating the 40th anniversary of the GDR (7 October 1989)

The regime's official celebration of the 40th anniversary of the founding of the GDR took place on 6–7 October 1989. Honecker was joined by the Soviet head of state, Mikhail Gorbachev and his wife, Raisa, and the 'party' began with speeches from both leaders.

Honecker proudly proclaimed, '*Today the GDR is an outpost of peace and civilisation in Europe. We will never forget this fact. Forty years of the GDR mark a totally new chapter in the history of our people. The GDR has paved its way with achievements serving to strengthen our people. Socialism and peace are, and remain, key words for that which we have achieved up to now, as well as that which we will continue to accomplish.*'

Gorbachev replied: '*Like every other country, the GDR, of course, has its own problems of development which must be considered and for which solutions must be found. We do not doubt the capability of the Socialist Unity Party of Germany, with all its intellectual potential, its rich experience and its political authority, in cooperation with all social forces, to find answers to the questions.*'

■ Question

How did the two speeches given on 6 October differ? Can you account for this?

The following day, Gorbachev stood alongside Erich Honecker and Willi Stoph, the GDR Prime Minister, in front of a banner proclaiming '40 Years of the GDR' on a specially erected grandstand on the Karl-Marx Allee in East Berlin. From here they witnessed the march past of GDR soldiers and missiles displayed on large trucks indicating the Republic's strength. Honecker revelled in the programmed cheers and probably believed that the carefully orchestrated performance was a sign of popular support. Despite the economic stagnation, the refugee crisis, the new exodus, the growing reform movements and the demonstrations, one of which occurred in East Berlin that very night and which was crushed with brutality, Honecker had his day of glory.

Gorbachev's visit and the 40th anniversary speeches failed to stabilise the regime and, if anything, made Honecker's position even more vulnerable. In the eyes of many East Germans, the staged celebrations merely exemplified his inability to face up to reality. Gorbachev's clear lack of support for the ageing leader – the Berlin reform demonstrations and arrests signalled his loss of Soviet endorsement, as well as the loss of internal support. Consequently, even some SED politicians came to accept that Honecker had to go.

However, Honecker, while stung by the criticism, seemed to have no intention of stepping down, nor of dropping his hardline approach. He reacted angrily to Politburo proposals for reform, forcing his deputy, Egon Krenz, to defend himself, saying, *'Erich, this is not directed at you – I am concerned about our country.'*

■ **Key profile**

Egon Krenz, (born 1937)

Egon Krenz joined the SED in 1955 and became leader of the Ernst Thälmann Pioneers (1971–74) and the Free German Youth (1974–83). He entered the SED Central Committee, the *Volkskammer* (People's Chamber), and finally the Politburo. He served as Secretary of the Central Committee from 1983 and was Honecker's deputy. He led the GDR from October–December 1989, but was forced to resign. In 1997 he was sentenced to 6.5 years in prison for the deaths of Berlin Wall would-be escapees and electoral fraud but he never renounced his political views.

Fig. 5 *Egon Krenz*

There was no mechanism for replacing a leader in power, so there had to be a 'plot' within the Politburo to remove him. This involved those who had convinced themselves that the GDR would be better off without him. They could hardly have been described as 'reformers'. Indeed, when their leader, Egon Krenz, had visited the FRG in June, he had been described by an SPD politician there as *'utterly unsympathetic'* and a typical product of the GDR system. However, they knew the party's authority was in danger and believed in a more flexible socialism, so, overcoming their natural inclination to submit to the elder statesman, Krenz, Stoph (the Prime Minister), Mielke (Head of the Stasi), Tisch (Head of the Unions) and Schabowski (the Berlin district chief) prepared a coup.

When the agenda for the closed Politburo meeting of 17 October was handed to him, Honecker found an additional item had been added – that he resign as General Secretary of the SED and associated state offices. He was both stunned and deeply hurt that his closest advisers could do this to him, but he did not try to fight. Although he later claimed he was the victim of a 'grand conspiracy', he was prepared to offer his resignation on 18 October to the plenary session of the Central Committee giving the 'official' reason as ill health.

Few mourned Honecker's political passing. In a sense he was a victim of his own political success. Honecker had built up a personal power base in the GDR, making all high-profile appointments himself, taking personal control over policy decisions and media broadcasts. In this deliberately cultivated isolated position he had acquired a false sense of security and this left him vulnerable as the tide turned. He never understood the implications of *perestroika*, nor the degree of public dissatisfaction with the GDR regime. Nor did he understand his state's appalling economic position. He had left the country leaderless in the summer months of 1989 while he was ill and, after his return, had been so preoccupied with the anniversary celebrations that he had failed to see how pressure from below had begun to affect the very men on whom he relied. His naivety was astonishing. He had said to a confidante: *'We have to go our own way. We cannot permit what is happening in Russia. We must deal with the few crackpots which are concerning us now.'*

The end of divided Germany

The opening of the Berlin Wall

With Honecker's departure, Egon Krenz assumed control. In his first address he stated:

> The first requirement is a realistic appreciation of the position we are in. In the past months it is clear that we haven't always paid sufficient heed to the nature of the social evolution of our country and we haven't always drawn the appropriate conclusions at the right time. From today we shall be taking a different course, we are going to win back the political and ideological initiative.

6

Krenz opened discussions with Church leaders and with Neues Forum. On 27 October, the ban on visa-free travel to Czechoslovakia was lifted and an amnesty given to all those convicted of trying to escape to the West. After a trip to Moscow at the beginning of November, Krenz spoke with Solidarity leaders in Poland and returned with a raft of reforms:

- The right to travel to the West (although only for 30 days in a year and with no guarantee of sufficient currency) – the legal committee of the Volkskammer initially refused to ratify this.
- Freedom to leave for the refugees in the Prague embassy.
- The establishment of a constitutional court.
- Democratic elections (although the leading role of the SED was not renounced).
- The legalisation of Neues Forum.

These measures were accompanied by the resignations or sackings of key figures associated with old-style rule such as Margot Honecker, Minister

Activity

Thinking point and essay question

'Honecker had no one but himself to blame for his downfall.'

In groups make a list of points for and against this view. Nominate speakers to present the case for each side and debate which you feel is the more convincing. You could then write an essay assessing the validity of the view.

of Education (Erich's estranged wife); Harry Tisch (Union leader); the leaders of the CDU and NPDP; some district SED and trade union leaders; Erich Mielke (Stasi chief); and Kurt Hager (Politburo member in charge of ideology).

However, much of this had come too late and the proposed measures were not extensive enough to satisfy the protest groups. Other meetings had also been taking place at a local level, where district party bosses were keen to find their own solutions, and weakening the national initiative was the way that SED officials responded differently in different areas. This caused a dangerous fragmentation within the party. Not all were happy to see Krenz as their head – even in the Volkskammer 52 members had voted against his becoming Head of State on 24 October. Younger and more reformist elements of the party favoured Hans Modrow, the first secretary in Dresden, who, although not a Politburo member, had views more in line with Gorbachev.

Fig. 6 *Hans Modrow*

Key profile

Hans Modrow, (born 1928)

Hans Modrow joined the SED in 1949 after release as a prisoner-of-war. He became the First Secretary of the SED in Dresden in 1973 and a member of the Volkskammer. He became Premier following the resignation of Willi Stoph on 13 November 1989 and was the unofficial leader of East Germany from 7 December after Krenz's departure. After the reunification elections of 18 March 1990, he became a Bundestag politician and member of the European Parliament. He was found guilty of electoral fraud in the May 1989 Dresden municipal elections in 1993 and fined.

Nor did the general public show much confidence in Krenz. He was widely believed to have authorised election fraud, supported repression in China and ordered force against demonstrators at home. His speeches were peppered with the same old SED vocabulary and while he spoke of a *Wende* (turn) this seemed merely to imply a different route to the same end. Such was the level of distrust that many feared the promises were simply a trap. A Leipzig newspaper commented, '*They could hardly have found anyone worse*'.

Krenz appeared on television on 3 November outlining an SED action plan of political reform, human rights, economic restructuring and changes in education. However, he did not reverse the statements he had made in a press conference two days earlier when he had rejected opening the Berlin Wall, moving towards reunification or giving up the SED's claim to leadership. On 4 November, between 500,000 and 1 million people crowded on to the streets of East Berlin, calling for free elections, freedom of speech, and hearing speeches in the Alexanderplatz by prominent intellectuals such as Christa Wolf. A further 500,000 marched in Leipzig on Monday 6 November. Furthermore, the relaxation of travel controls had encouraged the exodus west to continue, with even more following the route over the Czech border. It has been estimated that around 9,000 people a day or 375 an hour left this way, in early November.

The situation had reached breaking point and on 7 November the entire East German government led by Willi Stoph resigned. Berlin marchers cheered and shouted, '*All power to the people and not to the SED.*' On the following day, 8 November, the remainder of the Politburo resigned and a new, smaller Politburo was created which included Hans Modrow and a number of moderate reformers, as well as some old hardliners.

Fig. 7 *Schabowski's response to a reporter's question was to bring down the wall*

On the evening of 9 November, at a lengthy press conference in East Berlin, a weary Günter Schabowski, government spokesman and Politburo member, was asked a question by Riccardo Ehrman, the East Berlin correspondent for the Italian news agency. It was 6.53pm and the question was to have momentous repercussions. The question related to the new regulation, allowing GDR citizens to spend 30 days a year abroad, but only after going through a lot of official bureaucracy. Ehrman began: *'Mr Schabowski, don't you believe that it was a big mistake to introduce this travel law several days ago?'* Schabowski sidestepped the question but then added, *'We have decided today to implement a regulation that allows every citizen of the GDR through any of the border crossings.'* Asked when this new regulation would come into effect, he replied *'Immediately, without delay.'* It later transpired that the regulation had only been a draft proposal, but once the word out, they could not be retracted.

By 9.30pm, a few hours after the first reports, Berliners had started to congregate at the border crossings and a crowd of approximately 1,000 had gathered at the Bornholmer Strasse crossing. At 10.42pm the West German news programme *Tagesthemen* reported that the border was open and thousands more East Berliners, alerted to the situation by watching the West German news, rushed out to swell the gathering throng.

By 11.30pm there was a crowd of several thousand at the Bornholmer Strasse crossing and at midnight the border guards were at a loss at what to do. No one had expected the announcement and they were not prepared for the ever-increasing crowds. They were, however, ordered to avoid bloodshed at all costs and so, around midnight they gave up trying to control the crowds and let them through.

> ### Did you know?
> 9 November has played a key role in modern German history. It is the date of the founding of the Weimar Republic in 1918, the date of the launch of Hitler's November pogroms in 1938 and, more happily, the day the Berlin Wall came down.

Fig. 8 *Young West Berliners were able to scale the wall without fear of reprisals*

The Western political journal *Newsweek* later described the opening of the Berlin Wall:

> At the Brandenburg Gate, on the eastern part of the wall, thousands burst into the old square that was once the heart of an undivided Berlin. East German border guards watched, first with detached amusement and then with undisguised glee. Nearby a young man beat on the wall with a hammer and handed out fragments to the crowd. 'The wall is gone' the people chanted deliriously, 'the wall is gone'. At crossing points around the city, the police laughed and talked with passers-by. 'When we got the word,' one cop cheerfully explained, 'we were as surprised as anyone else.' All vestiges of the totalitarian past seemed gone. No one checked identity papers, no one probed under car seats for would-be escapees. There were no escapees.
>
> East Germans shouted, 'We'll be back' and most of them kept their promise. Some returned within hours, talking excitedly about their voyage into a suddenly brighter future, 'It's fantastic', 'it's incredible', 'The eighth wonder of the world!' 'I never believed I would be able to do this!' Such were the joyous reports of the people.
>
> 'It was wonderful,' said a 22-year-old East German student. 'It is amazing how warmly we were greeted. We were applauded. They cried. They were just as happy as we were.'
>
> The next day the newspaper headlines screamed – 'Berlin is Berlin again.'

7

The final attempts to reform and preserve the East German regime and their failure

Within the first four days of the opening of the border, 5.2 million Easterners had set out to visit the West; within a week it was 9 million. Over the following weeks and months, thousands more made the trip – to visit relatives or simply see what life was like 'on the other side'. Most returned, but those who chose to stay and take up permanent residence in the West continued to average over 2,000 per day through December, January and February – leading to the loss of nearly another million from the East in this period. This weakened the East German economy further, as well as placing huge burden on the FRG which had to house, feed and provide for its new citizens.

The opening of the border, coupled with Krenz's liberalising reforms, encouraged new opposition demands in the GDR, and the SED leadership desperately tried to curb these with yet another programme promising free elections, freedom for the media and economic reform. However, according to surveys, Krenz's personal approval rating was less than 10 per cent and few were satisfied by his promises. Many party members thought such changes too radical, but many in the population at large felt they were not enough. If the Berlin Wall could go, it seemed that nothing was impossible any more. Calls for the reunification of the two states became the new rallying cry. 'We are the people' (Wir sind das Volk) was replaced by 'We are one people' (Wir sind ein Volk).

On 13 November, the Volkskammer met and chose the moderate Hans Modrow as prime minister, while the CDU members voted in a new chairman, Lothar de Maizière, who was not tainted by collaboration with the old regime. Modrow's appointment temporarily stabilised the government. He offered concrete reforms rather than vague promises and although he rejected reunification, he did talk of strengthening 'cooperative existence' and establishing links to the EEC. Modrow also insisted on the separation of party and state power, which meant that power shifted from the SED back to the Volkskammer and the newly appointed cabinet of government ministers, comprising 16 SED ministers and 12 from other parties.

Hundreds of SED district leaders and lesser officials were also replaced and many citizens – SED functionaries as well as 'ordinary' Germans, 200,000 of whom returned their party membership cards in November – were left confused and angered by new and sometimes sensational revelations being spread by the newly liberated media. Party corruption was exposed, the activities and brutality of the Stasi brought to light and mind-boggling pictures broadcast of the former state leaders' luxurious holiday homes, well-stocked hunting preserves and the opulent lifestyle they enjoyed at Wandlitz, while their people queued for food. It is no wonder the credibility of the SED was terminally damaged from both within and outside the party.

On 1 December the Volkskammer formally deleted the SED's leading role from the constitution and on 3 December, Krenz gave up the struggle to harness the party and people to a programme of SED-led reform and stepped down as Chairman of the Council of Ministers. However, it is not quite true to say that this was the end of the dictatorship in the GDR. Over the following winter months, Round Table talks took place between the Modrow government and the leaders of the main opposition groups, the Churches and other parties. Throughout this time, there were still considerable suspicions – bred during the years of communist domination – that the changes could still be reversed, and this slowed progress.

■ Cross-reference

Hans Modrow is profiled above, on page 154.

■ Cross-reference

The opulent lifestyle enjoyed by the elite at Wandlitz is described on page 132.

■ Activity
Creative thinking

Produce a newspaper headline and leading article as might have appeared in the newly liberated East German press about the corruption that had existed in the GDR. You may wish to refer back to Chapter 8 to help you.

At the first meeting they set up four working groups to consider reforms and agreed that the GDR's first free elections would be held on 6 May 1990. However, most of those who participated in the Round Table talks were still committed to a 'third way' – a society that was half way between communism and capitalism. This was increasingly out of touch with the public mood. While in November 1989, 86 per cent of the population favoured socialist reform, by February, this was down to 56 per cent, with 31 per cent wanting a return to capitalism.

Fig. 9 *Last session of the Round Table talks in the GDR, March 1990*

Furthermore, the hated Ministry of State Security was replaced by the Office for National Security, but there was an alarming continuity of personnel and organisation. Only after the Normanenstrasse Stasi headquarters were stormed and occupied by disgruntled Berliners in January 1990, did the Modrow government climb down and dissolve the force entirely, although even then there were suspicions of continuing underground networks and control.

In the GDR, the economy was on the brink of collapse, and the early months of 1990 were ones of readjustment. True details about the state of the economy began to emerge, including a vast budget deficit of 17 billion marks. The government had huge foreign debts of around £12.9 billion (a higher rate of debt, per head of population, than in any other country except Poland) and an estimated £72 billion was needed to clear up energy and heat production. Workers established independent unions and tried to exploit the labour shortage by demanding higher wages and benefit increases. There were strikes and a flourishing black market – particularly in Berlin. Public order in the GDR seemed on the verge of total collapse. In February, an interim coalition government, the 'government of national responsibility', was created, bringing together 13 different parties and groups, including Round Table members and the old SED, renamed as the PDS (Party of Democratic Socialism).

The SED might have gone but the situation was still far from stable as the country prepared for its first free and democratic elections which, to appease the opposition, had to be brought forward from 6 May to 18 March 1990.

Modrow's mounting difficulties were not helped by the attitude of the FRG Chancellor Helmut Kohl who, sensing the mood of the East Germans, refused Modrow's requests for aid in the face of bankruptcy and rejected Modrow's own proposals for unification and the creation of a neutral German state.

In effect, the Federal Chancellor turned his back on the struggling East German government as it tried to haul itself forward to democracy, preferring to seek his own solution to the social and political consequences of the collapse of SED rule.

By mid-February, East Germany had approximately 160 'parties' competing to take part in the election campaign although only 24 finally took part. The real power came from the West German political parties, which backed different Eastern parties, and some of the groups which had led the November Revolution, such as Neues Forum, were swamped. Although it had been widely predicted that the reborn SPD would win the elections on 18 March, the result was an overwhelming endorsement for Helmut Kohl's 'Alliance for Germany'. With 48.1 per cent of the vote, in contrast to the SPD's 21.9 per cent, this was an overwhelming endorsement for the social market economy and, above all, for German reunification. The CDU leader, Lothar de Maizière, was elected the new head of the East German government and set about the task of *'democratising the GDR in order to dissolve it'*.

Key profile

Lothar de Maizière, (born 1940)

Lothar de Maizière began his career as a musician and member of the Berlin Symphony Orchestra before studying law and entering politics. In 1990, he was elected to the Volkskammer as leader of the CDU and became Premier from 12 April to 2 October 1990. He signed the 'Two plus Four' treaty which ended allied control over Berlin and Germany, and forwarded the German reunification of 3 October 1990. He was subsequently appointed Minister for Special Affairs under Kohl, but resigned on 17 December 1990 following rumours that he had worked for the Stasi.

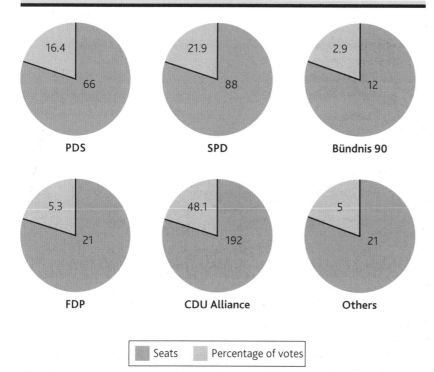

Fig. 10 *East German election results, March 1990*

Summary activity

Make a spider diagram to illustrate why Modrow's attempts to reform and preserve SED rule in the GDR had failed by February/March 1990. Differentiate between reasons specifically linked to Modrow, those linked to Kohl and other reasons.

Exploring the detail

Bündnis 90

Bündnis 90 was formed in February 1990 by Neues Forum, Democracy Now and The Initiative for Peace and Human Rights. It received 2.9 per cent of the vote in the March 1990 Volkskammer elections. For the first all-German elections in December 1990 it formed a joint list with the Green Party and received 3.9 per cent of the vote. This coalition merged with its Western counterpart to become the German Green Party in 1993.

Exploring the detail

East German parties in the election of March 1990

Kohl's CDU gave its support to the 'Alliance for Germany' – made up of Democratic Awakening, the German Social Union (the sister party of the Bavarian CSU) and the old German CDU. The West German SPD supported the East German SPD while the old SED took part as the PDS – Party of Democratic Socialism. It had no Western support. The East German Greens were supported by the West German Greens and made an electoral alliance with a women's party. The 'Alliance for Germany' was nearly derailed when the leader of Democratic Awakening was revealed to have worked for the Stasi and had to resign. However, Kohl's popularity saved the day.

The final months of the GDR's history were dominated by reunification negotiations which sometimes sidelined the GDR itself, as outside powers stepped in to steer the sinking ship. A currency union on 1 July only speeded up the GDR's collapse. This was followed by the reconstitution of the East German Länder and a treaty of accession in October whereby the Eastern states were merged into the Federal Republic. Although de Maizière conducted some hard bargaining over the draft treaty, the huge disparity in power between the weak disintegrating Eastern state and the dominant Western one made the act of reunification more of a takeover than a merging of equals.

 Activity

Revision thinking point

The collapse of the East German state is actually quite hard to pinpoint and can cause confusion. It would be helpful to think about the following:

When and why did

1 the SED collapse?

2 the East German dictatorship collapse?

3 the GDR collapse?

 Summary question

'The collapse of SED rule in East Germany was entirely the result of the party's own failings within the GDR.'

Assess the validity of this view.

(You should find the spider diagram prepared in the activity on page 159 helpful for the planning of your answer.)

10 Reunification and its Aftermath

Fig. 1 *Citizens from FDR welcoming the 'Trabis' across the border from the East*

On 3 October 1990, the GDR vanished for ever. The previous evening, the Leipzig conductor, Kurt Masur, had dedicated a Berlin performance of Beethoven's 'Ode to Joy' to freedom. *'We are one people who are becoming one state,'* he declared. Thousands had gathered in front of the old Reichstag building near the Brandenburg Gate where, at midnight, 14 athletes had raised a huge red, black and gold flag, 60 metres square. As the freedom bell began to toll, fireworks lit the sky and people danced in the streets. 3 October had been declared a national holiday. There were thanksgiving services and a festival atmosphere, but no marches or gun salutes as reminders of the past. Politicians made speeches; the media played classical music. This was the beginning of a new democratic united Germany.

Helmut Kohl's Germany

Kohl and the 10-point plan

The credit for German reunification is usually given to Helmut Kohl. On becoming West German Chancellor in October 1982, he had continued the tradition of Ostpolitik, although with less enthusiasm than Brandt. Nevertheless, it was under Kohl that Honecker visited the FRG in September 1987, marking the first visit by an East German head of state to West Germany. Agreements had been made on environmental and scientific cooperation, as well as measures of nuclear security, and they had issued a joint statement which declared that war must never again be allowed to emanate from German soil. However, as communist control in eastern Europe began to collapse, Kohl was as hesitant as anyone else about what this meant for the future of Germany.

In October 1989, Krenz had spoken of closer long-term relations between the GDR and FRG. He had suggested the need for more economic, ecological, political, cultural and humanitarian ties between

Activity

Constructing a timeline

As you work through this chapter, construct a timeline with details of the moves towards German reunification and their significance.

the two states. However, this was not reunification and there were still plenty of intellectuals in East Germany who feared any hint that its wealthy and powerful neighbour might be about to 'swallow it up'. They were intent on a socialist path to reform.

The events of November 1989 changed this position. With the opening of the border, grass-roots support for reunification grew in the East while there was also clear support for reunification in the FRG. An opinion poll of 20 November suggested that 70 per cent of West Germans supported unification and just 15 per cent rejected it. However, only a slim majority thought it might be possible within the next 10 years.

There was more hesitancy among the politicians. In East Germany, Modrow emphasised the need for an independent GDR in order to preserve stability in Europe. Within West Germany, while the CDU, FDP and SPD moderates all favoured unity, the left-wing Socialists and Greens wanted to retain an independent GDR, to prevent a nationalist resurgence. Some Western intellectuals, such as Günter Grass, also feared that talk of reunification would frighten Germany's European partners and urged caution.

It therefore came as a surprise when, on 28 November 1989, Kohl presented the Bundestag with a five-year programme of ten cautious steps to reunification – the so-called '10-point plan'. Kohl had maintained the secrecy to head off any foreign opposition, which he feared might have scuppered his plan. Even his FDP coalition partners had not been consulted beforehand. Kohl had seized the initiative and although the programme had no fixed timetable, he had committed himself to the active pursuit of reunification.

A closer look

The 10-point plan

The 10 points were:

1. Immediate medical assistance and foreign currency for travel.
2. Ecological, postal and railroad cooperation.
3. Further help given provided that the GDR held free elections and moved to a free market economy.
4. Common institutions to be set up.
5. Moves towards a federation with federal institutions – a joint government committee and a common parliamentary body.
6. Joint policies in the interests of international cooperation.
7. Strengthening European integration and bringing the GDR into the EEC.
8. New institutions for security cooperation in Europe.
9. Disarmament.
10. 'A situation of peace in Europe in which the German people can regain their unity in free self-determination'.

The Bundestag gave the plan overwhelming support, with the CDU/CSU referring to it as a 'historical contribution', but Kohl was swiftly accused, by his left-wing political opponents in the FRG, by the USSR, by Modrow in the GDR and by Margaret Thatcher in the UK, of being too hasty. The French too were offended at not having been informed, while smaller neighbours such as Holland, Denmark and Czechoslovakia were fearful of having a new large Germany on their borders. In Britain, Margaret Thatcher declared that reunification *'was not on the political agenda'*. Even East German reform groups repeated that they didn't want a 'Western takeover.'

Nevertheless, Kohl found an ally in America, which was more concerned with ensuring Germany's continuance within NATO, and the European Community as a whole favoured Kohl's attempts to place reunification within a European framework. The practical problem of coping with the East Germans who were again flooding the West, at a rate of up to 2,000 a day, made the unification argument stronger. Unification appeared to offer a way forward to equalise living standards and integrate the economies of the two states.

Kohl's plan turned vague talk of unity into what Jarausch has referred to as *'a topic of practical politics.'*

The 'rush to unity'

On 19 December 1989, Kohl visited Dresden and was taken aback by the welcome he received from the people. As he stood behind a microphone in front of the bombed Frauenkirche, he was greeted by a sea of German flags and chants of *'Helmut! Helmut! We need you!'* His speech was cheered at every turn and when he declared, *'My goal remains – if the historic hour permits – our nation's unity.'* The listeners exploded into frenzied cheering.

The strength of feeling made Kohl reconsider his timetable. He was convinced that reunification was not only desirable, but possible, and possible within a shorter timescale than he had originally envisaged. Others too received the message. Brandt, for the SPD, which had formerly opposed Kohl's plans, moved cautiously in favour of unity 'within the context of a peaceful Europe' and even the USSR, which had staunchly supported Modrow's plea to retain two Germanies was forced to reassess the situation. In December, Gorbachev moved from an outright refusal to consider unification, to a simple warning, *'History shall have to decide what the fate of the continent shall look like in the future.'*

Fig. 2 *Kohl and Modrow at the opening of the Brandenburg Gate, December 1989*

The Brandenburg Gate was symbolically opened on 22 December and a festive spirit reigned as politicians on both sides made speeches and walked through the breach in the 12-foot thick wall. There was a party atmosphere, which continued over the Christmas period and was marred only by some anti-Soviet graffiti that mysteriously appeared on the

Soviet war memorial in Treptow Park and which raised new fears of neo-Nazism and a fascist revival.

Amid the confusion and growing disillusionment within the GDR, Kohl's leadership was welcomed by the pro-unity demonstrators. Crowds of 500,000 plus continued to protest in Leipzig, Dresden and Chemnitz, chanting, *'Neither brown nor red, Helmut Kohl is our bet!'* Such grass-roots support convinced Kohl that he should cease negotiations with Modrow and instead work to win over international support for reunification. Among his supporters, he was described as the 'Chancellor of Unity' but for the struggling East German leadership his attitude was seen at best as thoughtless and at worst as offensively arrogant.

Kohl promised the French a commitment to European integration and although Gorbachev was still concerned about a future Germany being attached to NATO, Kohl's decision to send economic aid to ease the Soviet food shortage paid off.

On 30 January, Gorbachev made the surprising comment, *'German unification has never been doubted by anyone'* and Kohl's visit to Russia in February confirmed this Russian reversal. Triumphant at this success, Kohl announced on 6 February that his proposal for monetary union would come into effect after the March elections in the GDR.

In the GDR elections in March, Kohl gave his support to the 'Alliance for Germany' and mounted a fierce campaign to prevent a socialist vote, attacking the SPD as a communist party in disguise. Kohl took to the campaign trail himself, promising East Germans instant prosperity and winning audiences of tens of thousands who raised placards such as *'God protect our Chancellor, the architect of German unity'*. In his speeches Kohl declared that new entrepreneurs would invest in the East, pensioners and those unable to work would be supported by the 'proven safety net' of the West and unification would be *'liberation from suppression and want, a gateway to a better life'*. He also promised the fastest possible route to unification – in contrast to the SPD's preferred slower route.

The Alliance's overwhelming success was a vindication of Kohl's reunification plans, permitting the currency union to proceed and winning over international support for a policy which had a democratic endorsement.

Exploring the detail

The route to unification

Kohl wanted rapid unification – in effect a takeover by West Germany under Article 23 of the West German Basic Law which would allow the reconstituted Länder of East Germany to apply to become part of an expanded West German federal state – with the West German constitution and laws still applying. The SPD wanted to adopt a potentially slower route under Article 146 of the Basic Law which involved bringing the two German governments together to devise a new constitution for a united Germany. This would have meant a genuine merger and an opportunity to safeguard certain East German rights.

Fig. 3 *The wall was soon demolished and Berlin became one city again*

The currency union

The Currency Treaty was signed on 18 May and took effect from 1 July 1990. It was symbolic and psychological as well as practical. Since the separation of the currencies that had played a major role in the division of the two Germanies (the Eastern mark being a symbol of the division), currency reform was seen as a sign that reunification was around the corner. Against the advice of the president of the German federal bank, Kohl agreed that the West German Deutschmark (DM) would be exchanged for the East German currency at the favourable rate of 1:1 for salaries, wages and pensions. Debts were to be converted at 2:1 and savings (on a rather complex scale according to age, to favour the elderly), at 1:1 up to a certain amount and on less favourable terms thereafter. Foreign accounts exchanged at 3:1.

Fig. 4 *With the currency union, the East German mark disappeared*

■ A closer look

The currency conversion

In the final days before the conversion, the East Germans hastened to ensure that every family member had a separate bank account, in order to be able to take advantage of the differing rates for savings. Stores offered huge sales on GDR products, anxious to be rid of them at any price, and there was a rush to spend the last remaining Eastern marks with affluent West Germans travelling east to snap up bargains. This drained the stores, leading to food shortages, as wholesalers had held back produce in the hope of higher returns from the new currency. Western salesmen also flooded the East trying to persuade shopkeepers to sign deals to become outlets for Western chain stores and others tried to reclaim property lost in the division. (A legal agreement had been made that property taken after 1949 would be returned but not property taken between 1945 and 1949.) Overnight, East German shops were stocked with Western products – but at West German prices. Subsidies disappeared from the food supplies.

The result of the currency and economic union

Although the currency reform increased Western investment in the East (from 48.3 to 88.3 billion DM 1990–92), real income rose by approximately 28 per cent between 1989 and 1991 and 175,000 new businesses were founded. Nevertheless, the currency conversion initially left many East Germans worse off as income declined while the price of food and services increased. Furthermore, with the opening up of East German businesses and factories to Western competition industrial production fell by two-thirds within two years and the Eastern gross national product (GNP) declined 13.4 per cent in 1990 and another 20 per cent in 1991. With falling production came growing unemployment and women, particularly those who had formerly relied on state childcare provision, were particularly vulnerable.

Table 1 *Social impact of the currency union, 1990*

	GDR	Change	FRG	Difference
Income				
Gross pay	1,170 Mk	none	3,000 DM	+ 1,830
Net pay	1,000 Mk	– 150 DM	2,200 DM	+ 1,350
Expenses				
Food	822 Mk	+ 106 DM		
Industrial products	838 Mk	– 226 DM		
Services	166 Mk	+ 128 DM		
Monthly total	1,826 Mk	+ 8 DM		
Rent (as percent of income)	3%	+ ?	20%	+ 17%
Per capita wealth	11,022 Mk	–3,500 DM	40,747 DM	+ 33,225 DM
Income dissatisfaction	44%		19%	

With hindsight it is possible to see that the exchange rate for the East German mark against the Deutschmark had been set too high. It made much of the GDR's production uneconomic with devastating results. Many of the problems that followed the reunification were the result of this rather hasty, economic measure and in the longer term, the West was forced to prop up East German industry with subsidies, grants and retraining schemes.

The attitude of outside powers

Of the four allied powers of the Second World War, America, the USSR, Britain and France, only America showed any inclination to look favourably on the moves towards German reunification and then, only if the enlarged Germany retained its NATO membership. While Gorbachev had allowed the GDR to collapse, after the fall of the Berlin Wall, his attitude to reunification hardened. A new strong Germany, within the NATO alliance, was not in his thinking and he insisted that reunification should only happen as part of a general rapprochement or more conciliation within Europe. Although West German economic aid persuaded him to concede the 'possibility' of reunification, he remained opposed to the way Kohl was hurrying discussion along in the early months of 1990.

Britain and France too were hostile and went to some lengths to try to persuade the USSR to take a stand against reunification. The minutes of a meeting between the British Prime Minister, Margaret Thatcher and Gorbachev in September 1989 – two months before the fall of the wall – have recently come to light and make it clear that Britain did not want reunification at that point. *'We do not want a united Germany,'*

■ Cross-reference

The problems that followed reunification are covered at the end of this chapter, pages 169–174.

■ Activity

Creative thinking

Write a speech on the issue of reunification as might have been given in May 1990 by:

■ Kohl

■ de Maizière

■ President Bush

■ Gorbachev

■ Margaret Thatcher

■ President Mitterrand.

Mrs Thatcher said, *'That would lead to a change to post-war borders, and we cannot allow that because such a development would undermine the stability of the whole international situation and could endanger our security.'* Thatcher also assured Gorbachev that US President Bush wanted to do nothing that would be seen by the Russians as a threat to their security.

According to Anatoli Chernayev, a Kremlin aide at this time, politicians across western Europe *'say in unison that nobody wants a unified Germany'*, and he noted in his diaries that President Mitterrand of France had even considered a military alliance with Russia to stop it, *'camouflaged as a joint use of armies to fight natural disasters.'*

A month after the Berlin Wall came down, it was the turn of Jacques Attali, personal adviser to Mitterrand, to meet a senior Russian official in Kiev and reinforce the point: *'France by no means wants German reunification, although it realises that in the end it is inevitable.'* In April 1990, Attali repeated that the spectre of reunification was causing nightmares among France's politicians and he quoted Mitterrand as saying that he would *'fly off to live on Mars'*, if this happened. Thatcher too tried to slow things down, *'I am convinced that reunification needs a long transition period,'* she told Gorbachev. *'All Europe is watching this, not without a degree of fear, remembering well who started the two world wars.'*

It is little wonder, therefore that, from the fall of the wall, it took nearly another year of tough negotiations, involving both Germanies and the four ex-wartime allies, before a deal was finally reached.

Fig. 5 *Margaret Thatcher, who was unenthusiastic about the prospect of a reunified Germany, looked to Gorbachev to slow the pace of change*

The 'Two plus Four' agreements

The 'Two plus Four' negotiations began at the Ottawa 'Open Skies' Conference on 13 February 1990 and the six Foreign Ministers involved met four times in the ensuing months in: Bonn on 5 May; Berlin on 22 June; Paris on 17 July; and Moscow on 12 September. The Polish Foreign Minister participated in the Paris meeting in the parts that dealt with the Polish-German borders.

One of the key issues was to overcome the USSR's objections to a united Germany's membership in NATO. The Western powers wanted Germany to remain in NATO (possibly with concession of no NATO troops on former East German soil) but the Soviets wanted a neutral united Germany. There were also issues relating to the EEC, and Poland's western border with Germany.

Activity

Pairs or group task

Hold your own 'Two plus Four' conference with individuals or small groups representing America, the USSR, Britain, France, the FRG and the GDR. Each country should prepare a report stating their nation's position with regard to German reunification. The report should aim to convince others, explaining the importance of each state's standpoint. The countries could then question each other and see if they could produce an acceptable compromise.

On 6 July after a two-day NATO summit, the alliance, led by President George Bush, issued the London Declaration which changed NATO so as to make it appear more a political than a military alliance. This opened the way for Kohl to meet Gorbachev in Moscow on 15 July to discuss the issue of German membership of NATO. With promises of economic help for the ailing USSR, Gorbachev was persuaded to agree that NATO was transforming itself and that if Bonn accepted its existing frontiers and removed nuclear, biological and chemical weapons, then membership of NATO should not be an obstacle to unification and Four Power control could be lifted. This declaration, issued on 16 July, was hailed as the 'Miracle of Moscow' and Kohl could triumphantly declare, *'It's all in the bag!'*

The Kohl-Gorbachev meeting was continued in the Caucasus mountains at Gorbachev's *dacha*, where it was agreed that the Germans would renounce all claims to former eastern territories, provide financial assistance and make military cuts. In return, the Russians offered to withdraw troops in phases over a four-year period, and allow NATO membership and full and unimpaired sovereignty to a united Germany. The media hailed this as Kohl's 'coup' and pictures of the two relaxed statesmen strolling over the mountains and calmly discussing events of such momentous importance were emblazoned over the world press. Headlines proclaimed. 'Gorby sets the world free', 'Lucky Kohl' and 'Unity on credit'. The Chancellor was said to have *'achieved his lifelong goal'* and had become a *'political giant'*. Such international approval killed any remaining internal opposition to unity as opponents could no longer use the argument of foreign hostility.

Did you know?

A dacha was a country home or villa, whose size depended on the wealth of its owner. It was common for prosperous Russians to have a second home in the countryside or, for those who could afford it, in a particularly scenic spot, to act as a weekend and holiday retreat.

Exploring the detail

The resulting treaty was 1,000 pages long and covered a multitude of issues including: property claims, conditions for investment, transfer of social security, future state funding, ecological improvements, renewed federalism and cultural support. There had been much debate over the safeguarding of welfare rights, but this had eventually to be shelved as the fiscal collapse of the GDR after the currency reform forced immediate accession. Intellectuals were disappointed that there was no time to consider alternatives or involve the broader public in the details.

Fig. 6 *The signing of the final reunification treaty, 31 August 1990*

The deal was approved by the 'Two plus Four' negotiators in Paris a few days later and after the East and West Germans had negotiated its more specific details a treaty was signed on 31 August for *'the completion of German unity in peace and freedom as an equal member of the international community'* to come into effect on 3 October.

The five East German Länder were incorporated into an enlarged Federal Republic of Germany as the 'Berlin Republic', while the capital of the united state remained in Bonn. Ceremonies duly took place in the centre of Berlin at the Brandenburg Gate and the Reichstag, marred slightly by anti-unity demonstrations which had to be dealt with by the police. Certainly the mood was less euphoric than in November when the wall fell, but it was a significant day nevertheless, opening a new chapter of German and European history.

Did you know?

In June 1991 – after much heated discussion in the German parliament and beyond – it was decided to move the political capital back to Berlin. This was not actually fully achieved until 1999.

Cross-reference

The celebrations in Berlin are described in the opening of this chapter.

Activity

Thinking point

Why do you think the mood in October 1990 was 'less euphoric' than it had been when the wall came down? Do you think the celebrations would have been viewed differently by Easterners from Westerners? Is it fair to describe the reunification as an 'anti-climax'?

Fig. 7 *United Germany, showing the Länder and the former GDR/FRG border*

The impact of reunification

The political impact

The new all-German government had to be expanded to accommodate the Eastern Länder and on 4 October five new ministers, including Lothar de Maizière, were sworn in, while a further 144 Eastern deputies were added to the federal parliament. De Maizière became Kohl's CDU deputy and the overall government majority was maintained. However, the completion of the unification process required an all-German election to give it democratic legitimacy and before this could take place, elections had to be held in the Eastern State Länder. On 14 October, Kohl's party once again recorded an impressive victory, with the CDU topping the table in all states except Brandenburg, where it was beaten by the SPD.

In December 1990 the first all-German free election since November 1932 was held. The election was fought on the unification issue and another Kohl/CDU victory, together with a stronger FDP, led to a CDU/FDP coalition government. It was the final endorsement for Kohl's policy, showing approval in both East and West for the dramatic changes he had brought about. Kohl claimed it was *'the best result for a party since there have been free, secret and direct elections in Germany'*.

Reunification did not, however, help the SPD which performed surprisingly poorly in the East and whose numbers fell. The Green Party also lost out, winning no seats (although an Eastern Green coalition group of parties was more successful). For the first time since 1949, communists were returned to the Bundestag (in merger with the PDS) but the NPD (extreme right wing) won insufficient votes to gain representation.

Reunification had altered the party balance although this only became clear in later years.

Table 2 *Election results, December 1990*

	Percentage of votes			No. of seats in Bundestag
	West	East	Total	
CDU/CSU (Christian democrat – centre)	44.1	43.4	43.8	319
SPD (Socialist)	35.9	23.6	33.5	239
FDP (Liberal)	10.6	13.4	11.0	79
Greens/Bündnis 90	4.7	5.9	3.9	8
PDS/DKP (Communist left wing)	0.3	9.9	2.4	17
NPD/Reps (right wing)	2.6	1.6	2.4	Party failed to overcome the 5% barrier

Cross-reference and further explanation

The West German political parties of 1949 are summarised in the glossary.

The NDP was founded in 1964 and replaced the DRP.

The REP (Republican Party) was founded in 1983 by ex-CSU members; it comes from the German *Die Republikaner*. It is a nationalist and national conservative political party.

The PDS (Party of Democratic Socialism) was the successor of the Socialist Unity Party, the SED, which ruled the communist GDR.

Bündnis 90 was formed in the GDR in February 1990 (see Chapter 9, page 159) and formed a joint list with the Green Party in the December 1990 all-German elections.

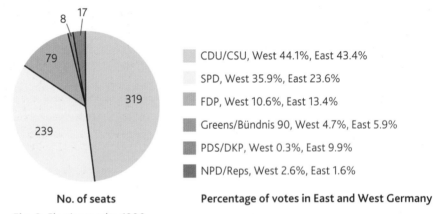

- CDU/CSU, West 44.1%, East 43.4%
- SPD, West 35.9%, East 23.6%
- FDP, West 10.6%, East 13.4%
- Greens/Bündnis 90, West 4.7%, East 5.9%
- PDS/DKP, West 0.3%, East 9.9%
- NPD/Reps, West 2.6%, East 1.6%

No. of seats   Percentage of votes in East and West Germany

Fig. 8 *Election results, 1990*

Activity

Thinking and analysis

Can you explain the election results of December 1990? (You will probably want to look back at the policies of these parties towards reunification.)

The economic impact

Following the currency union, huge changes were set in motion to extend the free market economy to the East and make up for years of under-investment and over-regulation. The GDR's economic and ecological problems were found to be worse than had been imagined and Kohl's vistas of 'instant prosperity' proved little more than dreams.

By the terms of the union, the GDR became subject to all the economic, social and labour laws of the FRG and had a banking system controlled by the Bundesbank. The huge task of privatising all the *Kombinate* (state monopolies) through the *Treuhandanstalt* (state holding trusts) was carried through but, since outside investment was limited because bigger profits were to be found elsewhere, many ailing industries simply collapsed. It soon became clear that the economic integration of the two states would take far longer than originally expected and since the Kohl government had promised not to raise taxes, in order to win support for unity, it was slow to institute the 'Eastern recovery programme' that the former GDR so needed.

Exploring the detail

CDU dominance in Germany

In 1998, Helmut Kohl's CDU coalition was defeated and replaced by Gerhard Schröder with an alliance of SPD and Greens. Kohl was damaged by scandals over party finances which may have brought about the suicide of his wife, and was replaced by Angela Merkel – a scientist from East Germany who won the 2005 elections at the head of a CDU/SPD coalition.

Fig. 9 *As factories were taken over by Western companies there was considerable dislocation. The Wartburg works in East Germany was taken over and modernised by Opel, the German subsidiary of US General Motors*

This investment programme was finally launched in March 1991 and government money was at last put into housing, agriculture and services, as well as the industrial infrastructure. New roads, phone lines and shopping centres appeared, railways were upgraded and buildings renovated or replaced, However, this all took time and money, and the initial damage done when the economy of the old GDR was confronted with West German and EEC competition left large areas suffering structural long-term unemployment.

Gradually, the formerly drab urban landscape was transformed, but in the short term, reunification certainly failed to perform the economic miracle that the Easterners had hoped for.

The social impact

Socially, reunification had a massive impact, although again some changes took time. Ridding a people of forty years of communist propaganda and repression meant changing more than their outward way of life. It meant changing mindsets and the old behavioural patterns that had characterised the 'niche society'. Compliance, passivity and withdrawal into a private world had to give way to new qualities like initiative, drive, competitiveness and a willingness to undertake responsibility. For the middle-aged and older generation in particular, this aspect of reunification was to prove one of the hardest.

Those who were compromised by their former political sympathies lost their positions and the judiciary and education system were reformed along Western democratic lines. There was a new encouragement to free-thinking – in the universities, in the workplace and in political life.

Cross-reference

The 'niche society' is discussed in Chapter 7, pages 130–132.

There were also massive adjustments to be made in the world of work, where, within six months of unification, 21 per cent of the workforce had moved to a new job, 8 per cent were unemployed and 10 per cent had taken an early retirement. There were new skills to be learnt and new competition in the market place. Work proceeded at a faster pace and there was less need for unskilled manual labour, which particularly hit at female employment.

For some, reunification brought immense rewards. The highly trained could do well and the independently minded could set up their own businesses. There were new opportunities for the young and those who wanted to travel had their horizons suddenly opened up. However, living standards did not immediately rise to meet those in the West and others lost out and were only saved by the Western safety-net of unemployment insurance and retraining schemes.

The international impact

As compensation for bringing about the new unified Germany, Kohl had tried to appease the French, with promises of greater European integration. However, when EEC leaders met in Maastricht to reach agreement on a 'Draft Treaty on Political Union' in December 1991, it became clear that many ordinary German citizens were less convinced about Germany's 'European future', given the EEC's reputation for bureaucracy and lack of democracy. In fact, reunification cooled rather than encouraged grass-roots German enthusiasm for Europe.

However, the German leaders pressed forward with plans for greater political union as a way of reassuring European neighbours of Germany's trustworthiness as an international partner, even if Margaret Thatcher continued to fear a Europe dominated by the Germans. Germany played a full part in the 1991 discussions leading to the Maastricht Treaty in 1992 and also supported moves towards a common European currency, although once again the politicians' commitment was not fully supported by the German people who viewed the Deutschmark with affection as the symbol of the FRG's post-war success.

Germany's relationship with the USSR and former Soviet states had also to be defined. Germany's main concern was the stability and prosperity of neighbouring central and eastern Europe states. Consequently, in the early 1990s, Germany offered aid, and became the single largest investor and the most important trading partner for the former Soviet bloc. In addition to assisting democratic and market reforms, the expansion of these economic and commercial ties was of direct benefit to German industry. Germany established bilateral agreements and treaties with the Soviet Union, Poland, Czechoslovakia, and Bulgaria. However, there was some criticism of Germany's 'economic imperialism' by Western opponents who were still uncertain about the united Germany's intentions.

The new Germany had to rethink its international role. The FRG had grown accustomed to a Basic Law which had prohibited the use of armed force outside Germany and this, together with the strong pacifist inclinations which had characterised the opposition and pro-unification movements in the GDR, left the country uncertain how to react to international crises.

When the Gulf War broke out in August 1990, to the annoyance of America, Germany refused to get involved although it did send monetary aid. However, when the Germans adopted a stronger line in the Yugoslav crisis of 1991, they were condemned for *'the flexing of united Germany's muscles'*, something that the British and French were particularly wary of.

■ Exploring the detail

The Maastricht Treaty

Negotiations on the Maastricht Treaty were complete by the end of 1991 although the final treaty was not signed until February 1992. The name European Economic Community (EEC) was replaced by 'European Union' (EU) and the treaty opened the way to extend cooperation into areas of foreign policy, the military, criminal justice, judicial cooperation and monetary union.

■ Exploring the detail

The First Gulf War, August 1990–February 1991

The Gulf War came about after Iraq's occupation and annexation of Kuwait in August 1990. A coalition force led by America but drawn from 34 nations was sent, with United Nations authorisation, to fight to expel Iraqi forces from Kuwait. Germany did not contribute any forces, but made financial contributions of $6.6 billion.

■ Exploring the detail

Yugoslavia 1991

Germany wanted to see the principle of self-determination applied in Yugoslavia. There were several hundred thousand guest workers from Croatia in Germany and many Germans who had holidayed in this area were sympathetic to their cause. However, Germany's unilateral recognition of Croatia and Slovenia in 1990 annoyed EEC members and America, whose own recognition ultimately followed suit in the spring of 1991.

Certainly reunification had altered power relationships. As the EU's largest and economically strongest state, united Germany was, as Thatcher feared, set to play a dominant role in Europe. Nevertheless, the Germans were determined to act responsibly and the country was wary of stirring resentments and careful in its approach.

1991

Reunification had solved some problems and created others. The initial euphoria wore off quickly and East–West divisions were not removed overnight. Within months some of those same Westerners who had partied and celebrated with a glass of champagne at the fall of the wall, were beginning to moan about the burden the eastern states were placing on the rest of the country, and in particular the financial drain. The economy of the old GDR failed to undergo an 'economic miracle' and according to an opinion poll in the summer of 1991, a large majority on both sides believed that *'only since unification has it become evident how different Eastern and Western Germany are.'* Resentment grew with the tax rises needed to support Eastern economic development, most particularly the so-called 'solidarity tax' levied on all Germans from 1991 which, according to the journalist, Allan Hall, *'often seemed the equivalent of throwing money at an alcoholic to keep the bar open.'*

The pride they had felt in welcoming the Eastern Länder was also tempered by reports of rising crime rates and youth delinquency there. This is perhaps explained by the collapse of Eastern youth organisations, the growth of unemployment and new 'freer' standards, which turned bored teenagers into skinheads and disillusioned adults into criminals.

Fig. 10 *After German reunification, neo-Nazi groups flourished as a result of the economic difficulties and high unemployment in the former East Germany. These neo-Nazi followers are giving the Nazi salute in Cottbus in May 1991*

Cross-reference

For more on the Gastarbeiter, look back to Chapter 3, page 57 and Chapter 7 page 120.

Did you know?

Students who visit Berlin will be well aware of the commercialisation of everyday objects from the former GDR, not least the red and green traffic men symbols which have been made into appealing tourist gimmicks. A feeling for this 'Ostalgie' can also be found through the films *Sonnenallee* by Thomas Brussif and Leander Haussman and *Goodbye Lenin* (Wolfgang Becker) which provides a 'comical' view of the GDR. These can be contrasted with the more serious *Lives of Others* (Florian Henckel von Donnersmarck) or Anna Funder's book *Stasiland* – although be aware that such works may well exaggerate the role of the Stasi.

Activity

Summary task

Prepare a balance sheet to quantify the success and failures of German reunification by 1991. On one side list the successes and the positive factors and on the other the failures and negatives. You might like to consider whether any of the 'failures' could have been avoided and whether the positive factors outweigh the negative ones.

However, the West itself was also experiencing growing racism – particularly directed at the 'guest-workers' whose labour was no longer in high demand and who were regarded as a burden rather than a help for the economy. Asylum seekers, whose numbers grew markedly from 1991, were also the victims of a worrying growth in racist extremism – encouraged to some degree by right-wing party activism. This bred fears of a new German 'nationalism', but with hindsight, it would appear that the incidents were more the product of the social dislocation of the early 1990s, rather than anything more sinister and the German democratic system proved able to cope.

There is no doubt, however, that German unification permitted a new type of national pride. This was to be seen in the trials of the former GDR state officials and Germany's greater confidence within the EEC and in international relations. However, a strange outcome of the two-state merger was the emergence of a new sense of GDR identity – a strange nostalgia for the old securities and the social cohesion of the communist state, once the restrictive and repressive aspects of the regime were no longer feared. This rose-tinted memory – *Ostalgie* – was to be deliberately encouraged by those who sought commercial gain from a preservation of the old, but, more importantly, its emergence only increased the distinctions between the 'Wessis' and 'Ossis'. There was soon a quip circulating that the Germans 'never felt more apart than when they were united'.

Even the question of where to place the capital of the reunified Germany illustrates the East-West conflict. Kohl could not decide whether to keep the capital in Bonn – favoured by many Westerners – or return it to Berlin – which was supported by those from the East. He waited until 20 June 1991 before Berlin won a crucial Bundestag vote by 17 votes, but the move did not take place until September 1999. With the establishment of the 'Berlin Republic', the history of post-war Germany from 1945 had turned full circle.

Activity

Overview debate

Now that you have looked at the history of Germany from its division to reunification, you should think about the broader issues of whether the GDR was always doomed to fail and whether reunification was inevitable. There are big and fundamental questions to be asked here. Why was the GDR unable to reform itself? Did the collapse in the East mean reunification was the only way forward? Debate some of these issues in class and look back over this book to provide evidence to support your opinions.

Learning outcomes

In this section, your study of modern German history has come full circle. You have seen how the GDR collapsed, the Berlin Wall came down and the East and West Germans were finally reunified. You have witnessed how these momentous events took place in the short space of two years and have considered the problems and issues raised by each stage of the process. You have looked at both internal pressures and external forces and have seen how the unification of October 1990 was far from the end of the process. Your examination of the immediate aftermath of reunification has encouraged you to reflect on the problems of reconciling peoples whose ways have diverged. By 1991 Germany was once more a large united European state – but its reunification was not entirely a success story.

Practice questions

1 How far was Helmut Kohl responsible for the reunification of Germany in 1990? *(45 marks)*

To answer this question you will need to identify and evaluate Kohl's particular contribution and balance this against other reasons for reunification in 1990. You might include Kohl's 10-point plan in November 1989, his reception at Dresden in December 1989, his negotiations leading to the 'Two plus Four' agreements of February – September 1990, and his crucial meeting with Gorbachev in July 1990. The currency union of July 1990 and Gorbachev's promises, approach and speeches would be all worthy of mention. However, you will also need to consider factors such as Gorbachev's policies and the events in eastern Europe between 1989–1990; Ostpolitik and the contribution of Brandt; the part played by the US and, to a lesser degree, Britain and France; Modrow and Lothar de Maizière and the importance of the GDR's economic collapse. You may also wish to criticise the way Kohl approached reunification, questioning whether he could have been more 'responsible' in the way he set about the task.

2 'It was the actions of America that determined the developments in the two Germanies in the years 1945 to 1991.' Assess the validity of this view. *(45 marks)*

This question is asking you to balance an external force – America – against other forces which moulded the development of Germany in the years 1945 to 1991. This is a broad question, so you need to be selective in your examples, but you should give some indication of relevant developments across the whole period and draw some conclusions from these. In 1945–49, the position of America had a huge impact on the emergence of the two Germanies and you would want, in particular, to highlight the importance of America in breaking the Berlin Blockade. American Marshall Aid helped fuel the West German 'economic miracle' and it was American influence which encouraged the West to turn its back on the East, aligning itself to NATO and promulgating the Hallstein Doctrine. You could consider whether Germany was just a pawn in the Cold War and whether Kennedy let the Germans down by failing to take action over the building of the Berlin Wall. The importance of détente for the success of Ostpolitik and America's reaction to moves towards reunification are, of course, significant here too. Other influences worthy of consideration are the German leaders themselves, economic forces, the USSR and eastern bloc states and western Europe. You might also consider whether the 'German people' had any control over their own destinies.

Fig. 1 *The Reichstag building in Berlin – left in ruins in 1945 – became a sad reminder of Germany's past, but it was to rise again; it came to symbolise the newfound unity and the strength of German democracy*

It is not easy to appraise the history of Germany between 1945 and 1991. Indeed, it is hardly possible to speak of 'Germany' at all in this period since there were, in effect, two Germanies between 1949 and 1990. To study this period is to study a unique attempt to establish two very different states on the soil of the defeated Nazi Germany – one a Western capitalist democracy; the other a Soviet communist state. This book has looked at how both evolved, survived for 40 years and then came back together again.

In trying to provide an overview of the period, it is tempting to think of it in terms of the inevitable 'success' of the democratic and capitalist West over the communist East, but such an approach is both dangerous and over-simplistic. The Federal Republic and German Democratic Republic were both founded as conscious attempts to create a new type of German state and society. In the West, democracy, the free market and Anglo-American values were the guide; in the East, Marxist doctrines of social equality. However, the ultimate success of the former over the latter in 1989/90 was not simply a matter of the 'better ideology' inevitably winning.

Both ideologies had their flaws. The 'freedom of choice' offered in the West was no freedom for those who could not afford it, while the restrictions imposed in the East might be justified in the interests of ultimate economic and social equality. In any case if repression brought about the GDR's collapse, it may be asked why that collapse occurred at the very point when the repressive capabilities of the SED were at their strongest. Democracy had failed in Germany between 1919–33 and capitalism had not brought freedom during the Third Reich. At the same time, material discontent stemming from the planned economy was present in the GDR throughout its history, so it is hard to explain why, if that is taken to be the reason, the regime failed to collapse before 1989. It is not, therefore, simply the case that the Western values were bound to triumph. When 'communism' collapsed in the GDR in 1989/90, it was not so much the collapse of the ideology as the collapse of a regime that had perverted communist theory. It was the downfall of the SED rather than of communism as such.

The overall conclusion must be that the history of both Germanies in this period can only be understood in relation to the wider political situation in which they were born and grew.

Their relative success and failures were moulded by the circumstances of Cold War division and since they sat on the front line, on either side of the iron curtain which divided Europe, their development was the product of the fears, tensions, misunderstandings and reconciliations of the directors of that Cold War: the superpowers – America and the USSR. Neither the FRG nor GDR were ever truly their own masters.

The social market economy and constitution of West Germany flourished because of the favourable international circumstances which nurtured it. The stability of West German democracy was at least in part made possible by the American rebuilding after the war and the role West Germany was able to play in developing post-war markets and within the EEC. The GDR's longevity and ultimate end similarly had much to do with the USSR's interests and capabilities. The history of the two Germanies was so intimately bound up in the wider conditions of Europe and the world that the success and failures of neither state can be fully analysed in the abstract, simply by appraising their own record.

There is also another difficulty with the study of this recent period of German history. It is one of perspective. You have been reading about events that occurred no more than 65 years ago. Your parents and grandparents are likely to recall at least some of the episodes mentioned and they may well have their own views on who was to blame or to praise. To step back and view such comparatively recent events objectively requires a determination to challenge assumptions and a readiness to dip into the works of scholars who have only been able to look closely at GDR records since the 1990s.

The histories of the two Germanies pre-1990 were highly influenced by what appeared to be a permanent division. Historians in the GDR sought to justify SED rule, denouncing the West for its capitalist imperialism, while those in the West presupposed the horrors of the Eastern regime and the superior values of their own. Even today, analyses of recent German history can be heavily influenced by political associations. In your study of this period you have been introduced to eye-witness accounts, documents, interviews, memoirs, journalism and case studies. It is important to distinguish between such sources of evidence and to formulate your own judgements, leaving aside the political prejudices of the Cold War era.

The history of Germany does not, of course, really end in 1991. The division had not entirely gone, since it was still there in people's minds and visible in the physical differences that remained between East and West. It certainly proved easier to destroy a boundary than recreate one people, but in 1990 a fundamental change had taken place. Finally Germany was a single sovereign state once again and there was, at the top, a determination to carve out a better future. For the first time since 1945, Germans were responsible for their own destiny. It was the end of another era.

Glossary

A

Amnesia: an inability to remember the past.

Apparatchik: a loyal member of the Communist Party establishment, employed by the party and entrenched in the system.

B

Balance of payments: the difference between payments made by a country for imports and the money earned by that country in exports (and through services and overseas investments). If the former is lower than the latter there is a balance of payments surplus. If not, there is a deficit.

Bundestag: is the elected parliament of Germany (also known as the Federal Diet). It was established by the German constitution of 1949 to replace the earlier Reichstag. It met in Bonn in West Germany until it transferred to Berlin in 1999.

C

The Christian Democrat Union Party or CDU (*Christlich Demokratische Union Deutschlands*): is a moderate conservative political party. The party was founded in West Germany after the Second World War by members of the former Catholic Centre Party (the Zentrum), to include all those with similar conservative interests. The CDU (along with its Bavarian 'sister party', the Christian Social Union of Bavaria [CSU], with which it formed the CDU/CSU alliance) was the dominant party in West Germany between 1949–69, under the leadership of Konrad Adenauer until 1963 and Ludwig Erhard until 1966. Following this, a grand coalition with the Social Democratic Party (SPD) took over government under Kiesinger, who was himself a member of the CDU. With the SPD's increase in popularity, the CDU went into opposition until 1982 when Helmut Kohl became the new chancellor for West Germany, a position he retained until after reunification. An East German CDU was also founded in 1945, but was forced into becoming part of the national bloc of parties under the Socialist Unity Party (SED) until 1990 when its leader, Lothar de Maizière, cooperated with Kohl and the Western CDU to win the first free East German elections in March 1990. In October 1990 it merged with the Western CDU.

Chancellor: the head of government in Germany and the position is the equivalent of that of a prime minister in other countries. The German term for prime minister is *Ministerpräsident* or minister-president, and it is used exclusively for the heads of government of the Länder (states). The chancellor is the leader of the party (or coalition of parties) holding a majority of seats in the Bundestag and, according to the 1949 Federal German constitution, can initiate government policy and direct government in conjunction with their cabinet of ministers.

Cold War (1945–91): the continuing state of political conflict, military tension, and economic competition existing after the Second World War, primarily between the USSR and its satellite states, and the powers of the western world, including the US. Because of the alliance systems that were created, this is sometimes expressed as NATO versus the Warsaw Pact countries. Tension was the product of these military alliances and influence blocs, manifested in the deployment of conventional forces, a nuclear arms race, espionage, wars by proxy, propaganda and technological competition as seen in the space race.

Collectivisation: farming the land as a joint, or 'collective', group. Targets for production would be laid down and workers paid wages for fulfilling their allocated work.

Council for Mutual Economic Aid (COMECON): set up in Moscow in 1949 in response to the Marshall Plan.

Constitution: a set of laws by which a country is governed.

Council of Europe: an organisation founded in 1949 to develop common and democratic principles based on the European Convention on Human Rights throughout Europe.

D

The East German Democratic Peasants' Party or DBD (Demokratische Bauernpartei Deutschlands): founded in 1948 as an attempt to establish a party loyal to the SED in the rural community. It was committed to land reform and forging closer links between farmers and urban workers. Its leadership came mainly from the ranks of the SED and it participated in government as one of the members of the national bloc. After the fall of Berlin Wall, the party initially tried to rebrand itself as an ecological agrarian party, but after poor results in the March 1990 elections it merged with the Western Christian Democratic Union.

Détente: a French term, meaning a relaxing or easing, and it is used to describe a time when previously hostile nations reduce tensions through diplomacy and by working together. It is used to describe the reduction in tension between the USSR and the US, bringing about a thawing in the Cold War from the late 1960s until the start of the 1980s.

Deutschmark (German mark or 'Deutsche Mark'): the official currency of West Germany, first issued under allied occupation in June 1948 to replace the Reichsmark. This had been the currency since 1924 but had become grossly inflated during wartime. The Deutschmark was the FRG's official currency and was used by the reunited Germany from 1990–99, when it was replaced by the euro.

E

Eastern Policy or Ostpolitik: a term for the efforts of Willi Brandt, who as Chancellor of the FRG tried to improve his country's relations with eastern European nations (including the GDR). Its official title was *Neue Ostpolitik* (New Eastern Policy), as a contrast to the former eastern Europe policy of Konrad Adenauer, who tried to ignore and isolate the GDR. Brandt hoped to improve East-West relations and win more freedom for East Germans by a certain degree of collaboration.

The East German Liberal Democratic Party or LDPD (*Liberal-Demokratische Partei Deutschlands*): originally it used the name Liberal Democratic Party (LDP), in October 1951 it was ordered to add the 'D' for 'Deutschland' into its name in order to serve the SED's all-German propaganda of that period. It was founded by a group led by Waldemar Koch on 5 July 1945. It was initially opposed to nationalisation and strongly anti-communist. However, under pressure from Soviet authorities, Waldemar Koch was replaced with the pro-Soviet Wilhelm Külz in November 1945 and he took the party into the SED-sponsored ruling bloc. Like the other allied parties of the SED in the 'National Front' it had 52 representatives in the Volkskammer, but as a *Blockpartei* (bloc party) the LDPD was subordinated to the SED. This ended attempts of western liberals to create an all-German liberal grouping. At a party congress in Dresden on 9–10 February 1990 it returned to its original liberal policies and restored its name to the LDP. On 12 February 1990, it joined the Association of Free Democrats which finally merged into the Free Democratic Party in August 1990.

Economic recession: a slow-down in economic activity, usually characterised by falling levels of investment and a decline in business profits, bringing lower levels of public spending and growing unemployment.

European Economic Community (EEC): an international organisation created to bring about economic integration and a single market which was free from customs barriers. The founding members were Belgium, France, Germany, Italy, Luxembourg and the Netherlands who signed the Treaty of Rome in 1957. However, it gradually grew up to 1993, when, in accordance with the Maastricht Treaty of 1991, it became part of the European Union. This currently has 27 members.

F

Fait accompli: something that has already been done and which therefore has to be accepted.

Final Solution: a euphemism for the extermination of the Jewish race, as practised in the Nazi gas chambers.

The Free Democratic Party or FDP (*Freie Demokratische Partei*): a socially and economically liberal political party. The FDP was founded in the West on 11 December 1948 through the merger of nine regional liberal parties that formed in 1945. The FDP's first chairman was Theodor Heuss. The FDP has held the balance of power for most of the federal republic's existence. It was the junior partner in coalition governments with the CDU from 1949–56, from 1961–66 and from 1982–98, and with the Social Democratic Party (SPD) from 1969–82. In all federal election campaigns from the 1980s to reunification, the FDP sided with the CDU and CSU. Following reunification in 1990, the FDP merged with the liberals from East Germany and participated in the federal government by representing the junior partner in the government of Chancellor Helmut Kohl of the CDU.

Federal Republic of West Germany or FRG: set up in May 1949, the FRG originally consisted of 12 states formed from the three Western zones with a capital city in Bonn. The number of federal states changed in the 1950s, when three south-western states merged to form Baden-Württemberg and the Saarland joined the FRG. On 3 October 1990 the five Länder of the GDR were incorporated into the FRG raising the number of Länder to 16. The expanded FRG is usually known simply as 'Germany' today.

G

Gastarbeiter: a name for workers invited to Germany from foreign countries (particularly Turkey) at a time when the German economy was thriving and in need of a bigger labour force – most particularly in the 1950s and early 1960s. Many were unskilled and provided valuable manual labour at that time.

Gestapo: the Nazi secret police and a branch of the SS.

The German Communist Party or KPD (Kommunistische Partei Deutschlands): a party founded in 1918 and represented in the Reichstag during the Weimar Period (1919–33). It was banned by Hitler, but revived after the Second World War. It won seats in the first Bundestag elections in 1949, but its support collapsed with the establishment of the communist state in the Soviet zone. In East Germany, the party merged with the SPD to form the Socialist Unity Party (SED), which ruled East Germany until 1990. It was banned in West Germany in 1956 by the Constitutional Court and ceased to exist from 1969, when a new, legal German Communist Party (DKP) was formed.

German Democratic Republic or GDR: a communist state that originated from the Soviet zone of occupied Germany and Berlin and which existed from 7 October 1949 until 3 October 1990. Upon reunification, the five East German Länder were incorporated into the FRG and is usually known simply as Germany today.

The German Socialist Party or SPD (Soziale Partei Deutschlands): established in 1869. Banned by the Nazis, the SPD was re-established, along with other political parties, in the western zone in 1945. However, in the Soviet zone, the SPD were forced to form a common party with the KPD to create the SED. After the Godesberg Programme of 1959, which aimed to move the party's political position away from Marxism towards the centre ground, the SPD changed from a socialist working class party to a social democratic party with a broader voter base. This ensured the future of the SPD as one of the two major parties in the FRG, (the other being the CDU).

J

Jugendweihe: literally means 'youth consecration' and was a secular ceremony introduced in 1955 for 14-year-olds. It was a socialist alternative to Christian Confirmation but even young people who attended Church were expected to take part in the Jugendweihe ceremonies. Those who refused met significant disadvantages and repression. For a year before the actual Jugendweihe, 'youth courses' were held, consisting of visits to workplaces, lectures on sexuality and politics, balls and similar social pursuits. At the ceremony, in a local town hall, the participants were given a speech, took a pledge to the Soviet State, were presented with flowers by the Young Pioneers and received identity papers. Until 1874, the state gave every participant the book *Weltall, Erde, Mensch* (Universe, Earth, Man), which

contained general knowledge in addition to propagandistic sayings. After 1974 everyone received the purely propagandistic book *Der Sozialismus – Deine Welt* (Socialism – Your World) and in the last years of the GDR the book *Vom Sinn unseres Lebens* (Of the Meaning of Our Lives) was presented. There was also a certificate.

Junkers: the traditional aristocratic landlords who lived in eastern Germany.

Jusos: an abbreviated from of *Junge Sozialisten* (Young Socialists), which was the youth movement of the SPD. Many Jusos were radical in outlook and attracted to the student movement. They forced intense debate within the party over its place and future – for example, in response to terrorism threats, Brandt increased surveillance of foreigners, tightened screening for applicants for jobs in government and permitted, where necessary, for mail to be opened and telephones tapped. Such measures were at odds with his political philosophies and much opposed by the radical Jusos.

L

Land (plural Länder): a German state.

Lignite: a form of brown coal. It is deemed the lowest rank of coal and has a high moisture content, which produces a particularly unpleasant smoke. This had adverse effects on the environment and public health.

M

Marxist-Leninism: the German philosopher Karl Marx had put forward the view that history was the product of class struggles, and a society in which all were equal would be created through revolution. Lenin had adapted Marxist theory to emphasise the need for the Bolshevik/Communist Party to lead the proletariat in bringing about this state of equality. It is this Marxist-Leninist theory that is generally

implied in references to the practice of communism.

N

North Atlantic Treaty Organisation or NATO: set up in April 1949 to provide a system of collective defence for states in Western Europe, together with Canada and the US. West Germany joined the organisation on 9 May 1955 to strengthen it against possible Soviet aggression at the time of the Cold War. Germany's accession led to the formation of the Warsaw Pact, signed on 14 May 1955 by the Soviet Union, Hungary, Czechoslovakia, Poland, Bulgaria, Romania, Albania, and East Germany, as a formal response, thus confirming the two opposing sides of the Cold War.

The National Democratic Party of Germany or NPDP (Nationaldemokratische Partei Deutschlands): a nationalist political party in East Germany, founded as a liberal nationalist group in 1948 and absorbed into the SED to become one of the bloc parties. It re-emerged in 1990 but after performing disastrously in the elections of March 1990 was eventually merged into the FDP. In West Germany, an NPDP was founded in 1964 as a successor to the German Reich Party (DRP) and was on the far right of the political spectrum. The party campaigned for German reunification and nationalist aspirations and won local government seats across Germany in the late 1960s. However, it went into decline in the 1970s and despite a small recovery when immigration issues became acute from the mid-1980s to the early 1990s, it never received the minimum 5 per cent of votes needed to obtain a seat in the Bundestag.

O

The Organisation for European Economic Cooperation or OEEC: came into being on 16 April 1948. It emerged from the Marshall Plan and the Conference for European Economic Cooperation, which sought to establish a permanent organisation to continue work on a joint recovery programme and to supervise the distribution of aid in particular.

Ostpolitik: a new eastern policy intended to reduce tensions between East and West and to enable West Germany to work with eastern bloc states (including the GDR) for their mutual benefit.

P

People-owned enterprise or VEB (Volkseigener Betrieb): the official form of industrial enterprise in the GDR. VEBs were publicly owned and were often combined in groups called *Kombinate*.

R

Real income: the income received after any price changes are taken into account and indicates a person's standard of living.

The Reichswehr: the German army of the inter-war years. It was a proud and powerful independent force. In a famous incident in 1920, some Reichswehr soldiers refused to fire on others that were staging a coup, known as the Kapp putsch. The army was virtually beyond the control of the civilian authorities.

S

SA: a Nazi paramilitary force used to intimidate opponents – the 'brownshirts'.

S-Bahn: Berlin's above-ground railway network.

SD: the Nazi security service under the control of the SS.

Separation of powers: the separation of the law-making or legislative body (parliament) from the executive (which carried out the laws) and the judiciary (which judged people according to the laws).

The Socialist Unity Party of Germany or SED (*Sozialistische Einheitspartei Deutschlands*): the governing party of East Germany from 1949 to March 1990. It was created in 1946 when the Soviet Union forced members of the SPD and KPD in the eastern zones to merge. After 1990, the party reformed itself as the Party of Democratic Socialism (PDS).

Socialist realism: the name given to art which expressed socialist values. Socialist Art was meant to help the state fulfil its ideological purpose.

The Soviet Military Administration or SMAD: had its headquarters in Karlshorst, Berlin and ruled the Soviet occupation zone of Germany from May 1945 until November 1949. It helped bring about a communist-style regime and supervised the formation of the SED in 1946; controlled the movement of refugees; carried through the 1945 land reform, which confiscated the land of German nobles; nationalised banks and heavy industries; and introduced the 1946 (secular) education reform. The SMAD also set up internment camps for the detention of 'suspect' Germans. After the establishment of the GDR, which took over administrative responsibilities in East Germany, the SMAD was replaced by the Soviet Control Commission.

SS: originally Hitler's personal body guard, these were the Nazi 'blackshirts' who ran the concentration camps.

Stasi (*Ministerium für Staatssicherheit*): a nickname for the Ministry for State Security, derived from *Staatssicherheit*, literally 'state security'. It was the official secret police of East Germany with its headquarters in East Berlin. Its motto was '*Schild und Schwert der Partei*' (Shield and Sword of the Party), showing

its connections to the SED. It was founded on 8 February 1950 and Wilhelm Zaisser was the first Minister of State Security with Erich Mielke as his deputy. It was run by Wollweber 1953–57 and then by Mielke until his resignation in 1989. In November 1989, the ministry was renamed as the 'Office for National Security' under popular pressure. Modrow was forced to dissolve the organisation in January 1990.

Status quo: things as they stand.

T

Trabi: a nickname for the East German Trabant car. West Germans tended to look down on these inferior cars, which had none of the style or power of the popular West German models. The body of the car was made from a material comprising cotton fleece and plastic and was therefore easily damaged!

W

The Weimar Republic: Germany's only experience of a genuine democratic constitution with a figurehead president, an elected central (federal) government and local state governments pre-Second World War. The Weimar Republic had lasted from 1919–33, although its multiplicity of competing political parties, encouraged by a system of proportional representation, weakened it and was ultimately destroyed by Hitler's rise to power and exploitation of its constitution.

Work norm: refers to productivity goals and lay down rules on how much output is expected within a given time. In the GDR during 1953, a 10 per cent increase in work norms meant that workers were expected to do 10 per cent more work for the same money.

Bibliography

For student use

Fulbrook, M. (2000) *Interpretations of the Two Germanies 1945–1990, 2nd Edition*, Palgrave Macmillan

For student reference

Childs, D. (2001) *The Fall of the GDR*, Longman

Fulbrook, M. (1991) *The Fontana History of Germany 1918–1990, the Divided Nation*, Fontana

Laver, J., Rowe, C. and Williamson, D (1999) *Years of Division: Europe Since 1945*, Hodder Murray

Thomaneck, K. and Niven, B (2000) *Dividing and Uniting Germany*, Routledge

For teachers and extension

Berghahn, V. R. (1987) *Modern Germany, 2nd Edition*, Cambridge University Press

Carr, W. (1991) *A History of Germany 1815–1990, 4th Edition*, Hodder Arnold

Fulbrook, M. (1997) *Anatomy of a Dictatorship: Inside the GDR 1949–1989*, OUP

Garton Ash, T. (1994) *In Europe's Name: Germany and the Divided Continent*, Vintage

Geiss, I. (1997) *The Question of German Unification, 1806–1996*, Routledge

Jarausch, K. and Gransow, V. (1994) *Uniting Germany: Documents and Debates, 1944–1993*, Berghahn Books

Jarausch, K. (1994) *The Rush to German Unity*, OUP

Judt. T, (2006) *Postwar: A History of Europe since 1945*, Penguin

Kettenacker, L. (1997) *Germany Since 1945*, Oxford Paperbacks

Kirk, T. (2002) *Cassell's Dictionary of Modern German History*, Weidenfeld and Nicolson

Kitchen, M. (2005) *A History of Modern Germany 1800–2000*, Blackwell

Pulzer, P. (1995) *German Politics 1945–1995*, OUP

Winkler, H. (2000) *Germany: The Long Road West 1933–1990*, OUP

The FRG

Fulbrook, M. (1997) *German History since 1800* (contains many useful essays including Mark Roseman, Division and Stability – the Federal Republic of Germany), Hodder Arnold

Glees, A. (1996) *Reinventing Germany: German Political Development since 1945*, Berg Publishers

Klein, H. (ed) (1996) *The German Chancellors*, Edition Q.

Kramer, A. (1991) *The West German Economy 1945–1955*, Berg

Prittie, T. (1979) *The Velvet Chancellors*, Holmes and Meier

The GDR

Childs, D. (1988) *The German Democratic Republic: Moscow's German Ally*, Routledge

Dennis, M. (2000) *The Rise and Fall of the German Democratic Republic*, Longman

Funder, A. (2004) *Stasiland: Stories From Behind the Berlin Wall*, Granta Books

Grieder, P. (1999) *The East German Leadership 1946–73*, Manchester University Press

Maier, C. (1999) *Dissolution: The Crisis of Communism and the End of East Germany*, Princeton

McCauley, M. (1986) *The German Democratic Republic since 1945*, Palgrave Macmillan

Biographies/First hand accounts

Adenauer, K. (1966) *Memoirs*, London

Brandt, W. (1978) *People and Politics: The Years 1960–1975*, Little, Brown and Company

Garton Ash, T. (1999) *We the People: The Revolution of '89*, Penguin

Grass, G. (1991) *Two States, One Nation*, Harvest

Heneghan, T. (2000) *Unchained Eagle: Germany after the Wall*, Reuters

Klein, H. (1996) *The German Chancellors*, Edition Q

Leonard, W. (1979) *Child of the Revolution*, Pluto Press

Marshall, B. (1997) *Willy Brandt: A Political Biography*, Palgrave Macmillan

Molloy, P. (2009) *The Lost World of Communism*, BBC Books

Schwartz, H. P. (1995–97) *A German Politician and Statesman in a period of war, Revolution and Reconstruction (2 Vols)*, Berghahn Books

The Berlin Wall

Hilton, C. (2002) *The Wall: The People's Story*, Sutton

Smith, K. (1991) *Berlin: Coming in From the Cold*, Penguin

Taylor, F. (2007) *The Berlin Wall*, Bloomsbury

Tusa, A. (1996) *Berlin and the Wall: The Last Division*, Coronet Books

Non-written Sources

Films

The Lives Of Others (*Das Leben Der Anderen*)

Goodbye Lenin

Popular Music

David Bowie: The Berlin Trilogy

Pink Floyd: The Wall live in Berlin – Roger Waters (1990 Benefit Concert)

Play

Democracy (about Günther Guillaume) by Michael Frayn

Photographs

DDR Design, 1949–1989, Taschen, 2004

Michael Sturmer, The German Century, Weidenfeld and Nicolson, 1999

■ Non-written Sources

Video

Cold War – Taylor Downing and Jeremy Issacs

The End of the System in 'People's Century' series

Atlas

Crampton, R. J. (1996) *Atlas of Eastern Europe in the Twentieth Century*, Routledge

Site visits

For an 'in depth' understanding of post-war German history, a visit to Berlin is strongly recommended. To see the remains of the wall, the Brandenburg Gate, the Stasi, DDR and Checkpoint Charlie museums and to visit the Stasi prison, helps invoke an appreciation of events which is hard to obtain from mere reading. *Berlin 1945–1989* by Maik Kopleck, Verlag (English edition available from Amazon) provides a valuable guide book to the post-war sites and useful factual and visual resources are published by and, are on sale at, such Berlin Museums.

Useful websites

www.dailysoft.com/berlinwall
For outline History, photographs, reminiscences.

www.h-net.org/~german Provides some useful links including a propaganda archive and unification case study for classroom use.

www.bbc.co.uk
Has various interesting links to the opening of Stasi files. (Search 'Stasi files')

Has recorded excerpts of reactions to the building of the Berlin Wall. (Search 'Berlin Wall')

Acknowledgements

The author and publisher would like to thank the following for permission to reproduce material:

Source texts:

p11 extract from *End of a Berlin Diary 1944-1945* by William Shirer 1947. Reprinted with kind permission of Don Congdon Associates; p13 extract from *Memoirs: 1925-1950* by George F. Kennan, published by Little Brown and Company, USA. Reprinted with permission; p28 extract from Winston Churchill's speech at Fulton, Missouri, USA on March 5th 1946. Reprinted with permission of Curtis Brown UK; pp36, 51 extracts from *The Americanisation of Germany 1945-1949* by Ralph Willett, Routledge UK 1989 © 1989 by Ralph Willett. Reprinted with permission of Cengage Learning Services Ltd; pp51, 52 short extracts from *Postwar: A History Of Europe Since 1945* by Tony Judt copyright © 2005 by Tony Judt. Used by permission of The Penguin Press, a division of Penguin Group (USA) Inc and The Random House Group Limited, UK; pp52, 56 extracts from *A History of Germany* by Mary Fulbrook 2009, published by Wiley Blackwell; p66 (4) short extracts from *German Post-War History In Selected Articles 1949-1993* by Rainer Hildebrandt, edited by Alexandra Hildebrandt, 2002. Reprinted with permission of Alexandra Hildebrandt, Mauermuseum; p68 extract from *Protest Movements in 1960s West Germany: A Social History of Dissent and Democracy* by Nick Thomas, 2003, Berg Publishers. Reprinted with permission of A & C Black; pp70, 86, 125, 135, 146-7 extracts from *The Lost World Of Communism* by Peter Molloy, BBC Books 2009. Reprinted with permission of The Random House Group Limited; pp85, 141 (2), 142 extracts from *Anatomy of a Dictatorship: Inside the GDR 1949-1989* by Mary Fulbrook, 1995, reprinted with permission of OUP; pp93 (both), 141 (1) extracts from *Divided City: The Berlin Wall* by Christian Bahr, © Jaron Verlag GmbH Berlin 2010. Reprinted with permission; p98 extract from *East Berlin: Life before the Wall fell* by Harald Hauswald, Lutz Rathenow. © Jaron Verlag GmbH Berlin 2010. Reprinted with permission; p112 short extracts from *The Sixties Unplugged* by Gerard De Groot, Macmillan, 2008. Reprinted with permission of Pan Macmillan, originally published in Detlef Siegfried 'Don't Trust anyone older than 30' Voices as conflict and consensus between generations in 1960s West Germany, Journal of Contemporary History, 40, 2005 SAGE; p134 short extract from *The Failed Experimental East German Communism* by Mark Allinson, in *German History Since 1800* by Mary Fulbrook, Arnold 1997. Reprinted with permission of A & C Black Publishers Limited; p138 extracts from *The German Chancellors* by Hans Klein, translated by Edna McCown published by Edition Q, 1996. Reprinted with permission of be.bra verlag GmbH, Berlin; p156 short extract from 'Is it possible?' Newsweek. 20 November 1989. Reprinted with permission of PARS International Corp.

Photographs:

Cover photograph: Rex Features

Chris Niedenthal/Time Life Pictures/Getty Images p171; Cotton Coulson/National Geographic/Getty Images p131; Druszcz Wojteic/AFP/Getty Images p144; Edimedia pp17, 28, 36, 103, 167; Germania Collection pp11, 12, 14, 19, 24, 25, 29, 32, 46, 48, 55, 59, 61, 65, 83, 95, 102, 125, 152; Getty Images pp84, 90, 113, 126, 133, 151; Jonathan S. Blair/National Geographic/Getty Images p120; Photo12 pp34, 39, 41, 43, 50, 51, 54, 56, 60, 62, 68, 70, 75, 76, 79, 94, 96, 99, 110, 112, 117, 121, 123, 136, 138, 155. 158, 161, 164, 168; Public Domain: pp116, 148, 154, 163; Tom Stoddart/Getty Images: p173; Topfoto pp53, 64, 71, 91, 100, 156; United Archives pp2 (both), 143, 176.

Photo Research by *www.mediaselectors.com*.
Researchers: Alexander Goldberg & Jason Newman

Every effort has been made to contact the copyright holders and we apologise if any have been overlooked. Should copyright have been unwittingly infringed in this book, the owners should contact the publishers, who will make the corrections at reprint.

Index